Sacred
Fragments

SACRED FRAGMENTS

Recovering Theology
for the Modern Jew

NEIL GILLMAN

The Jewish Publication Society
Philadelphia · New York · Jerusalem
5750 · 1990

Copyright © 1990 by Neil Gillman
First edition   All rights reserved
First paperback edition, 1992
Manufactured in the United States of America

Library of Congress Cataloging in Publication Data
Gillman, Neil.
    Sacred fragments: recovering theology for the modern Jew /
Neil Gillman.
        p.   cm.
    Bibliography: p.
    Clothbound ISBN 0-8276-0352-5
    Paperback ISBN 0-8276-0403-3
    1. Judaism—Doctrines.   2. Judaism—20th century.   3. Philosophy,
Jewish.   I. Title.
BM601.G55   1989
296.3—dc20   89-11204
                                                           CIP

Designed by Jonathan Kremer

10   9   8   7   6   5   4   3   2   1

For Abby and Debby
with abiding love

Contents

Acknowledgments xi

Introduction xv

I REVELATION: WHAT REALLY HAPPENED? 1

II RELIGIOUS AUTHORITY: WHO COMMANDS? 39

III KNOWING GOD: HOW AND WHAT? 63

IV TALKING ABOUT GOD: SYMBOLIC LANGUAGE 79

V SENSING GOD'S PRESENCE: EMPIRICISM 109

VI PROVING GOD'S EXISTENCE: RATIONALISM 139

VII ENCOUNTERING GOD: EXISTENTIALISM 163

VIII SUFFERING: WHY DOES GOD ALLOW IT? 187

IX RITUAL: WHY DO WE NEED IT? 215

X THE END OF DAYS: WHAT WILL BE? 247

Afterword: Doing Your Own Theology 275

Index 281

"Thereupon the Lord said to me, 'Carve out two tablets of stone like the first, and come up to Me on the mountain; and make an ark of wood. I will inscribe on the tablets the commandments that were on the first tablets that you smashed, and you shall deposit them in the ark.' "

—Deuteronomy 10:1–2

"Rabbi Joseph taught: '. . . that you smashed, and you shall deposit them . . .' teaches us that both the tablets and the fragments of the tablets were deposited in the ark."

—Babylonian Talmud, Tractate Baba Bathra 14b

Acknowledgments

IT WAS PROFESSOR GERSON D. COHEN, THEN CHANCELLOR AND NOW
Chancellor Emeritus of The Jewish Theological Seminary of
America, who first suggested to me that I incorporate the Jewish
philosophy course material that I had been teaching at the Seminary into a volume directed specifically to the Jewish lay person.
Indeed, it has been my good fortune, these past thirty-five years,
to have studied and taught at the Seminary under the leadership
of three chancellors, all giants of Jewish scholarship. Professor
Louis Finkelstein gave me my first opportunity to teach Jewish
philosophy, and Professor Cohen's successor, Professor Ismar
Schorsch, has been a steadfast source of encouragement and support. I acknowledge my debt to them all.

I can not think of a more exciting place to study and teach
than the Seminary, and that is largely because of the constant
stimulation of an extraordinary community of scholars and students of Judaica. My colleagues on the faculty have been unfail-
ingly generous with their time and scholarship on the issues that
have found expression in this volume. And every teacher knows
that much of the hard, critical work of scholarship takes place in
the classroom. Generations of students have challenged me to
sharpen my thinking, refine my reasoning, and clarify my conclusions. From them, I have learned infinitely more than I have
taught. Their imprint is on every page of this book.

I would be remiss if I didn't also acknowledge my gratitude to adult education classes in synagogues around the country for confirming my impression not only that is there an audience for a book of this kind but that there is an extraordinary intellectual sophistication and curiosity about theological issues in our congregational membership. I am grateful to my former students, now rabbis in these congregations, for giving me the opportunity to teach my material to their congregants. If I single out my students in the various classes I have taught under the auspices of the Women's League for Conservative Judaism, it is because they have been exposed to the twists and turns of my thinking longer than any other group. I invariably come out of these classes with renewed astonishment at their knowledge, their seriousness of purpose, and their unflagging enthusiasm for study.

Professors Elliot Dorff of The University of Judaism in Los Angeles and Gordon Tucker of the Seminary, friends of many years, were gracious enough to review the entire manuscript of this volume, correct my reading of texts, and make numerous specific suggestions regarding my formulation of the issues. I need not add that whatever inadequacy this inquiry may contain is entirely my own responsibility.

The manuscript of this volume has gone through many different stages. I am grateful to Florence Green, who served as my secretary when I was in the Seminary administration, for having typed earlier versions of much of my material. Donna Fishman and Amy Lederhendler helped with the editing chores of those early drafts. Stephanie Coen assembled the bibliographical data included in the "For Further Study" sections accompanying each chapter. Jay Sales helped with reading the proofs of the volume and prepared the index. The last major decision affecting this book was the choice of a title, and I am grateful to Adrienne Weiss for helping me clarify just what I wanted the title to say.

Sheila F. Segal, former Editor-in-Chief of the Jewish Publication Society, provided more support than any author has the right to expect from his editor. She had confidence in me and in my book at a time when I needed it most. She edited the manuscript thoroughly and sympathetically, and provided advice and unfailing encouragement throughout the process of bringing it into print. To her and her associates at the JPS, I express my unbounded gratitude.

There are simply no words that can adequately express my appreciation to the members of my family—my wife, Sarah, and my children, Abby and Debby—for their patience and support during the years it took me to complete this manuscript. I have dedicated the volume to my children because, in many ways, it was written for them. I am particularly grateful that my father will be able to see this project come to fulfillment.

Finally, I consider myself singularly blessed by God in that I am able to spend my waking hours doing what I love to do most, simply to study and teach Jewish philosophy and theology. If I have been able to convey even a touch of that excitement to my readers, I will feel amply rewarded.

New York
Erev Pesah 5749
April 1989

Introduction

IN 1952 I WAS AN UNDERGRADUATE STUDENT AT MCGILL UNIVERSITY
in Montreal. I had been raised in a small town in French Canada.
Opportunities for serious Jewish education were almost nonexistent. My home was moderately observant and I had accumulated
many positive experiential associations with Judaism—Shabbat
dinners at home, Passover *seders* with my grandmother, synagogue with my father. But I had almost no Jewish peers, and
Hebrew school at the end of the school day and on Sunday
mornings was a joke.

Whatever Jewish observances I brought with me to McGill
quickly went by the boards. I reveled in the heady intellectualism
of the college experience and majored in philosophy and French
literature. Judaism, by contrast, seemed to be an intellectual
anachronism, an old wives' tale suitable for my parents and
grandparents and their rabbis but utterly irrelevant to any modern, educated Jew. I was comfortably on my way out of any
serious involvement with Jewish life when one day, quite by
chance, I wandered into the B'nai B'rith Hillel Foundation and
attended a lecture by the late Will Herberg.

I did not know then that Herberg had quite recently found
his own way back to Judaism. He had been a Marxist, had edited
Communist publications, and had served as director of educa-

tional activities for the New York division of the ILGWU. After breaking with Marxism and the Party, he turned to the eminent Protestant theologian Reinhold Niebuhr, who guided him to the study of Judaism. Under the aegis of the late Milton Steinberg, then rabbi of the Park Avenue Synagogue in New York and one of the most eminent Jewish thinkers of his generation, Herberg began his odyssey of return. The outcome was his book, *Judaism and Modern Man* (1951), a personal reworking of Jewish philosophy in terms of Buberian and Rosenzweigian existentialist thought. His visit to Montreal was part of a nationwide tour of synagogues and college campuses devoted to teaching his book.

I had studied existentialism in philosophy classes at McGill. I had read Kierkegaard, Tillich, Sartre, Camus, and their critics. But this was the first time in my entire experience that Judaism was presented as worthy of serious thought. Suddenly, under Herberg's tutelage, Jewish philosophy became part of that agenda: Maimonides was related to Plato and Aristotle; Yehudah Halevi, to David Hume and John Locke; Martin Buber and Franz Rosenzweig, to Kierkegaard; Abraham Joshua Heschel, to Rudolf Otto and the continental phenomenologists; and Mordecai Kaplan, to John Dewey, William James, and the American pragmatists. Most important, for the first time, the Bible came alive for me. Every chapter concealed an implicit theological claim. I began to read it as if for the first time.

I have since discovered that I was but one of many young Jews who were "turned on" to Judaism by Will Herberg during the 1950s. In my own case, this encounter led to rabbinical studies at the Jewish Theological Seminary, to doctoral work in the philosophy of religion at Columbia University, and to a career in teaching and writing on Jewish thought.

Of course, I am not so naïve to believe that Herberg's book is solely responsible for my return to Judaism. My studies at the Seminary introduced me to the field of Jewish intellectual history, and particularly to the thought of two of our century's theological giants, Mordecai Kaplan and Abraham Joshua Heschel, with whom I was privileged to study and whose influence will be found on every page of this book. Nor do I believe now that *any* statement of Jewish theology or philosophy alone, no matter how cogently or dramatically presented, could do the same for my students. In fact, throughout this volume I distinguish between the intellectual (i.e., theological or philosophical) dimension of Jewish religion and its experiential or existential dimension, and I seek to delineate the legitimate functions of each of these. But my own reassessment of the more limited role of theology and philosophy in Judaism is quite recent and results from my exposure to the literature on religion from the perspective of the social sciences, particularly religious anthropology. Despite this, my primary field remains Jewish philosophy and theology, and I continue to believe that for many of my contemporaries, the Jewish "head work" has to be done if Judaism is to be at all relevant in their lives.

For me, the issue of determining the legitimate role of theology and philosophy in Judaism was posed quite starkly by Mordecai Kaplan. Kaplan used to teach that there are three possible ways of identifying with a religious community: by behaving, by believing, or by belonging. Kaplan himself insisted that the primary form of *Jewish* identification is belonging—that intuitive sense of kinship that binds a Jew to every other Jew in history and in the contemporary world. Whatever Jews believe, and however they behave as Jews, serves to shape and concretize that underlying sense of being bound to a people with a shared history and destiny. When that connection disappears, Judaism too will disappear.

Very few of Kaplan's teachings escaped controversy and this claim is no exception. His most vociferous critics—largely, the more traditionalist of contemporary Jewish thinkers and the masters of the talmudic and halakhic literature—are the proponents of behaving as primary. Belonging by itself, they argue, is empty, a mere emotional attachment that makes no demands. What really concretizes Jewish identity is an idiosyncratic lifestyle, a code of behavior that touches every moment of the day.

This dispute is clearly a matter of emphasis, of priorities, for both parties would agree that authentic Jewish identity demands a measure of both belonging and behaving. But disputes over priorities can frequently have genuine and profound implications. Kaplan's emphasis on the primacy of belonging is precisely what enables him to view the Jewish behavioral pattern as forged *by the community* in order to express, concretize, and communicate that sense of distinctive peoplehood. It also gives him the right to allow the community to "reconstruct" traditional patterns of behavior (and belief as well), in order to make belonging possible for a new generation of Jews. His critics, on the other hand, see the Jewish behavioral code as God's immutably revealed will. It comes first; it is assumed by any definition of Jewish identity; and no one can tamper with it—even in the interest of promoting belonging.

What is particularly striking about the dispute is the absence of any prominent modern thinker who is willing to make the case for the primacy of believing. The Jewish theologian contemplates this dispute with a mixture of amazement and unease. Amazement, because how is it even possible for anyone to belong *or* to behave without a coherent, underlying justificatory ideology? Unease, because what does this glaring vacuum say about the very legitimacy of theology in the Jewish enterprise?

Looking back over Jewish history, there is of course one clear candidate for the championship of believing: that towering medieval figure, Moses Maimonides. It was Maimonides, for example, who articulated the Thirteen Principles of Faith which, he insisted, comprised the minimal belief system for every Jew. Maimonides also composed a code of Jewish law, the *Mishneh Torah,* and scandalized his contemporaries by opening this treatise with an extended codification of the content of Jewish belief that he claimed *also* has the force of law. Finally, toward the end of his monumental *Guide of the Perplexed,* Maimonides delineates a hierarchy of Jewish religious authenticity. Who appears at the very top of the hierarchy—above those whom he contemptuously dismisses as "the ignoramuses who observe the law"? Precisely the Jew who has mastered mathematics, logic, the sciences, and the literature of philosophy, primarily metaphysics. In other words, the Jewish philosopher.

But Maimonides is a lonely voice, at least on this issue. Survey the history of Jewish thought—from Philo in first-century B.C.E. Alexandria through Martin Buber, Franz Rosenzweig, Mordecai Kaplan, and Abraham Joshua Heschel in our own century. Add the authors of Genesis, Job, Ecclesiastes, and Proverbs, and the homiletical material in rabbinic literature, as well as some of the mystics and Hasidic masters who deal with theological issues in their own characteristic way. We still have a relatively small group of thinkers, and a meager body of theological or philosophical literature, compared with what the Jewish legal tradition produced in the same period.

For over 2,000 years, the very enterprise of systematizing the belief content of Judaism has been regarded by Jews as somewhat alien; in fact, most of the thinkers who engaged in this enterprise wrote in a language other than Hebrew. They borrowed not only the language of their respective outside worlds but even the reigning philosophical idiom: Philo, from Plato; Maimonides, from medieval Aristotelianism; the moderns, from the continental existentialists or the American naturalists. Their influence, then, was remarkably transient: Maimonides' legal code, the *Mishneh Torah,* is considered authoritative to this very day; but his *Guide* is hardly consulted by the perplexed among our contemporaries.

Further, whereas the Jewish legal tradition—not surprisingly for a system of law—exhibited a great deal of inner consistency and coherence, Jewish theological positions have been wide-ranging and diverse. Take any issue, even as central an issue as the nature of God. Without going much beyond the Bible itself, it is quite clear that the God of the Genesis narratives is remarkably different from the God of the classical prophets; the former, to take one example, knows nothing of the possibility of repentance as a means of atonement for sin, while the latter is infinitely compassionate and pleads for repentance. There is also little in common between either of these and the God of Maimonides, of the medieval mystics, and in our century, of Kaplan and Heschel. Is it not thoroughly reasonable, then, to ask how important this entire enterprise can really be if all of these can pass for a Jewish concept of God?

In the final analysis, the suspicion that seems to have haunted Jewish philosophy most throughout its history stems from an almost intuitive feeling that the philosopher's preoccupation with clarifying and systematizing what Jews are supposed to believe is simply not as intrinsically important to Judaism, as it is for Christianity. A Christian is not a Christian unless he or she *believes* that Jesus of Nazareth was God who became a human being, was crucified and resurrected, and will return at the end of days. Christians are required to hold these beliefs in order to be Christian in the first place and thereby "justified," or in an authentic relationship with God. Christianity is the paradigm of a religion that affirms the primacy of believing. The Roman Catholic Mass, recited daily, includes a portion entitled the Credo—literally "I believe"—which delineates the essential doctrinal content of Christianity. Its incorporation into the daily liturgy testifies to its centrality.

There is no parallel statement of belief for the Jew. Most Jews, even the most authentic among us, have never given much thought to clarifying just what we believe about God, nor do we feel that our religiosity is any the worse for it. The "religious" among us observe the Sabbath, the dietary laws, the Festivals, thrice-daily prayer, and the ethical teachings of the tradition. What else do we need? If challenged, we would say: "Of course we believe in God!" But pressed to go much beyond this, to answer *why* we believe or *what* precisely we mean by God, most of us retreat. Maimonides' Thirteen Principles of Faith are frequently published in Jewish prayer books, but usually *after* the end of the formal morning service of worship—an instructive contrast to the centrality of the Christian Credo. Recitation of Maimonides' text is clearly optional.

But it is also clear that there have been periods in Jewish intellectual history that were marked by a great deal of concern for believing, periods that were marked by a flowering of Jewish philosophical creativity. If the past is in any way instructive, we must consider two sets of conditions that seem to guarantee such a development. The first is an ideologically open social setting. Whenever Jews participated in a cultural setting where a wide range of ideologies competed for allegiance, they began to engage in philosophy. The Middle Ages, from the tenth through the fifteenth centuries, provides the most instructive paradigm. During this period, the three major claimants to exclusive truth—Judaism, Christianity, and Islam—all interacted with each other. Each religion had its more liberal and more conservative wings. Oriental religious cults also abounded. Casting a shadow over all of this religious activity was a powerful and seductive "secular," or rational-skeptical, philosophical movement embodied in the writings of Aristotle. This last tradition insisted that a human being could attain all possible knowledge by simply cultivating natural experience and reason alone. Who, then, needed the revealed truths of any religion? The social setting was remarkably open and since Arabic was the *lingua franca* of the age, all of this literature was accessible to everyone. Jews were eager to jump into this stimulating social and intellectual milieu.

It was an exciting age, but it was also threatening to the defenders of religion. For many Jews, the tradition was simply no longer self-validating; the other options, especially Aristotelian rationalism, were too alluring. In such a context, the case had to be made for Judaism. Someone had to provide a systematic, coherent, and intellectually compelling statement of the content of Jewish belief, precisely because Jewish identity had become problematic. The philosopher wrote in Arabic, not only because he wanted to be read by the entire community, but also because his audience may well have become so alienated from Judaism that it was no longer comfortable with Hebrew. And he wrote with an eye on Aristotle, either appropriating his thought (Maimonides) or challenging it (Yehuda Halevi), in both cases because it was Aristotelian rationalism that posed the challenge.

The second condition that has stimulated an outpouring of Jewish philosophy was a major turning point in Jewish history, frequently, alas, a historical trauma. The destruction of the Temple, both in 586 B.C.E. and in 70 C.E., the Crusades, the expulsion from Spain at the end of the fifteenth century—events of this magnitude shook established ideologies and called the most primitive commitments of the community into question. Again, what had been easily taken for granted no longer seemed so clear. Again, the tradition had to be looked at afresh and defended in a new and compelling way, or stretched to accommodate a new reality. In the process, Judaism's validity became reestablished and the community was able to move on.

If there was ever a moment in Jewish history when these two sets of conditions coincide, it is our own era. We too live in an open culture. Contemporary Jews are intellectually sophisticated and socially mobile. Jewish identity is entirely voluntary. We are challenged daily by the most virulently fundamentalist readings of religion on one side and by an aggressive secularism on the other. Assimilation and intermarriage, the almost inevitable trade-offs of open social settings, are rife. We also live in the wake of two monumental historical events: the Holocaust and the reestablishment of Jewish sovereignty in the State of Israel. Either one of these alone would have transformed the terms of Jewish existence; together they pose a formidable challenge. Our situation thus compels us to pursue Jewish philosophy—that is, to examine anew the content of Jewish belief in terms of our own historical situation.

That is precisely what Will Herberg did for himself, my contemporaries, and me. We were all young Jews living in an open, exciting social setting, in the wake of the Holocaust and the establishment of the State of Israel. In this specific historical context, he made the case for Judaism in an intellectually cogent and compelling way.

In some ways, contemporary Jewish philosophers continue in the footsteps of our predecessors. We write in English, and with an eye on Freud, Einstein, the technological explosion, the nuclear age, and the analytic school of modern philosophy. Our theologies have to explain the Holocaust and struggle with the implications of Jewish power and self-determination. We too write for the Jew who is not "at home" with his Jewishness, who feels the attraction of other ideological options, who cherishes the freedom and individualism that are the hallmarks of modernity, or who is overwhelmed by the Holocaust. Our audience is made up of Jews who insist that their children attend the best universities and become "movers and shakers" in the world outside the Jewish community—but then lie awake at night wondering if these same children will be seduced by cults, marry Jews, come home for Passover, or check into the Hillel program on campus. We write in order to tell these Jews that it is totally legitimate for them to hope that their children can embrace the best of the surrounding culture, and yet remain caring, committed, serious, and learning Jews. In fact, we try to provide a model for how this subtle and complex synthesis can be achieved.

It is almost inevitable, too, that our attempts to create a contemporary philosophy of Judaism will displease those Jews who *are* "at home" with their Jewishness and who do not feel the strains and tensions of modernity. Our work testifies to the fact that for some of us, the received tradition is no longer self-validating, that it has to be rethought, reformulated, stretched anew. In fact, one of our major concerns is how much stretching the tradition can take and still remain recognizably Jewish. For example, is it legitimate for a *Jewish* theologian, such as Harold Kushner, to account for the fact that "bad things" can happen to "good people" because God is simply not powerful enough to prevent this from happening? Ironically, our work is almost doomed to be unsatisfactory—not radical enough for the modernist who would insist that only a major transformation of the categories of Jewish thought can account for our experience, and inauthentic to the traditionalist who wonders why any change is necessary in the first place!

We take some consolation from the awareness that even Maimonides, today surely as hallowed a figure as Judaism has ever produced, was bitterly criticized during his lifetime, and that his books were banned and even burned because of their "heretical" content. Still, no one wants to be totally at odds with the community, especially if our ultimate purpose is to make it possible for that community to cohere in the face of multiple challenges.

Yet, in significant ways, our situation is different from that of our predecessors. One of the "gifts" of modernity is historical self-consciousness. From our vantage point today, we know that Maimonides "Aristotelianized" the biblical image of God, that the rabbis of the Talmud borrowed liberally from Plato and Hellenistic thought, that Jewish mystics were influenced by an ancient, pagan tradition rooted in oriental religions, that, in fact, the Bible itself reflects the rich and complex culture of the ancient Near East within which it was composed.

We are aware of the *fact* of history. We see change and development everywhere. The God of the Genesis narratives *is* very different from the God of the later prophets, of the medieval philosophers and mystics, and of Mordecai Kaplan. A story that captures our enigma perfectly is the familiar talmudic homily that places Moses in Rabbi Akiba's classroom, listening to Akiba expound a point of law that Moses simply does not recognize but, Akiba insists, was taught by Moses at Sinai. In one sense, it *is* the Torah from Sinai; we copy it painstakingly onto a scroll and read meticulously from it in the synagogue. But in another sense, it is also an eternally new text, read anew by every generation as Jews seek to uncover another of its infinite layers of meaning. Was Maimonides aware that he was radically transforming the plain sense of the biblical text? The answer to that question is not clear, at least to this writer. But *we* surely are aware—both of what Maimonides did, and of what we do as well. Therein lies our peculiarly modern challenge.

It is startling to find an anticipation of the challenge of modernity in a rabbinic homily on Deuteronomy 10:1–2: "Thereupon the Lord said to me [Moses], 'Carve out two tablets of stone like the first, and come up to Me on the mountain; and make an ark of wood. I will inscribe on the tablets the commandments that were on the first tablets that you smashed, and you shall deposit them in the ark.'"

The rabbinic homily (Babylonian Talmud, Tractate *Baba Bathra* 14b) reads the last two phrases of the passage very carefully and draws our attention to the precise referent for the word "them" in the last phrase of the verse. What is to be deposited in the ark? Apparently, that which is immediately juxtaposed to the word "them." (We know, from Exodus 40:20, that the new set of tablets was deposited in the ark.) Hence, the verse from Deuteronomy teaches us that the fragments of the first set of tablets were also to be placed in the ark together with the new and carried by the Israelites through their desert wanderings into the Holy Land. Those first tablets were shattered in Moses' rage at seeing the Israelites dancing around the golden calf (Exodus 32:19). Yet their fragments retained their inherent sanctity and could not be abandoned. They too were to be preserved and deposited in the most sacred spot in Israelite religious life.

For many of us, the traditional set of images that characterized Judaism from antiquity on has been irreparably shattered. The new individualism, our historical awareness, and the critical temper of our time have done their work. The belief system that our ancestors carried with them—and that carried *them* through to modernity—doesn't work for us. Nor do we have any powerful desire to recapture that mental set in its classical form.

In this situation, we too have to carve out our own new set of tablets. But we also know that we can never discard the fragments of the old, however inadequate they may seem to us. To do so would be to lose our link with our community—and without a community, where and who would we be? In fact, an extended modern homily on both the biblical verse and its rabbinic interpretation might teach that we must refashion our new tablets precisely out of the fragments of the old.

The Hebrew term for the process we are describing is *midrash.* A *midrash* is traditionally understood to be a talmudic homily that expands on a biblical word, verse, or narrative in order to give it a new, more comprehensive meaning. But Mordecai Kaplan also used to teach texts such as Maimonides' *Guide* and his own *Judaism as a Civilization* as *midrash,* global rereadings of the entire received tradition up to their day. In turn, Maimonides' work and Kaplan's now have become part of the "text" for the *midrashim* of future generations.

Every *midrash,* then, is a temporary consolidation, a plateau, the outcome of a struggle to rethink a tradition that has become, at least to some Jews, irrelevant. It is then inherently transitory, itself easily becoming anachronistic, lingering until we are shocked out of our complacency when our children tell us that we no longer "speak" to them.

There is one further sense of the term *midrash* that is central to this volume. *Midrash* can also be understood as a process or activity, rather than an outcome. It denotes the process of encountering a text, challenging it with an ever-new set of questions, and struggling to extract from it equally new answers. If we emphasize the process over the outcome, it is because of our peculiarly modern concern with the tentative, individualistic, and even fragmentary nature of the entire enterprise. We can never boast that our readings of Judaism are secure and permanent. We are all, more or less, always "on the road"; our work is always in process.

Two questions will haunt just about every page of this study: What makes any one theological statement "true," or at least "authentic"? And who decides?

In actuality, everyone decides—at least, everyone who shares the sense of a tradition that has become problematic and yet holds out the promise of renewed meaning. Everyone who cares about the issues, who is willing to read, study, and think. Everyone who has a stake in the outcome, which is nothing less than the continuity of Judaism. It is one of the glories of the Jewish philosophical tradition that there never was one ultimate authority—a pope, chief rabbi, or panel of philosophers—who had the power to declare one statement of Jewish belief authentic or another heretical. The concerned community decides—by its very willingness to study and teach, appropriate and transmit, that statement to its children and students. The very readiness to do all of this is itself testimony to its truth. It is this concerned community that lends coherence and integrity to the process of *midrash,* however individualistic it may be.

That openness, flexibility, and pluralism is what made and continues to make Jewish philosophy such a powerful teaching instrument. Today, in twentieth-century America, it is once again an enterprise whose hour has come. There is no difficulty finding Jews who feel the urgency of the problems. The challenge is to persuade them to join in the struggle for answers. This volume is designed to encourage and enable them to do just that.

I

Revelation:
What Really Happened?

WHY DOES A BOOK ON JEWISH PHILOSOPHY BEGIN WITH A DIS-
cussion of revelation? First, because it is revelation that
creates Judaism as a religion. Revelation is what brings God
into relationship with a community of human beings. Without
God's revelation, however we understand it, God would be
irrelevant to the human enterprise, and Judaism would be purely
a matter of peoplehood and culture alone.

Second, what distinguishes one religion from another is the
revelatory event that it accepts as authentic, or primary, as opposed to others that it dismisses as illusory, or secondary. When,
where, and how did God reveal Himself, or His will? To the
biblical community at Sinai? Through Jesus of Nazareth in first-
century Judea? To Mohammed in the Arabian desert in 610 C.E.?
To Joseph Smith in upstate New York in 1820? All of the above,
or only some? And how do we know? Our answers to these
questions determine our religious identity.

Third, how we understand revelation determines how we
deal with the issue of religious authority. Why do Jews, for
example, believe in a messianic age to come or observe the
Sabbath and Festivals of the Jewish year? Partly, because we
accept the authority of a body of traditional teaching that we call
Torah. But what gives this teaching authority over us—its antiquity? The community that has transmitted it over the centuries?

Or the notion that somehow it records or reflects God's "revealed" will? If the last of these, then how did God's will become embodied in a set of books? And if it is recorded in a set of books, how can the contemporary Reform and Conservative movements assert their own authority to reject or modify portions of that tradition?

Finally, though it is tempting to claim that any theological inquiry must begin with the nature and existence of God, it is clear that the "revealed" Torah is a primary source of information about how this God was construed by our ancestors. Yet on this issue the Torah speaks in diverse and frequently contradictory voices. In the early Genesis narratives for example, God is portrayed as harshly punitive, but in Jonah, as infinitely compassionate. Which of these images should be authoritative? Why should any of them dictate the content of our belief? To what extent can we listen to our own experience instead?

All of these issues bring us back to revelation. They can be reduced to three broad, interrelated questions. First, how, *in principle,* is it possible to believe in revelation? Second, did any revelatory event *in fact* take place? How do we know which of these events is, or are, authentic and which are not? Finally, *what* was revealed—God's very presence? His will? And how—in a book? In nature? Or in historical events?

It is impossible to deal with all of these questions simultaneously, but it is also clear that how we deal with any one of them will affect our discussion of the remaining two. For example, it might be easier to accept revelation in principle and in fact if *what* was revealed was God Himself in intimate relationship with a community (as existentialist thinkers such as Martin Buber would claim), rather than His will as recorded in a book that He dictated (as thinkers such as the nineteenth-century German traditionalist Samson Raphael Hirsch would insist)—or, for some of us, vice versa.

But we must begin somewhere. With the understanding that our initial discussion will have to be provisional, we begin, then, with the first of the three questions.

Is Revelation Possible?

To question the very possibility of revelation is to address the nature of God. If we postulate that God exists, the further claim that God reveals Himself, or His will, affirms that this God also relates to realities beyond Himself, specifically to human beings. In fact, the claim that this God reveals is simply an extension of the claim that He also creates. We could just as easily ask: Why does God have to create—the world, or anything? Couldn't He have been content with remaining alone? Is His own existence not self-sufficient?

The Bible portrays a God who both creates *and* reveals, and thereby tells us something significant and also disquieting about this God: that He is not at all content with being alone and self-sufficient. This God "needs" a world, human beings, and a relationship with a specific community as well.

What is disquieting about this image of God is that it contradicts much of what most of us believe about God, that He is perfect, omnipotent, absolutely transcendent—in short, that God, at least, is supposed to "have it all together." The Bible feels no such discomfort. Genesis 1, at least, assumes His power, His ultimacy, and the supremacy of His will. But as the narrative continues, it also portrays Him as intimately involved with His creation, particularly with human beings, and caring deeply about how they conduct their lives and what kind of social order they create on earth. Paradoxically, this concern is more often than not frustrated; from Genesis 3 through the last pages of the Bible, God's disappointment is constant. Yet He never stops caring, so powerful is His stake in what happens on earth.

The scope of His involvement with human beings begins with individuals but soon focuses on one man, Abraham, his family, and ultimately his posterity, the people of Israel. The *brit,* or covenant, that defines His relationship with this community is only a formal rendering of a far more intimate relationship. Exodus 6:7 captures this intimacy: "I will take you to be my people, and I will be your God." Jeremiah 31:20 stresses the emotional bond: "Truly, Ephraim is a dear son to me, a child that is dandled! Whenever I have turned against him, My thoughts would dwell on him still. That is why My heart yearns for him; I will receive him back in love."

Not only love and yearning but also anger, pleasure, sorrow, disappointment, and frustration—a veritable outpouring of God's emotions flashes through the pages of the Bible. This is a God who changes His mind, who wills destruction and then saves, who wills security and then destroys. He is personally involved in the events of history. He desires certain historical outcomes. But because He created human beings free—nothing in His creation matches that for surprise—His plans for history are always tentative and conditional. Yet there is never the slightest question of God's own freedom or of His power. The source of His frustration is His reluctance to use either of these because of commitments that He Himself has entered into.

This is hardly the perfect, self-sufficient God of the Western philosophical tradition. We are tempted to read the biblical account as somewhat primitive in comparison with that other tradition. But is it?

One fact is clear: God reveals because He cares passionately about human civilization. Our task is to decide how we feel about this image of a caring God.

Images of God

The problem here goes far beyond the question of revelation. It is nothing less than the methodological question that haunts every page of theology. Simply put, how can human beings think or speak of a reality that transcends the limits of human perception? The Bible cautions us against making graven or sculpted images of God. The issue, however, is not sculpted images but conceptual images. Here the Bible is extraordinarily permissive, as it has to be, for the only alternative would be silence—and then there would be no Bible and no Judaism.

The solution to the dilemma is the recognition that all of our human thinking and speaking about God uses our familiar human experience in a metaphorical way. All of our characterizations of

God are human creations, never literal photographs, never objectively true or false. They are shaped by human communities, products of the cultures in which they arose, of the explicit and implicit value systems of the age, of the psychic make-up of the thinkers themselves. The God of the Western philosophical tradition—perfect, unchanging, self-sufficient, emotionless—stems from Greek philosophy, particularly from the writings of Plato and Aristotle, which shaped all of Western thought. The biblical God—passionate, caring, involved, changeable, frustrated, but also infinitely hopeful—grew out of the culture of the ancient Near East and early Israelite experience. Both conceptions are metaphorical—created out of the stuff of human experience. One is no more objectively true or false than the other, one no more primitive than the other. They represent different perspectives on the world and on the human being. We may choose between the two, but the choice is always between contrasting metaphors.

Admittedly, the claim that none of our "God talk" is literally true is not universally accepted by contemporary Jewish thinkers. Traditionalists among us would agree that some of the more blatant physical descriptions of God in the Bible are clearly metaphorical; God does not literally have a "right hand" with which to shatter Israel's enemies (Exodus 15:6). But when we move beyond these crude anthropomorphisms and portray God as having an inner life characterized by thought, intentionality, or emotion, the literalness of the biblical material poses less of a problem, at least to these thinkers.

Above all, many traditionalists would insist that the biblical claim that God "spoke" to the biblical community, or to Moses, and that His words are recorded in the Torah is literally true. The claim that the Torah records God's explicit, verbally revealed will for the Jewish people provides these thinkers with the theological grounding for its authority. In fact, they would insist that the fact that God did speak is precisely what makes Him God. To deny that God could speak if He wanted to is to deny Him a power that even human beings have. It is, in effect, to deny the biblical God.

Others among us—call us "modernists" or "liberals"—are

far more thoroughgoing in our denial of literalism. Paradoxically, we too would insist that we do so in order to preserve the biblical God. For us the traditionalist position is uncomfortably close to idolatry, which is to construe God as a natural object, here a human being. Human beings speak. If God speaks, it is only in a metaphorical sense. That God can be characterized only through metaphors is, for us, precisely what makes Him God. We then, of course, have to redefine just what God did reveal if it wasn't His will in words.

One of the distinctive claims of this entire study is that all of our theology is centered about a set of humanly created metaphors. The fact that God "reveals" anything is one of these metaphors, intrinsically tied to His equally metaphorical "caring" for human society. This approach alone helps dissolve the resistance we intuitively feel against the notion that God relates to human beings and involves Himself in the drama of history. There is no underestimating the significance of that step. As we shall see, it opens the way for everything else we want to do in theology.

To return to our original question: Is revelation, then, in principle possible? That depends on our image of God. But certainly, if we accept the biblical image of God, revelation is not only possible but actually demanded.

Events, Not Processes
The leap from affirming the principle of revelation to affirming the authenticity of a specific revelatory event raises a host of new questions. How do we reconcile our image of God as beyond time with the biblical notion of a God who reveals Himself at specific moments in history? How do we discriminate between specific revelatory events, accepting some and dismissing others. And how do we decide?

Most of us would be more comfortable with the fact of revelation if we could understand it in a more natural way, as the gradual emergence in human consciousness of a set of timeless truths about ourselves and our world—something on the model of an extended scientific inquiry. That model of attaining truth is familiar to us; it makes no extraordinary demands on our ways of understanding the world.

This is clearly not the biblical model. The Bible understands revelation as an event, not a process, as occurring at a specific point in time, not as a gradually emerging pattern. In general, the Bible takes time and history very seriously. It takes discrete events occurring at specific moments and shapes them into a pattern charged with meaning, into an expression of God's concern. Scattered throughout the Bible are mini-surveys of the history of the Israelite community, but, like all historical narratives, the events are selected, organized, and interpreted to "reveal" God's hand and His plans. Some of these narratives were introduced into the liturgy. Nehemiah 9:6–11 together with Exodus 14:30–31, for example, are recited daily. As part of our morning service of worship, we tell the story of God's relationship to the world and to our ancestors, beginning with Creation, through God's promises to Abraham, the enslavement in Egypt, and His miraculous act of deliverance at the Red Sea. Deuteronomy 26:5–8 provides the narrative basis for the retelling of the Exodus story at our Passover *seder*. Psalms 105, 106, and 136 are striking examples of story-telling in liturgical form.

Simply telling the story is itself a form of worship because the events that are narrated are revelatory. Furthermore, the story is *our* story. That's why *we* recite it daily. That's why *we* are commanded to remember the day of the Exodus (Exodus 12:14) and the day of Sinai (Deuteronomy 4:10). We eat unleavened bread and bitter herbs as we recount the story of the Exodus because, as the Passover Haggadah reminds us, if God hadn't taken our ancestors out of Egypt, we would still be slaves. That classic statement is historically both naïve and profound. Our ancestors' enslavement in Egypt would have ended eventually, one way or another, but at the same time, their liberation has clearly shaped our national and personal destiny. Their story is our story and that's why we must remember and recount it.

History, understood as events shaped into a pattern, is very much the creation of a community. Our ancestors knew well that God is beyond history. But they viewed Him as able to distinguish certain moments in which He becomes manifest, and cause certain events through which He reveals His concern. God also sets apart or "sanctifies" a day of the week as the Sabbath (Genesis 2:3) and a month of the year as "the beginning of the months" (Exodus 12:2), just as he "sanctifies" a people (Exodus 19:6) and "chooses" a place "to establish His name" (Deuteronomy 16:2). These interventions into nature and history, taken together, create what the twentieth-century Jewish theologian Will Herberg called "the scandal of particularity" in biblical religion.

Particularity is "scandalous" because we are intuitively trained to look at the world through Platonic as opposed to biblical spectacles. Plato—and most philosophers after him—insisted that only that which is timeless, unchanging, eternal, universal, and abstract is real. Plato called these eternal realities "ideas," "forms," or "universals," and assigned them some kind of reality in another world beyond the senses and accessible only through reason. The time-bound, changing, particular existents of our familiar world are, to use Plato's own metaphor, but a "shadow" of reality. Plato's thesis, designed to solve a host of philosophical problems, is also a clear statement about how he and his culture viewed the concrete world of objects and events in which he lived. The Bible, on the other hand, says that this world, the world of our everyday experience, is of primary significance, even to God. That's why He relates to particular people at particular moments and in particular places on earth.

Again we see contrasting metaphors, neither literally true nor false, both created out of the stuff of human experience, both attempts to capture an elusive or hidden reality, both attempts to explain human experience. The biblical model understands the world of everyday experience as potentially charged with meaning, rather than paling in significance in favor of a timeless "other world." That is the heart of the claim for the fact of revelation as the Bible understands it.

Which Revelatory Event?

A well-groomed man appears on national television and testifies that one day, while driving along a highway, he saw Jesus of

Nazareth standing by the side of the road and beckoning to him. He took the next exit, drove to the nearest church, fell on his knees, and "accepted Jesus as Christ." From that moment, he has felt himself to be "saved" for eternity.

Some of us would dismiss this story as at worst a deliberate fiction and at best an illusion. But others would relate personal experiences of a similar kind and accept this man's experience as perfectly genuine. After all, one of the central underpinnings of Christianity is the personal testimony of a group of men that Jesus appeared to them after his death on the cross. To question their claim is to question the very legitimacy of Christianity. Still, other Christians do question that claim and insist that its veracity is absolutely irrelevant to the legitimacy of Christianity today. How can such judgments be made? What criteria can we use in making them?

In the Middle Ages, three great Western religions—Judaism, Christianity, and Islam—confronted each other, each claiming to represent God's ultimate revelation for humanity. In this context, some notable Jewish thinkers such as the ninth-century Saadia Gaon and the eleventh-century Yehuda Halevi, appealed to the highly public nature of God's revelation to the biblical community at Sinai, and its subsequent transmission from generation to generation as the criterion that establishes beyond question the truth of Judaism. Both of the other religions accept Sinai as revelatory, even though they view the revelation at Sinai as superseded by later revelations. But to Saadia and Halevi, these later revelatory events were far more limited and private. Sinai remains *sui generis,* and hence ultimately authoritative.

The problem with using the public nature of the Sinai revelation as a criterion for its authenticity is that the argument is circular. Since all of our knowledge about Sinai comes from the Torah, we are actually appealing to the book to prove the book's authority. Our argument assumes what we are trying to prove; hence its circularity.

More generally, this highlights the problem of using criteria that are internal to the revelatory event to prove its validity as revelation. People who claim to have had a private revelation often appeal to its inherent content or to the quality of the experience as proof of its authenticity. "What I saw was Jesus," they will claim, "and the experience was so clear and vivid, not at all like a dream." What they are saying is that the experience was self-authenticating. But the only people who are really convinced by such claims are those who assume, from the outset, that their experience is absolutely veridical. Since the experience is totally private, there's no way it can be used to convince anyone else.

If internal criteria are illegitimate, can we then appeal to external criteria? Again in the Middle Ages, rationality was proposed as an external criterion of this kind. Since our faculty of reason is God-given, since it is the quality that distinguishes us from the rest of creation, and since all human beings share that same innate faculty, what better way to establish the veracity of a religious tradition than by demonstrating its inherent rationality? Note the shift, here, from the quality of the revelatory experience to its content. The only remaining question was: Which religion is the most rational? The race was on.

But here too problems abound, for it is precisely *God's* revelation that is being judged. Isn't it sacrilegious to submit God's will to any external criterion, even one as divine as reason? And if reason can yield religious truth, why do we need revelation in the first place? In fact, could we not claim that it is the very incompatibility of a religious doctrine with reason that is the best guarantor of its divine origins? It is precisely because the doctrine is irrational that God had to reveal it. We are back, then, to our original impasse.

Reasons for Belief and Grounds for Belief

The broad issue here is establishing the truth of a religious tradition. We have linked that broad issue to a more narrow one, the authenticity of a religion's core revelatory event. Is that linkage legitimate?

To a degree, it is. We would all agree, for example, that some religious or revelatory claims are patently "off the wall." We dismiss the ravings of a disheveled man on a street corner who is predicting the imminent end of the world. We are horrified by the mass suicide of a religious cult in South America in response to the private vision of the cult's founder. The line is not absolutely clear, for we might feel differently if the man on the street were a serious political commentator and his message related to nuclear disaster. But in large measure, most of us can recognize psychosis or drug-induced visions when we see them, and we dismiss them.

We can dismiss certain religious claims because they are simply not within our universe of discourse. They ignore the basic assumptions of social and intellectual exchange. But what we have not done as yet is to show how to verify and hence choose from among the claims that remain.

That second step is fraught with ambiguities, especially when we are dealing with the core revelatory events of the major religions. These events are buried in antiquity. What we have today is the event as it was perceived, understood, or interpreted—the event as it was seen through the spectacles not only of the intervening centuries but, more important, of the human participants in the events. These human beings perceived the event as revelatory and that perception led to its acceptance as the central founding event of the religious community.

Is there a historical basis for Sinai? In all likelihood, yes. Something probably did happen in the desert wilderness at the earliest stage of our historical awareness as a people that left its imprint on our ancestors' consciousness. But we can't go much beyond that highly minimalist claim. What really happened at Sinai can never be determined in a totally objective way. Such complex events can never be verified in that way, especially ancient events, especially events that are perceived to involve a reality not accessible to direct human perception (such as the biblical God), and even more especially, events that are understood as part of a complex pattern including nothing less than all of nature and human history. Many historians would insist that we will never know what really happened in the recent Vietnam War—so much is the observer tied to the interpretive structure he brings to the event. All the more so with the founding events of Judaism.

Even the biblical account of the revelation at Sinai, then, has to be understood as a creation of the later tradition. In fact, in the Bible itself, Sinai is never as central as it later came to be. Look, for example, at the brief review of the community's history in Deuteronomy 26:5–10, the text which serves as the basis for the liturgical telling of our story in the Passover Haggadah. This narrative knows of an enslavement in, and a redemption from Egypt, but there is not a word about any event at Sinai. Typically, in most religions, the site selected for the erection of a Temple for the worship of God is associated with the locus of God's prior revelation on earth. But in Judaism, the site of the Temple in Jerusalem was associated with Moriah, the place of God's appearance to Abraham at the binding of Isaac (Genesis 22:14 and 2 Chronicles 3:1), not with Sinai.

The quest for the historical Sinai, then, is fruitless. In fact, it may not even be a crucial issue for us today, depending on whether we seek reasons for belief, or grounds for belief. Members of a religious community who want to persuade others to accept their commitments need reasons for belief, compelling data that would lead someone to accept Judaism as true. But if we try, instead, to explain to others why we are comfortable with our religious commitments, we would more likely list grounds for our commitments. We might, for example, talk of Judaism's strong communal emphasis, the impact of its ritual patterns on a healthy family life, its messianism as a source of an ultimate dream that gives significance to all of our endeavors here on earth. Grounds are admittedly weaker than reasons, but they are employed in a less militant situation. We have been searching for reasons for belief. The search for grounds is easier to pursue.

The historical authenticity of Judaism's founding events is only one of a number of different factors that figure in that inquiry. People buy into and live within a religion community for many subtle reasons. Even the theologian, the one who is most concerned with the cerebral dimension of religion, with intellectual rigor, has to acknowledge the impact of psychological, sociological, emotional, and cultural needs as well. How all of these factors affect one's religious commitments varies from person to person. The historical facticity of a religion's account of its founding revelatory events will carry some weight for some people. How much will vary; only rarely will it be decisive.

What Was Revealed? The Traditionalist View

The almost intuitive answer to this question by most Jews who claim to speak in the name of classical Judaism would be that God dictated the words of the Pentateuch to Moses, and Moses recorded those words in one coherent and consistent text that is the Humash (literally the "five" books) or Pentateuch, the same text we have before us today. They would add that parallel to this written text, God revealed a supplementary Torah that is the authentic interpretation of the written Torah. Transmitted orally from generation to generation, this text was set down in writing by the rabbis of the Talmud. By the close of the Talmudic era then (ca. 500 C.E.), the Jewish people had a complete and authoritative written record of God's will for the community.

This position is founded on two dogmas: the dogma of verbal revelation and the dogma of the Mosaic composition of the Pentateuch. The first maintains a literal interpretation of the biblical statement that God "spoke" to Moses. The second maintains the internal unity, coherence, and consistency of the Pentateuch as interpreted by the oral tradition. For the traditionalist, to deny either of these dogmas is to deny the divinity of the Torah. It is to deny that God could do, or did do, what the Torah clearly insists He did. By extension, then, it is to deny the monotheistic God.

The thrust of the position is the claim that what God revealed was His unambiguous will for the Jewish people. The doctrine of the Oral Torah may suggest that the written text was not all that unambiguous since it did need interpretation. But in practice, the conclusions of the talmudic interpretation are accepted as revealed and hence authoritative. One who accepts this position knows unambiguously, or can learn from a rabbinic authority, what God expects of the Jew.

This is popular Jewish traditionalism. The two dogmas that are at the heart of the position were rarely formulated as such until the modern age, and then largely in reaction to the more liberal views that began to emerge in the course of the Jewish Enlightenment. One of the first major statements of this position was articulated by Samson Raphael Hirsch, the founder of German neo-Orthodoxy, in his attempts to oppose the radical reinterpretation of Jewish belief and practice by German Reform Judaism in the middle of the nineteenth century. In fact, there are statements scattered throughout talmudic literature that would contravene the notion that God literally spoke to Moses. In the Middle Ages, Rabbi Solomon ben Adret (13th century) and the biblical commentator Rabbi Abraham Ibn Ezra (12th century) explicitly deny that God can literally speak, and Ibn Ezra also expresses reservations about the Mosaic unity of the Pentateuch (e.g., in his comment on Genesis 12:6). The foremost medieval opponent of anthropomorphism was Maimonides, and, not unexpectedly, he too struggles with the literalness of the biblical account of revelation, even though he insists on the absolute authority of Torah as revealed.

In our day, this literalist understanding of revelation provides the theological foundation for Jewish traditionalism as embodied in the various wings of the Orthodox movement. It has been articulated in a vigorous and unapologetic way by Rabbi Norman Lamm, currently President of Yeshiva University. In a symposium on Jewish belief that was originally published in *Commentary* in 1966, Lamm insists that the Torah was revealed "in discrete words and letters." He dismisses the attack on the dogma of Mosaic composition raised by contemporary biblical criticism. An omnipotent God, Lamm claims, can certainly communicate His will to human beings in an unambiguous way if He chooses to do so. To deny this is "to impose upon Him a limitation of dumbness that would insult the least of His creatures."

Lamm is equally clear about the implications of his position: The entire Torah is binding on the Jew in all of its detail. It can not be subject to external criteria of contemporary relevance, intelligibility, or meaningfulness. Even those commandments that seem to be most understandable—for example, the prohibitions against theft, homicide, or adultery—must be accepted not because of their apparent rationality but simply out of obedience to God. In fact, it is the most arbitrary of the commandments—the dietary laws, for example, or the biblical prohibition against wearing cloth made of a mixture of linen and wool—that offer us the highest opportunity to serve God, precisely because they can not be performed for any humanistic reason. Finally, Lamm would be extremely reluctant to introduce changes in Jewish practice apart from those that have a clear precedent in past formulations of Jewish law.

The traditionalist position has the advantage of being clear and consistent throughout. It solidifies the tight authority of Torah over the life of the Jew. Torah is authoritative because it is the explicit word of God; nothing could be more authoritative. Any accommodation that has to be made between Torah and modern culture must come from the culture, never from Torah, for Torah is absolute. The Jew has only one decision to make: accept the Torah as God's will or reject it. On matters of belief and practice, its answers are clear cut and final.

But the position also raises significant questions, particularly in regard to its two central dogmas. First, the dogma of Mosaic composition flows less out of any biblical reference than out of the need to establish the absolute authority of Torah. The impulse behind it is more theological than historical or textual. There are only four references in the Pentateuch to Moses' writing anything: Exodus 24:4 (which probably refers to the law code in Exodus 20–23); Exodus 34:28 (which refers to the Ten Commandments); Deuteronomy 31:9 (which refers to the Book of Deuteronomy, or more likely, to parts of it); and Deuteronomy 31:22 (which clearly refers to the song in Deuteronomy 32). If we confine ourselves to the text itself, most of the writing of the Pentateuch remains unaccounted for.

To many of us, a far more serious challenge to the dogma comes from the findings of biblical criticism, the relatively recent attempt to apply historical and scientific methods to the study of the Bible. The earliest Bible critics were Christians (though Baruch Spinoza was one notable exception), and they may well have been motivated by an anti-Jewish animus. But within the past century, the discipline has moved into the broader field of humanistic studies, and many Jews—believing and practicing Jews among them—have joined the enterprise.

Traditionalist thinkers claim that the findings of biblical criticism are still in dispute. But they are mistaken. There is, in fact, widespread agreement on at least three broad conclusions that are fatal to the dogma of Mosaic composition.

The first is that the Pentateuch is a composite of a number of documents, each of which circulated independently, first orally and later in writing. The text of the Pentateuch as we know it today was spliced together out of these previously existing documents and canonized (i.e., accepted as Torah) well after Moses' death, in the time of Ezra (5th century B.C.E.). Second, many of the traditions in the Bible, including its narratives, laws, and even some of the most basic institutions of biblical religion such as the *brit* (covenant) are paralleled in the literature of the other ancient Near Eastern cultures that flourished prior to and contemporaneously with biblical Israel. These traditions may well have been revised in the process of Israelite appropriation, but the traces of their origin are beyond dispute. Finally, despite the care with which the text of the Bible was transmitted, numerous errors invariably crept in. Modern Bible scholars can discern these errors, emend them, and make the text yield a much more coherent meaning than ever before.

These conclusions also impinge on the dogma of verbal revelation. It is simply far-fetched to assume that God would use the common core of ancient Near Eastern materials in His verbal revelation to Israel—often quoting these texts verbatim! But as we have seen in the opening pages of this chapter, far more troublesome are the purely theological problems raised by the notion that God literally speaks at all. To many of us, this dogma reflects a crude anthropomorphic understanding of God. We deny it in order to preserve God's transcendence.

Some thinkers of the traditionalist school have been sensitive to this charge of anthropomorphism and have softened their version of this approach to revelation. In place of the dogma of verbal revelation, they propose the dogma of propositional revelation. In this view, God's communication with Israel was not through words but rather through ideas alone. What the Torah records, then, is not divine words but a divine content recorded in human words. In the final analysis, however, even in this view, the teachings of Torah correspond precisely with God's will for the community—as they do for those who accept verbal revelation. The second version of the traditionalist option may avoid the theological problems of the first, but it remains vulnerable to most of the others. Both versions minimize the human contribution to the shaping of the content of Torah and assign the overwhelmingly dominant and initiatory role to God. The alternative positions disagree. There is no reconciliation between these two stances. The individual must simply choose.

The choice is not simply a matter of theology. In most instances it will more probably be dictated by other considerations. Are we more comfortable with an authoritarian approach to Jewish belief and practice, or do we prefer a more flexible, pluralistic, even humanistic approach? Or, we may invoke more pragmatic considerations. Do we want more freedom in adapting Judaism to ever-changing conditions, or should we be more staunchly conservative and unyielding? How much do we want to accommodate Torah to the conditions of modernity? And what does the history of Jewish thought and law tell us about the historical authenticity of one or the other of the positions?

Considerations of this kind invariably impinge on the purely theological issue at stake here. But for those of us who can not dismiss theology out of hand, there are a number of other theological options.

The Naturalist Alternative: Mordecai Kaplan on Revelation

Norman Lamm's view of revelation reflects the supernaturalism of his entire theology. God is "super" nature, "beyond" the natural order. Since he is the source of Torah, its authority also lies beyond any natural (including human) foundation. Everything else in Lamm's position flows from this basic assumption.

The polar opposite to Lamm's supernaturalism is Mordecai

Kaplan's theological naturalism. We identify Kaplan (1881–1983) as a "naturalist," first, because he believes that there is no reality beyond nature. Nature—understood as not simply flowers and trees but as the order of all that exists—is simply all there is. But he is a religious naturalist because he views human nature as endowed with an innate religious impulse. Religion flows in a thoroughly natural way out of the everyday, intuitive activities of human beings and their communities, not out of the intervention of any Being from beyond. Human beings are religious, or function religiously, simply because they are human beings.

In Kaplan's view, the natural human impulse toward religion manifests itself less through the individual than through human communities. We are all intuitively social creatures, seeking bonds with other human beings. We group ourselves into extended families that gradually become nations or peoples. In Kaplan's chronology, then, there was first and foremost a Jewish people, and this people then created its own religion.

To say that religion is a creation of human beings and their communities in no way implies that religion is a fiction. Kaplan views all of this natural activity as informed by the work of God—not Lamm's supernatural Being, but a "naturalist" God, a God who functions as a process or power within the natural order. It is this God, functioning within us and throughout all of nature, that constitutes our religious impulse. Finally, our human "discovery" of how to live religiously constitutes God's "revelation" to us.

The term "discovery" conveys an entirely different image than "revelation." The latter term emphasizes God's active role. He "reveals." But human beings "discover." We are now in the active role. Kaplan, in fact, insists that these two activities—God's revelation and human discovery—are identical. What we experience as our discovery is God's revelation, which takes place in and through the human mind. In this scheme, human beings play an infinitely more decisive and aggressive role in shaping the content of revelation than they do in Lamm's traditionalist view.

To Kaplan, the experience of revelation is very much akin to other forms of human creativity. When we experience within ourselves, within our social order, or in humanity at large, a striving for ever-growing levels of perfection, when we devise means to reach these levels, and when we are personally impelled to put these means into effect, we have experienced revelation. Kaplan's comprehensive term for all of this activity is "salvation," what the Bible and our liturgy refer to as *geulah*. Salvation denotes the actualization of all of our values and the elimination of all evils that come in the way of personal and social fulfillment. Revelation is the process through which we discover how this state is to be brought about. And God is that process within the natural order—and within us (for we are part of the natural order)—that brings these visions to our consciousness and impels us to achieve them. Hence Kaplan's definition of God as "the process (or power) that makes for salvation."

Kaplan believed passionately in his naturalist God. That such a God is real, present, and revealed within him was beyond doubt. His act of faith is that this God is also revealed in the world at large. Since we are within the natural order, whatever is present within us is also present in the world beyond us. This God is not a being, not an entity of any kind—certainly not a "personal" God as a traditionalist would understand it. Kaplan argues that just because the word "god" is a substantive in English syntax, we are tempted to view it as referring to an object or entity, just as the words "watch" or "blood cell" refer to objects or entities. But there are syntactic substantives that refer not to objects but to processes or activities. Take the word "mind." "Brain" refers to an entity, but "mind" refers to a form of human activity. It is really an adverb parading as a substantive. When we deliberate, make intelligent choices, or act intentionally, we are exhibiting (or "revealing") that we "have" a mind, or, more accurately, that we are behaving "mindfully." "God" is the same kind of word; it too describes a certain kind of activity, Kaplan's "salvational" activity. When nature exhibits or reveals salvational behavior, it is behaving in a "God-ly" way, or revealing God within itself. Understood this way, God very much "exists" and is encountered daily by the believer.

Kaplan's religious naturalism was the end result of a number of currents of thought that influenced his thinking in the early decades of this century. His early exposure to biblical criticism led him to rethink the notion of revelation as the explicit "word" of God. He was one of the first Jewish thinkers to master the emerging social sciences, particularly the work of Emil Durkheim and William James, who studied the way in which psychological, sociological, and anthropological considerations inform the development of religion in human communities. His philosophical idiom was strongly influenced by John Dewey's philosophical naturalism, functionalism, and humanism. Throughout, he was driven by the need to make Judaism intellectually respectable for the growing population of young Jews who were being exposed to modern science and philosophy and who, Kaplan felt, would be repelled—as he himself was—by the primitiveness of Jewish theological speculation at the turn of the century. Of course, all of these theoretical considerations both implied, and in turn were demanded by, Kaplan's programmatic concern: his sense that Jewish belief and practice had to be radically changed if it were to be in any way acceptable in a twentieth-century, democratic, American setting.

Religious naturalism has its own inevitable limitations. If revelation and Torah are processes and outcomes of natural human activity, what makes them unique and authoritative? Kaplan includes artistic creativity, scientific research, the striving for peace, the moral impulse, the search for truth and knowledge—all within the realm of revelation, for they are all forms of salvational activity. This makes revelation easily accessible to our human intellect, a natural and familiar human experience. But it also deprives Torah of the unique hold it has on our lives. Whatever problems we may have with Lamm's theological supernaturalism, it readily accounts for the *sui generis* quality of Torah—for the fact that Jews have transformed their lives and have even been prepared to die for it. Is this kind of devotion possible under Kaplan's scheme?

Kaplan is very much aware of these problems. He argues, first, that Torah is unique because it is ours. It is Israel's characteristic and cumulative vision of what a person and the social order can become. True, other communities cherish their own visions as equally divine, even though none has any greater supernatural sanction than any other—as no one community is more or less "chosen" than any other—but every community will cherish its own wisdom as unique and will cling to it as its *raison d'etre.*

Second, Torah differs from other forms of human creativity because it deals with the ultimate questions of human existence: Where do I come from? Why am I here? What meaning does my life experience have? How should I live? Why do I suffer? How do I deal with my guilt? What happens after I die? What makes it distinctive, then, is not its origins but its intrinsic content and its comprehensiveness. Its vision is global, unifying nature and history, and touching every area of individual and communal life, informing the entire pattern with its salvational vision.

Yet the locus of the authority of the Torah has shifted radically, from the supernatural God to the human community, for it is out of Israel's collective life that Torah emerged. Moreover, Israel's original conception of Torah can be recast as Israel's salvational vision is refined. Hence, Jewish belief and practice change as the community changes. What identifies these ever-new formulations as Jewish is simply the fact that they emerge out of the collective life of the Jewish community. Judaism, then, is whatever the Jewish community says it is. Of course, the continuities are genuine and at least as powerful as the changes, but the authority to determine when and what to change lies within the community of people who call themselves Jews.

It is this theoretical framework that gives Kaplan the right to "reconstruct" Judaism for our day: Hence the name Reconstructionism for the movement inspired by Kaplan's teachings. The Jew who wants to enjoy that right will identify with Kaplan's position at the inevitable price of weakening the distinctive power of religious tradition. For one must ask: Who represents the community that makes these changes? Where do our reinterpretations stop? And if, theoretically, anything can qualify as "Judaism," how seriously can we take Torah and its hold on our lives? Kaplanians and their opponents have been arguing these issues for decades.

A Middle Ground: Rosenzweig and Heschel

Many contemporary Jewish thinkers remain dissatisfied with these two polar positions on revelation. It is possible, they insist, to deny the two dogmas of a supernaturalist view of revelation—verbal or propositional revelation and the Mosaic composition of the Pentateuch—and yet understand revelation as a unique experience that confers distinctive authority to Torah.

Middle-of-the-road positions are always more elusive than polar positions, and this one is no exception. Its characteristic thrust is to insist that both God and the Jewish community are equally involved in the formulation of what was revealed. Since it does recognize that the Jewish community is an active participant in the revelatory experience, it also legitimatizes the ongoing role of the community in shaping Jewish belief and practice. This view, then, is less authoritarian than the traditionalist view, more pluralistic, more conscious of the influence of history—hence its popularity in non–Orthodox circles. But it tends to take a more conservative view of how and when change in belief and practice takes place than Kaplan does, and it is also much more aware of the distinctive hold of religion in human experience. This approach also avoids blurring the secular-religious border in a way that Kaplan can not.

In our century, this middle-of-the-road position has been formulated in a variety of ways, but most of these are variations of two major statements articulated by two of our century's most influential Jewish thinkers, the German Franz Rosenzweig (1886–1929) and the Polish-born, later American Abraham Joshua Heschel (1907–1972).

Rosenzweig's existential theology was worked out in close collaboration with his friend and colleague Martin Buber (1878–1965) in the first decades of this century. Buber went on to become one of this century's most influential thinkers, but (for reasons that will become clear as we proceed), Rosenzweig had a much greater impact on Jewish thought. On revelation itself—though not on the further implications of the position—they are largely in agreement.

In fact, we can take the title of Buber's masterpiece *I and Thou* as the key to their understanding of revelation. Revelation is precisely the creation of an I-Thou relationship between the very personal God of the Bible and the biblical community, and later with any human being. The model is an intense, interpersonal relationship in which two people "reveal" primarily themselves to each other. This self-revelation creates the relationship and through the relationship each partner acquires a full-fledged identity. The relationship is mutual with each partner affecting the other. It is charged with meaning and emotion, transitory yet renewable. Finally, what is *not* revealed—neither at Sinai nor in any authentic I-Thou relationship—is any form of behavioral code, neither in the form of a book, nor in any specific content-filled document.

For Rosenzweig, the content of revelation is simply the fact of revelation, God's entering into a unique relationship with Israel. According to Rosenzweig, the biblical passage immediately preceding the giving of the Ten Commandments in Exodus 19 and 20, "He [God] came down [on Sinai]" (19:20) already concludes the revelation; the passage "God spoke . . ." (20:1) is the beginning of interpretation, and the verse beginning "I am . . ." (20:2) is totally interpretive. Torah, Rosenzweig explains, is Israel's classic *response* to the revelatory encounter, spelling out how Israel understood its relationship with God and how it determined to live in the light of its unique status.

Where Buber and Rosenzweig part company is over the relation between revelation and Jewish law. They agree that law is not part of the content of revelation—revelation is never legislation—but Rosenzweig insists that the sense of "being commanded" is. God may not *legislate,* but God *commands.* The difference between law and command is that a law is impersonal and universal, while a command is personal and subjective. Laws are written in books; commands are experienced.

In this sense, every relationship has a commanding quality to it. Every relationship compels the participants to behave in a way that is appropriate to the relationship. God's love for Israel is all that is needed to inspire Israel to live in a certain way. *Contra* the traditionalists, then, what was revealed was not the specific commandments but the fact of being commanded. But *contra* Kaplan, God is very much the authority—however implicit—for the commandments, just as a lover's expressions of affection are governed by the presence and implicit wishes of the beloved.

Abraham Joshua Heschel's version of this middle option moves in a different direction. Heschel too accepts the personal, transcendent God of the Bible. But, because of his roots in eastern European mysticism and Hasidism, he insists that God is totally beyond human conceptualization. We can never "know" God or use human concepts and language to describe him objectively and adequately. The most we can have are intimations of His presence, an awareness of His reality. What kind of a God would He be if we could understand Him?

The cardinal theological sin for Heschel, then, is literal-mindedness, the presumption that our theological concepts are literally true or objectively adequate. Thus Heschel's striking claim about revelation: "As a report about revelation, the Bible itself is a *midrash*." We understand *midrash* as a later interpretation of a biblical text. But according to Heschel, even the Bible itself is a human interpretation of some prior, or more primal revelatory content that is beyond human comprehension.

Heschel teaches that two events occurred at Sinai: God's giving of the Torah and Israel's receiving of the Torah. Both parties were active in the encounter, and what emerged is colored by both its divine origin and its human appropriation. To use another of Heschel's formulations, Judaism reflects "a minimum of revelation and a maximum of interpretation." Accordingly, "the source of authority is not the word as given in the text but Israel's understanding of the text." Yet, as we shall see, Heschel takes the Jewish legal system that emerges out of this revelation very seriously indeed.

Rosenzweig and Heschel clearly reject the two polar understandings of revelation as articulated by the traditionalists on one hand and the naturalists on the other. Yet they disagree in their understanding of *what* was revealed. For Rosenzweig, what was revealed was simply God's presence in intimate, commanding (though not legislating) relationship with Israel. For Heschel, it was the Torah as representing God's will for Israel, though what we have is not that Torah in its purity but rather, our ancestors' and our own understanding of its contents. Both maintain the unique authority of Torah, not as the explicit word of God but as a response to (Rosenzweig) or expression of (Heschel) His concern for Israel and humanity.

Both statements also avoid some of the more troublesome theological problems of Lamm's supernaturalism and Kaplan's naturalism. Both allow for the findings of biblical criticism. For both, pluralism, historical development, and ambiguity are inevitable. Judaism no longer speaks in clear-cut, authoritarian terms. That is why both positions will be rejected by the modern traditionalist and welcomed by other Jews who prize the individualism and freedom that Rosenzweig and, to a lesser extent, Heschel recognize. Of course, with freedom and individualism comes responsibility—and not a little anxiety.

The Jewish Myth

We have come full circle. We opened our discussion of revelation by noting that our three subissues—the principle, the fact, and the content—of revelation were inextricably intertwined, that the way we dealt with any of the three issues would inevitably predetermine how we would deal with the other two. Our review of the various attempts to define the content of revelation indicates that at least for three of our thinkers—Kaplan, Rosenzweig, and Heschel—the only way of approaching all of these questions is to reject the literalness of the biblical account of revelation and to posit that no human characterization of God and His activity can be understood as objectively true. Rather, all such characterizations have to be understood as metaphorical attempts to capture what is inherently beyond the range of human experience.

The primary metaphor, the metaphor on which the status of Torah rests, is the claim that God "spoke" to Moses and the children of Israel at Sinai. Acknowledge the metaphorical nature of that claim and you redefine Torah as to some extent the creation of a human community. That is precisely what Kaplan, Rosenzweig, and Heschel have done, each in his distinctive way. Each, then, has to struggle with redefining the uniqueness and authoritative character of Torah. But we should never minimize the gravity of the step that these thinkers have taken. The gap between these three positions and the traditionalist position is genuine and irreparable.

Yet a third version of the middle position—the position that strives to balance the complementary contributions of God and the human community in shaping the content of revelation— stems from the contemporary preoccupation with the status of theological language and conceptualization. The seminal statement of this position is in the writings of the preeminent Protestant philosopher/theologian of this century, Paul Tillich (1886–1965) who proposes that all religious language has to be understood as "symbolic" and "mythical." In popular parlance, a "myth" is understood to be either a fiction (the "myth" of the invincibility of the New York Yankees) or a legendary tale (the "myth" of Oedipus). But scholars in the social sciences and in religion use the term in a different, more technical way.

A myth should be understood as a structure through which a community organizes and makes sense of its experience. The world "out there" does not impinge itself on us in a totally objective way, tidily packaged and organized into meaningful patterns. Our experience of the world is a complex transaction between what comes to us from "out there" and the way we structure or "read" it. Myths are the spectacles that enable us to see order in what would otherwise be confusion. They are created, initially, by "reading" communities, beginning with their earliest attempts to shape, explain, or make some sense out of their experience of nature and history. Gradually, as the mythic structure seems to work, to be confirmed by ongoing experience, it is refined, shared, and transmitted to later generations. It becomes embodied in official, "canonical" texts and assumes authoritative power. In its final form, it becomes omnipresent and quasi-invisible, so much has it become our intuitive way of confronting the world.

Take, for example, the myth of the human psyche that is at the heart of Freudian psychoanalytic theory. Before Freud, students of human functioning were confronted by a confusing array of behaviors without any clear idea of how they were connected, what patterns they assumed, what meaning they had, which were pathological and which normal, and why people behaved the way they did. Scientists of human behavior didn't even know what to look for, which data were worth noting and which were irrelevant, or what constituted the "facts" that needed interpretation.

Freud's contribution was to organize this data into patterns. He identified what constituted the significant facts. He showed how these various behaviors assumed certain predictable forms. Finally, through his picture of the human psyche with its id, ego, and superego, its conscious, preconscious, and subconscious, its oedipal drive, and the rest, he proceeded to explain how and why people behave the way they do. To this day, even with all of its revisions, we invariably use the Freudian myth as a set of spectacles that enables us to "read" and understand human behavior.

Leaving aside, for a moment, the differences between the ways myths function in science and in religion, the Freudian example is instructive. A myth orders experience, explains how it reveals specific shapes, forms, and meaningful patterns. In general it explains overt experience by constructing an invisible or covert world that lies behind ordinary experience and is not itself directly accessible—that's why the myth often appears to be subjective or fictional. Is there really such a thing as an id or an ego? Is the subconscious a real dimension of the psyche? In short, did Freud invent these entities or did he discover them?

In fact, he did both. He was able to see certain patterns in human behavior because they were there in the first place, along with many other apparent patterns and much that didn't fit into any clear-cut scheme. But his creative, inventive, or imaginative contribution was to select and identify those patterns that were significant, and show how they cohered with each other to form a meaning-laden whole.

The more global the myth—the more it tries to explain—the

more inventive and imaginative it seems, and hence the more fictional it appears to be. But though a myth has an inherently subjective quality—for it can never be directly compared to the reality it represents, and objectively confirmed to be true or false—it is far from a deliberate fiction. We may never be able to stand outside of the myth to measure its correspondence with reality, for we can never have a totally a-mythical perception of that reality. The issue is never myth or no myth but which myth, for without a myth our experience would be literally meaningless. But every myth is dictated by experience, however much it shapes that experience in the very process of being constructed.

Myths are intrinsic to communities. In fact, myths create communities. When they assume narrative form, they recount the community's "master story," explaining how that community came into being, what distinguishes it from other communities, how it understands its distinctive history and destiny, what constitutes its unique value system. A myth provides a community with its distinctive *raison d'etre*.

Religious myths do all of this for a religious community. They also convey the community's distinctive answers to ultimate human questions: Why am I here? What is the meaning or purpose of my existence? How do I handle guilt, suffering, sexuality, interpersonal relations? What happens when I die? Myths promote loyalty to the community, motivate behavior, generate a sense of belonging and kinship. Because they emerge from and speak to the most primitive layers of our being, they are capable of moving or touching us in the most profound way. People die for their myths, so coercive is their hold.

Religious myths are canonized in Scripture, in the sacred books that record the authoritative version of the communal myth and become the text for communicating it to succeeding generations. They inspire liturgies, poetic recitations of portions of the myth, to celebrate significant events in the life of the community and its members. They also generate rituals, dramatic renderings of the myth, this time in the language of the body. Frequently, liturgy and ritual merge to create elaborate religious pageants which bring the myth into consciousness and give it a concrete reality in the life experience of the community. The Passover *seder* and the Jewish rites of passage are superb examples of such pageants.

If myths are subjective, impressionistic human constructs, in what sense are they "true"? Why should one be preferred to another? There is no simple answer to these questions. Myths are clearly not objectively true in the sense that they correspond to some reality out there. We simply do not have an independent picture of that reality against which we can measure the myth, for we literally can not see the world except through the spectacles of our myth.

But myths are also not capricious inventions. They emerge originally out of our experience of natural and historical patterns. They may select, identify, and organize these specific patterns, but they can do all of this because the patterns are there to be seen, selected, and organized in the first place. They can then be seen to be be roughly consistent with our experience of the world. To use our earlier language, we are able to falsify some mythic claims. For example, many of us would not want to account for the death of six million Jews in the Nazi Holocaust by invoking the traditional mythic explanation of suffering as God's punishment for sin. That explanation has been falsified for us; it does not cohere with our experience. It does not provide an adequate explanation. We may not be able to produce a better explanation, but we know this one can not be true.

It is one thing to falsify a myth but quite another to verify or confirm one. Though no single mythic claim may capture reality in a totally accurate way for everyone, some claims may be more or less accurate than others. Again an example. There is a clear difference between the Jewish and Christian explanations of why people behave in evil ways. The dominant Christian image is of the human being as forever tainted by the "original sin" that stems from Adam and Eve's rebellion in Eden and is transmitted throughout the generations by procreation. Judaism, in contrast, sees the human being as the arena of a conflict between two warring impulses, one good and the other evil, with the individual free and responsible for determining which dominates. This is an admittedly crude presentation of a complex issue, but it shows how two communities produce two different mythic explanations for a complex pattern of human behavior. Judaism's consistent rejection of the doctrine of original sin reflects this community's continuing intuition that its own explanation is closer to the real state of affairs.

Beyond this, myths can be subject to a pragmatic test that determines whether they work, whether they do what they are supposed to do: explain, motivate, generate loyalty, create identity, and so forth. The pragmatic test is frequently invoked by scientific myths. Freud's psychoanalytic theory, for example, will be judged "true" to the extent that it works to predict human behavior and cure pathology. It will be replaced if and when another equally mythic theory does all of this more effectively.

Finally, myths can be verified existentially. Existential truth is ineluctably personal and subjective. The more a mythic claim touches upon my personal, concrete existence, the less it can be "true in general," "true for everyone," "objectively true"—and the more it has to be "true for me" or "true for us." Mathematical truth, within a specific set of axioms, is objective; it is "true for everyone." But the further we move toward the issues that impinge deeply upon our humanness, the more our truths become personal and subjective. In effect, we make these existential claims true by living them, by committing ourselves to them, and by risking our lives for them.

Revelation in the Torah Myth

Freud's efforts were directed to understanding one small corner of our experience of the world, human behavior. In the course of its earliest experience as a people, the biblical community tried to do much more: understand the world in its entirety and its own place in that world. The classic Torah myth, embodied in Scripture and celebrated in liturgy and ritual, is the result of that inquiry. The only way our ancestors could make sense of their experience of the world was by invoking a supernatural, personal God who created the natural order, entered into a uniquely intimate relationship with a man, his family, and ultimately his progeny. He delivered this people from slavery, entered into a covenant with them whereby they pledged to constitute themselves into a holy people devoted exclusively to Him and His revealed will, punished them for their disobedience, rewarded them for their loyalty, guided them through the desert to their promised homeland, exiled them, and subsequently returned them there again. It is nothing less than astonishing that this classic mythic structure, elaborated and refined throughout the generations—notably by the addition of a vision of the end of days as the ultimate fulfillment of this community's hopes for itself and for mankind—remains in place to this day.

Is this structure objectively true? There is no way of establishing that. We can not prove, objectively, that God did or did not take our ancestors out of Egypt, destroy Jerusalem, save the Maccabean army, or, for that matter, guide the reestablishment of the modern State of Israel in 1948. But there is no denying that in large measure, the myth has withstood the attempts to falsify it. Nor is there any doubt that it has passed both the pragmatic and existential tests of truth for close to three thousand years.

As for revelation, if we are serious in affirming that no myth is a fiction, then we have in the same breath affirmed both the principle and the fact of revelation. Since there is an objective dimension to the myth, since the patterns are discovered, not invented, however much they may be shaped or "read" by the community, that objective dimension is what we call "revelation." In fact, the very use of that term is the best indication that the myth is at work.

The thesis that Torah contains the classic Jewish mythic explanation of one community's experience of the world, is clearly still a third version of what we have called the middle option on revelation. It most closely resembles Heschel's position that Torah is a *midrash,* but it uses a different idiom. A *midrash* is usually understood to be a reading of a text, but in an extended sense, it can also be taken as a reading of the world, of human experience. In this extended sense, myth and *midrash* share many characteristics. Both are culturally conditioned, human renderings of realities that lie beyond direct human apprehension. Both exhibit startling continuities and equally surprising discontinuities as they move through history. As long as the community that shapes them remains vital, it will determine what it wishes to keep and what it prefers to discard and reshape in the light of its ongoing experience.

Five Options: How Do We Choose?

Decisions between theological options should never be made on the basis of one issue alone, even as central an issue as revelation. It may yet be helpful, in a preliminary way, to suggest how various criteria figure in reaching such decisions.

In the course of this chapter, we have appealed to four such criteria: theological coherence, historical authenticity, programmatic implications, and psychological adequacy. First, is the position theologically coherent on its own terms? Second, does it have an authentically Jewish ring? Third, what are its implications for the decisions that face the Jewish community today? Finally, does the position meet the psychological needs of the individual believer?

It should not be disturbing that theological decisions are rarely made on the basis of internal theological criteria alone. The expectation that they should is neither realistic nor reflective of how human beings operate. The middle two criteria are invoked because we want our theology to resonate Jewishly because our context remains Judaism, and because theology is not an intellectual game. Its purpose is to make it possible for Jews to belong to the community and to function Jewishly.

Finally, since everything we do is informed by our individual psychic constitutions, we will naturally gravitate to religious positions that best meet our psychological needs. A person who looks to religion as a source of authority, who wants final and absolute answers to issues of belief and practice, who is impatient with pluralistic or indecisive answers to ultimate questions, will embrace the traditionalist position and view Torah as literally and verbally revealed. In contrast, someone who is prepared to live with ambiguity and indecision, who accepts the inevitability of different points of view on complex moral, theological, and spiritual issues, and who is prepared to become engaged in the issues and evolve a position that is personally adequate, however much it may differ from that of the religious establishment, will embrace one of the other options.

How any one of these options fares in regard to the four criteria remains a highly individual judgment. This author finds both the traditionalist option and Mordecai Kaplan's position problematic both on theological and programmatic grounds—though clearly for very different reasons. The middle position, though far from unassailable, remains the most satisfying of the group. It is this position, particularly in its third version, that will inform the remainder of this volume.

Religion is an extraordinarily complex affair. It is an organic unity of historical memories, theological doctrines, behavioral patterns, communal bonds, myths, rituals, and liturgies, all of which touch various levels of our being: intellectual, emotional, aesthetic, and psychological. What distinguishes the "insider" from the "outsider" is that for the former, the whole coheres in an ultimately satisfying way. Any one of us may feel vaguely dissatisfied with any of these dimensions; we may, for example, find some of the liturgy anachronistic, some rituals meaningless, or the approach to suffering thoroughly inadequate. Sometimes many small dissatisfactions will accumulate and outweigh the positives. But most of the major religions are rich and variegated enough—and/or have evolved procedures for discarding and replacing the outworn and the unsatisfactory—that as a whole, the tradition still works for many, though clearly not for all, in the community.

The process is messy and hardly quick and easy. One person may want intellectual sophistication, another, explicit guidance in ethical decision making. A third may seek emotionally and aesthetically pleasing worship experiences, a fourth, psychological support in traumatic life situations. How all of this works itself out in the life experience of any one individual is subtle and complex. But this is probably an accurate picture of how most of us do, in fact, reach decisions of this kind.

One final note. The decision can not be made from the outside. Religious commitments are probably the most existential issues we face. We have to be prepared to jump in and live within a tradition before we can appreciate its strengths and weaknesses. The convinced skeptic may be unwilling to take this initial step but this is a failure of will, and it is not our failure. Our responsibility is to address those who feel the urgency of the issues and are willing to struggle to find the answers.

FOR FURTHER STUDY

The bibliographies that follow each chapter of this volume make no claim to being complete or exhaustive. They represent a highly personal selection of books and articles that this author has found helpful in years of studying and teaching this material. They include what would typically be listed in footnote form, and can be viewed as supporting and expanding the discussion in the chapters that precede them.

NOTE: *Publisher and date of publication are listed after the first citation of the volume. Later citations refer you back to the listing in which the volume originally appears. "pb" indicates paper back edition.*

Except where noted, all translations of biblical passages are those of TANAKH *(The Jewish Publication Society, 1985).*

First and foremost, we are blessed with two encyclopedias that belong in the home of any serious student of Judaism. THE JEWISH ENCYCLOPEDIA *(12 volumes, Funk and Wagnalls, 1901) is, in some areas, out of date, but it contains the collective wisdom of the greatest minds in Jewish scholarship at the beginning of the century, and many of its entries continue to be classical summaries of the available scholarship. It is, of course, out of print, but it can frequently be found in used bookstores. If you find it, grab it.*

The ENCYCLOPEDIA JUDAICA *(16 volumes, Keter, 1972) is much more up to date and is simply indispensable, particularly for its entries on twentieth-century issues in Jewish life (e.g., the Holocaust, the State of Israel), and also for the conclusions of the best of current Jewish scholarship.*

Encyclopedias are, by their very nature, uneven in quality. But there is sufficient high-quality material in both of these collections to justify their place in your home library. We will make no further reference to them, but you should assume that the appropriate entries in both works should be consulted almost automatically.

Equally indispensable for any form of Jewish study are the Hebrew Scriptures and a SIDDUR SHALEM, or complete (i.e., daily, Sabbath, and Festival) prayerbook. For the first, there is no substitute for the one-volume TANAKH (Jewish Publication Society, 1985). The translation reflects the best of contemporary Bible scholarship while remaining both authentically Jewish and properly reverential. For the second, THE AUTHORIZED DAILY PRAYER BOOK, Hebrew text, English translation with Commentary and Notes by Dr. Joseph H. Hertz (Bloch, 1948), is bulky and its translation is antiquated. But it is all-inclusive, it includes all biblical references, and its commentary is frequently helpful.

The claim that our theories of revelation are extensions of our concepts of God is the central thrust of Abraham Joshua Heschel's THE PROPHETS (Jewish Publication Society, 1962; pb Harper Torchbooks, Vol. 1, 1969, Vol. 2, 1971). See in particular, chs. 12–14 (or chs. 1–3 of pb Vol. 2) which deal with Heschel's notion of God's "pathos." These three chapters are required background reading for anyone who wants to understand Heschel's personal theology. The seminal statement on the nonliteral quality of all of our God-talk is Paul Tillich's DYNAMICS OF FAITH (pb Harper Torchbooks, 1957), particularly ch. 3. See further references to the literature on religious myths and symbols after ch. 4 below.

Part 2 of Heschel's GOD IN SEARCH OF MAN (Jewish Publication Society, 1956; pb Harper Torchbooks, 1969) is a systematic inquiry into the biblical claim for the factual nature of revelation. Will Herberg discusses the "scandal of particularity" in Jewish religion in ch. 18 of his JUDAISM AND MODERN MAN (Farrar Straus and Young, 1951; pb Atheneum, 1983).

On the content of revelation, the literalist position is articulated by Norman Lamm in the symposium, THE CONDITION OF JEWISH BELIEF (compiled by the editors of COMMENTARY MAGAZINE, published originally in COMMENTARY, August 1966, Vol. 42, No. 2, and in book form by Macmillan, also in 1966, and republished by Jason Aronson,

1989). The propositional approach to revelation is in the contribution by Emanuel Rackman in the same symposium. The contributions by Eliezer Berkovits, Immanuel Jakobovits, Aharon Lichtenstein, M. D. Tendler, and Walter S. Wurzburger represent variations on one or the other of these positions. Samson Raphael Hirsch's seminal statement of the traditionalist position is in his "Religion Allied to Progress," reprinted in THE JEW IN THE MODERN WORLD, *edited by Paul R. Mendes-Flohr and Jehuda Reinharz (pb Oxford University Press, 1980), pp. 177–181.*

An excellent summary of the most recent conclusions of modern biblical scholarship is in Richard Elliot Friedman's WHO WROTE THE BIBLE? *(Summit Books, 1987).*

The naturalist alternative is represented in the COMMENTARY *symposium by Ira Eisenstein. Mordecai Kaplan's own clearest statement of this position is in Part 2 of* THE FUTURE OF THE AMERICAN JEW *(Macmillan, 1948; pb Reconstructionist Press, 1967).*

Franz Rosenzweig's version of the middle position (and his disagreements with his colleague, Martin Buber) is in the anthology, ON JEWISH LEARNING, *edited by N. N. Glatzer (Schocken, 1955; pb 1987), specifically in Rosenzweig's exchange of letters with Buber, "Revelation and Law: Martin Buber and Franz Rosenzweig." The claim that revelation is not legislation is on pp. 111–115 of that volume. Heschel's position is in Part II of* GOD IN SEARCH OF MAN, *in particular, chs. 19 and 27. Heschel's claim that the Bible is a midrash is on p. 185 of that volume; that Torah constitutes a minimum of revelation and a maximum of interpretation is on p. 274. See also Heschel's summary of some medieval views on God's "speaking," including that of Maimonides, on p. 188. In* THE CONDITION OF JEWISH BELIEF *the contributions by Eugene B. Borowitz, Emil Fackenheim, and Jakob J. Petuchowski echo the Rosenzweigian position; the essay by Seymour Siegel presents the Heschelian position. A systematic study of the philosophical assumptions in Heschel's work on revelation is Lawrence Perlman's* ABRAHAM HESCHEL'S IDEA OF REVELATION *(Scholars Press, 1989).*

On the mythical quality of theological and religious language, see Tillich's DYNAMICS OF FAITH, *cited above, and for a remarkably clear summary of the implications of the position for theology and in compari-*

son with science, see Ian G. Barbour's MYTHS, MODELS AND PARA-
DIGMS, *pb Harper and Row, 1974). My own "The Jewish Philosopher
in Search of a Role" and "Authority and Authenticity in Jewish
Philosophy" (*JUDAISM, *Vol. 34, No. 4, Fall 1985, and Vol. 35, No.
2, Spring 1986), and "Toward a Theology for Conservative Judaism"
(*CONSERVATIVE JUDAISM, *Vol. 37, No. 1, Fall 1983) explore the
implications of this approach for Jewish philosophy and theology.*

*Finally, the distinction between the objective truth of mathematics
and the existential truth of religious claims is elaborated by Franz
Rosenzweig on pp. 205–206 of the anthology,* FRANZ ROSENZWEIG:
HIS LIFE AND THOUGHT, *edited by N. N. Glatzer (Schocken 1953;
pb 1961). See also ch. 5 of Tillich's* DYNAMICS OF FAITH, *and ch. 7
of Barbour's* MYTHS, MODELS AND PARADIGMS.

II

Religious Authority:
Who Commands?

The Issue of Authority

HOW WE UNDERSTAND REVELATION DETERMINES THE NATURE and extent of the authority that the Torah, and particularly its laws, will have in our lives. If we take the traditionalist or Orthodox position that God revealed His will explicitly in words, then the authority of the Torah is strong and tight. If we locate the authority in the Jewish people, then this people can continually refashion Torah as its historical experience changes. If we adopt a middle position on revelation, then the issue of authority is much more complicated.

In Judaism at least, the authority of the Torah affects how we behave much more than what we believe. This is largely because the hallmark of religious authenticity in Judaism has always been adherence to God's law, much more than to a set of beliefs. Judaism has been prepared to tolerate wide variations in the formulation of its belief content, but its behavioral obligations have been analyzed and codified with all of the rigor that characterizes any code of law. Legal codes are omnipresent in the pages of Jewish literature from the Pentateuch through to our own day. The impulse to clarify and codify precisely how God wants the Jews to behave is absolutely intuitive to this religious tradition. Traditionally, the authentic Jew is the Jew who observes God's law.

The issue of religious authority in Judaism, then, comes to a focus in the law. Indeed, the very use of the term "law" says it all. "Law," however, is an all-purpose English term that covers a number of finer distinctions in the original Hebrew. For our purposes, the most authentic Hebrew equivalent would be *mitzvah* (plural *mitzvot*), literally "command" (or "commandment"). The common Hebrew term for the body of *mitzvot* taken as a whole is *halakhah,* from the Hebrew meaning "to walk" or "to go," and thus defined as "the path" or "the way" of Jewish living. The term *aggadah,* etymologically, the "telling," refers to all nonlegal instruction, preeminently in talmudic literature; by extension it can include the later philosophical, mystical, and homiletical literature as well.

A striking—and to the theologian disturbing—illustration of the primacy of *halakhah* over *aggadah* in Judaism lies in the commentary to the very first verse of the Bible by the classic medieval French exegete Rashi (acronym for Rabbi Solomon ben Isaac, 1040–1105). Rashi begins his commentary to the Bible by quoting a rabbinic passage that questions why the Bible opens with the story of Creation instead of with Exodus 12:1, which contains God's first commandment to the biblical community, to prepare the Passover sacrifice prior to the exodus from Egypt. The suggestion is dismissed, but the fact that a *prima facie* case could be made for excluding all nonlegal material from Scripture is dramatic testimony to the centrality of law as the authentic form of Jewish religious expression. Rashi's commentary on the Pentateuch, it should be added, always reflects the normative thrust of classical Jewish thought; here, that there is no authenticity in Judaism outside of the law.

Covenant in History

Why this centrality of required behavior? And why is it expressed in terms of law, *mitzvot* or *halakhah?* These questions can be discussed from two different perspectives, that of history and that of theology. The first deals with the historical and cultural background against which Judaism came to be in the first place; the second, with Judaism's pervasive views of the relationship between God and Israel, or between God and the individual Jew. Both perspectives are indispensable. The historical approach helps us understand how and why our ancestors came to conceptualize who they were and what role they were to play in God's plan for civilization. The theological dimension wrests that conceptualization from its historical roots and addresses the issue of its meaning to us here and now.

First, the perspective of history. When our ancestors tried to understand their distinctive identity and destiny on earth, they referred to an institution called a *"brit,"* or "covenant," which they saw themselves as having entered into with the God of their ancestors, Abraham, Isaac, and Jacob, after their redemption from slavery in Egypt. In fact, this communal *brit* was a reaffirmation of similar earlier covenants that God had made with each of the Patriarchs and, in each case, with their offspring. To be a member of this community, then, was to be a *ben brit,* or participant in the covenanted community. To this day, every Jewish male child is brought into the Jewish community on the eighth day after birth through the ritual of circumcision, which confers upon him the *ot brit,* the "sign" of the covenant.

There is no more central theme in Jewish self-perception than that of covenant. It is the single indispensable key to understanding the way Jewish religion evolved from its earliest beginnings. To use our idiom of the previous chapter, it is the linchpin of the Jewish myth, that structure that Jews use to lend meaning to their experience in the world and to locate their place in the flow of nature and history.

Our understanding of what a covenant meant to our ancestors has been immeasurably heightened by recent archeological discoveries of Hittite diplomatic treaties dating from as early as the twenty-third and twenty-second centuries B.C.E., but mainly from the fifteenth to the thirteenth centuries B.C.E. (The Israelite conquest of Canaan under Joshua is dated in the thirteenth century B.C.E.) These treaties, commonly concluded after a war and dictated by the conquering king, had to adhere to a standard form to be legally binding—much as today, a legally valid will must be phrased in a specific way. Typically, this ancient treaty form included: (1) a preamble that identified the name of the conquering king who dictated the terms of the treaty; (2) a historical prologue that narrated the events leading up to the treaty, mainly the recent war; (3) the stipulations or specific legal agreements, expressed in the form of laws, entered into by both parties, mainly by the now vassal kingdom; (4) provisions for the public deposit and reading of the treaty so that its terms would be known to all; (5) a list of divine witnesses to the treaty to be invoked if it were violated; (6) a list of blessings and curses that would devolve on the vassal kingdom if it fulfilled or violated the terms of the treaty; and (7) a ritual solemnization of the treaty in the form of a sacrifice or ritual meal.

That the Bible should be aware of this ancient institution is not surprising. What is startling is that it should adopt it in order to describe God's unique relationship with Israel. Of course the institution was transformed in the process of being adapted: The covenant was not preceded by a war, and, at least in the Bible, Israel is portrayed as entering willingly into the covenantal relationship. But these differences aside, the parallels are striking. The Hittite vassal treaty became the model for the biblical *brit*.

Look at the account of the Sinai covenant in Exodus 20–24, and at the later accounts of its renewal, first under Joshua at Shechem in Joshua 24, then in the reign of King Josiah in 2 Kings 22–23, and, finally, in the time of Ezra and Nehemiah in Nehemiah 8–10. The covenant is either dictated by God Himself (as in Exodus 20:1) or by a human representative who speaks in God's name (as in Joshua 24:2, 2 Kings 23:2, and Nehemiah 8:1). Each account is preceded by a historical prologue, either the Exodus alone (Exodus 20:2) or the more extended history of Israel (Joshua 24:2–13), or else of the world as a whole (Nehemiah 9:6–37). Each is accompanied by a set of stipulations, either in the form of an explicit code (the Ten Commandments in Exodus 20:2–14 and Exodus 21–23, commonly called the Covenant Code) or in more summary form (Joshua 24:25 and 2 Kings 23:3). The text of the covenantal treaty is read in a public forum (Exodus 24:3, 2 Kings 23:2, Nehemiah 8:3). The tablets of the covenant are deposited in the ark (Exodus 25:16) and the book of the covenant is placed next to the ark (Deuteronomy 31:26). The Bible could not appeal to other gods to serve as witnesses, but Deuteronomy 31:28 appeals to heaven and earth, and Deuteronomy 27:15–28:6 preserves a formula of blessings and curses. Exodus 24:7, Joshua 24:24, 2 Kings 23:3, and Nehemiah 10:30 record an oathlike formula by which the community binds itself to the covenant. Finally, Exodus 24:4–18 describes a ritual solemnization of the Sinai covenant in a particularly gripping way. The parallels with the ancient structure are undeniable.

This comparison illuminates much of the later structure of Jewish religion as it evolved out of the Bible. It explains, for example, why at crucial moments of the life cycle and the liturgical year we are asked to recite the history of our people, and, on Passover, to renew our membership in the community by reenacting the founding events of our community. It clarifies why the Jewish people has understood itself as standing in a unique relationship with God. It helps understand why the public reading of the Torah and the study of Torah occupy so central a role in the service of worship. Finally, it illuminates the Jewish sense of being irretrievably bound to a specific destiny.

Most significantly, for our purposes here, the comparison of the Sinai covenant and the Hittite treaties explains why, from the very outset, Jewish religion found its intuitive form of expression in the system of *mitzvot*. The *mitzvot* are the stipulations of the Hittite treaty translated into the language and conceptual scheme of biblical monotheism. They lend concreteness to the sense of being covenanted. To be a Jew is to be within the covenant, and that means to obey the stipulations of the covenantal treaty. Because the covenant is a juridical institution, its stipulations are expressed in the form of law.

The nexus between covenant and law is also reflected in the pre-Sinai covenants recorded in the Bible. The Bible records two versions of God's covenant with Abraham (Genesis 15 and 17). Neither of these is accompanied by a formal code of law, but in the second, Abraham is commanded to "walk in My ways and be blameless" (17:1). As a result, when God is about to destroy Sodom and Gomorrah, He feels compelled to inform Abraham of what He is about to do because "I have singled him out ("elected" him), that he may instruct his children and his posterity to keep the way of the Lord (as in 17:1 above) by doing what is just and right" (18:19). This sets the stage for the remarkable debate that follows (18:23–33) wherein Abraham challenges God: "Shall not the Judge of all the earth deal justly?" Doing what is "just and right," then, can be understood as the stipulation of this covenant. It is the "way" of the Lord and thus binds both Abraham and God. That's why Abraham can force God to account for His behavior toward the inhabitants of Sodom and Gomorrah. The same covenant is later renewed with Isaac (Genesis 26:1–5) and still later with Jacob (28:10–22 and 35:9–13). It is subsequently recalled when God appears before Moses and commands him to lead Israel out of Egypt (Exodus 6:1–8).

The redemption from Egypt is God's fulfillment of the stipulations of His covenant with Abraham. In turn, it becomes the historical prologue for the Sinai covenant. From then on, the Sinai covenant serves to define the mutual obligations of God and Israel. It is the basis not only for the prophetic castigation of the biblical community but also for Israel's challenge to God. From Moses (in Exodus 32:11–13) to Elie Wiesel, God can only be challenged from within the covenant. Abandon the covenant in anger at God's dealings with the Jewish people and you lose your right to challenge God. Thus the fateful paradox of Jewish destiny.

The contemporary traditionalist understands the covenant as a literal description of the God-Israel relationship, initiated by God with the biblical community and binding its descendants for all time. Those of us who do not accept a literalist view of revelation view it as the central symbol in the complex Jewish myth. The parallels with the Hittite treaties illustrate how a community uses institutions from its cultural milieu to understand its historical experience. To call the covenant a symbol in no way lessens its power. As long as we are human beings, we will invariably read our experience in terms of symbols or constructs. To the extent that we feel ourselves bound to the Jewish people in time and in space, to the extent that we feel its destiny to be ours, to the extent that we feel obligated to do whatever it is we do as Jews because of that bond, we are responding to the sense of covenantedness that has been transmitted to us from the past.

If we are to pinpoint the historical basis for whatever authority the classical Jewish reading of the world and human life has on us, it lies precisely in that vision of a people bound in covenant to God. Deuteronomy 29:9–14 reminds us that God's covenant was made not only with those who stood at Sinai but also "with those who are not with us here this day"—that is, with us, the descendants of that original community, to this very day.

Covenant in Theology

But *we* were not really at Sinai, and herein lies the problem of relying exclusively on history. History does illuminate the present. It helps us understand how Judaism came to be what it is, but it can not persuade us that it ought to remain that way today or that its institutions should have any claim on us. The historical approach has to be supplemented by a theological perspective that deals with Judaism's pervasive views of God and humanity, and their interrelationship.

Every tradition begins with a set of axioms or intuitive value claims that are implicit in its classical literature and shape its distinctive content. Typically these claims are never questioned, though their influence is pervasive. Take, for example, the claim that Judaism has no room for the distinction between the realms of the "religious" and the "secular." There is no dimension of life that is even potentially free from God's concern or from religious obligation. Hence the all-encompassing nature of the *mitzvot*. A claim of this kind is simply axiomatic to Judaism; it neither requires, nor can it be given, any justification beyond itself.

Now to pursue the implications of that axiom. If we were to attempt to delineate God's ultimate purpose in revealing the Torah, it would have to be His concern with creating a certain kind of social order on earth. This is Judaism's acclaimed "this worldliness" as opposed to the alleged "other worldliness" of other religions. Granted, the distinction is not absolutely clear-cut—no religion focuses solely on one or the other—but we are dealing with emphases or priorities, and Judaism's emphasis is that religion must transform the world of everyday human activity. We will have a great deal to say about Judaism's view of the afterlife and the "world to come" later on, but these doctrines never induced a sense of apathy about our responsibilities here and now, and in this world.

If the task is to transform the social order in the here and now, then the focus of activity has to be the infinitely complex range of relationships between human beings in concrete life situations. It is true that spirituality, purity of heart, and devotion are important, and many of the *mitzvot* involve ritual behavior with no obvious or primary interpersonal referent. But again, we are dealing with emphases and priorities. A mere glance at the first chapter of the book of Isaiah establishes that God's priority is the interpersonal *mitzvah,* the fate of the widow, the orphan, and the oppressed—not sacrifices and prayer. To use the distinction that became so central to Christianity, Judaism insists that we are "justified" (i.e., rendered authentic or legitimate in the eyes of God) by our "works," that is by our behavior and not, as Pauline Christianity would have it, by our "faith;" and among these works, morality is primary.

Judaism is pervaded by a basic confidence in our human ability to do the right thing. It is dangerous to speak in such broad strokes about a long and complex tradition, but again, it contains relatively little of the pessimism or fatalism about the human being that one senses in other traditions. The Bible (for example, Genesis 6:5 and 8:21) preserves a remarkably clear-eyed appreciation of our ability to do both good *and* evil, and it is never naïvely optimistic that we will inevitably choose the good. But in no way is the evil outcome predetermined by the fact of our humanness, by our intrinsic character. We do not believe, for example, that Adam's sin left its indelible imprint on all future generations, as the Christian doctrine of original sin teaches. Our freedom is real and unquestioned, as is our ability to repent and, even more striking, God's readiness to accept genuine repentance (as, in Jonah, He accepts Nineveh's repentance) so that we may start afresh.

What should be mistrusted, however, is our reliance on our own intuitive human judgment as to what is good and what is evil in any one concrete situation. This, finally, is what, under the traditionalist interpretation of Jewish religion, justifies God's revelation of *mitzvot*. Every moment of our lives can bring us into a complex interpersonal relationship where values are in conflict, and where it is not at all clear how we should act. Human intuition, the Bible assumes, is far from infallible. We are easily blinded by self-interest. The Jew confronts each of these situations with the question: What does God demand of me now? The answer is the *mitzvah*.

To be a member of the covenanted community, then, is to bind ourselves to be partners with God in creating a certain kind of world for ourselves and our progeny. The *mitzvot* are the means for bringing this about. Their formulation in the terminology of law is our tradition's attempt to lend them a dimension of authority, a binding or structuring quality that flows directly out of the assumptions of biblical theology and anthropology.

Autonomy vs. Theonomy

We return now to our five options on the issue of revelation: revelation as the communication of an explicit verbal (or propositional) content (traditionalism); as the communication of a content that Israel appropriates in midrashic form (Heschel); as God's (commanding) presence in an I-Thou relationship with Israel (Rosenzweig); as the objective or external dimension to Israel's classic mythic structuring of the world; and as the human discovery of an ever-developing vision of salvation (Kaplan).

The correlation between our discussion here and the traditionalist position as articulated by Samson Raphael Hirsch and Norman Lamm is clear-cut and straightforward. According to their views, God dictated the Torah in words and letters. He thus dictated the covenant and its stipulations. Their authority lies in God's explicit words, literally understood. The authority is tight and powerful. The contemporary Jew who accepts the package takes upon himself the entire system of *mitzvot* for one reason alone: because they represent the will of God for the Jewish people.

It is also clear what happens to this entire structure should one accept Mordecai Kaplan's theological assumptions. However much Kaplan's God, "the power that makes for salvation," can be said to be the source of revelation, the content of that revelation is thoroughly shaped by the human community. The community, then, becomes the source of authority on what was revealed, and as the community's perspective on that content changes over time, Torah changes with it.

It should not be surprising, then, that Kaplan is reluctant to speak of the *mitzvot* as "laws." Kaplan rejects the coercive quality implied by the term. However meaningful that dimension might have been in the past, allegiance to the *mitzvot* today is voluntary and consensual. Jews elect to accept whatever *mitzvot* they do observe, and it is the consensus of the community that determines which of the entire system continue to be valid expressions of our most mature religious commitments. Those that do not should be dropped. It is understandable, then, why Kaplan refers to the ritual *mitzvot* as "folkways." They are the characteristic behavior patterns of our community. They can function in many important ways, but they are not laws.

The polarization of Lamm and Kaplan on the issue of religious authority stems ultimately from the tension within all of us between two conflicting impulses. Part of us intuitively wants a religious tradition to be grounded in an authority that lies beyond anything human, in a Being that transcends any individual and any cultural setting. This impulse lies behind religion's ancient and honorable role as a critique of all temporal forms of human expression, of the transient "spirit of the age," in the name of authoritative moral and spiritual absolutes. But this "heteronomous," or "theonomous," impulse is frequently challenged by an equally powerful "autonomous" impulse, which insists that it is the right and proper task for us—indeed, for all human beings and communities—to figure out for ourselves what the world is all about and how to conduct our lives. How to balance these two impulses, what power to give to either of them, will change with the individual, the age, and the culture. Lamm clearly enthrones the theonomous impulse; Kaplan, the autonomous.

But note well. A religious or philosophical position that stresses human autonomy, then, in no way implies the *rejection* of all law or of a sense of obligation. It does, however, insist that the authority for determining the nature and extent of the obligation lies within the human "self" ("autonomy"), within communities, not in some "other" authority ("heteronomy"), even in God ("theonomy").

But note also that the contrast is not that sharp. First of all, even Mordecai Kaplan would insist that the human self never operates purely autonomously; in the final analysis, it *is* God who is the source of our sense of obligation—not an independent Being beyond us, but God nevertheless, God as the power within us that impels us to bind *ourselves* to moral and spiritual values. Second, even a traditionalist would acknowledge that the doctrine of the Oral Torah allows the community and its authorities considerable scope in determining the precise legal implications of the biblical text. In fact, Deuteronomy 17:8–13 urges the community to bring its disputes to the magistrates who are "in charge at the time," and their judgments are to be followed meticulously. The tension between the two impulses is present in the full range of the positions, however differently it may be resolved in each case.

The issue, then, is most emphatically *not* the very legitimacy of a religious or specifically Jewish sense of being obligated. Nor is it the legitimacy of behavioral obligations in the first place. What *is* at issue are the respective roles of God and human beings in grounding that sense of obligation and in shaping the specific content of what we are obligated, as Jews, to do. If modernity has wrought a single, decisive transformation in the terms of this discussion, it is the insistence not that we be free from religious obligation, but that we take the authority on ourselves, or more accurately, that we share the authority with God, for we perceive God as having shared His authority with Israel. Of course, with authority comes the obligation to care, to study, and to think seriously about the issues. Most important, authority brings a far greater share of the responsibility for what we do and don't do as Jews.

Why Mitzvot? Nontraditionalist Options

Between these polar positions on the authority of the *mitzvot* lies
a middle option which, as we have noted above, has been expressed in three ways. Of these, the one that is most explicit on
the authority of the *mitzvot* is that of Franz Rosenzweig. Recall
that for Rosenzweig, what was revealed was God Himself in
intimate relationship with Israel—no less and no more. There was
no additional content to that revelation itself. The Torah is
Israel's response to revelation. Above all, Rosenzweig is explicit
that "God is not a Law-giver." "But," Rosenzweig continues,
"He commands." There is a difference between "law" and "command." The former is impersonal, objective, universal; the latter
is personal, subjective, individual. Laws are written in books and
apply across the board to everyone who accepts the authority of
the book; commands are felt internally by the individual. Properly translated, then, *mitzvah* means "command," never "law."

This, then, is what happened at Sinai. God revealed Himself
in relationship with Israel. This covenantal relationship was itself
a commanding relationship, as are all intense interpersonal relationships. In all such relationships, the partner feels obligated to
respond, to live in terms that are appropriate to the condition of
relatedness. That sense of obligation was entirely spontaneous, a
totally natural yearning to acknowledge God and His covenant
with Israel.

Predictably, though, that original spontaneity faded and then
human beings, in their inveterate "inertia"—the word is Rosenzweig's—changed the commands into laws, into an impersonal
legal system, written in books and empty of the spontaneity and
the emotion that characterized the original response to God's
presence. The task of the modern Jew is to recapture, today, the
original sense of God's self-revelation, and with it the sense of
being commanded to respond. Only then are we obligated to act.

Another way of formulating Rosenzweig's position is to say
that the fact of *mitzvah,* the condition of being obligated, is
intrinsic to God's revelation, while the specific *mitzvot* are Israel's
attempt to infuse content into that sense of obligation. The fact

of authority is intrinsic to revelation; how that authority gets spelled out is subject to legitimate human interpretation in the form of *mitzvot.*

Rosenzweig's attempt to negotiate the tension between theonomy and autonomy has all of the hallmarks of existentialism: It flaunts subjectivity, spontaneity, passion—the centrality and responsibility of the individual. It derides the objective, the universal, the rational. It seems to approach the anarchic—as does any existentialist posture—but only because of its emphasis on the right and responsibility of the individual to determine for himself the structure of meaning that his life must assume. Within that individualist structure, the sense of obligation remains strong and genuine. What this does to Judaism's emphasis on community is another matter. But probably no other thinker has captured our very modern proclivity for individualism in matters that touch upon ultimate issues of value as well as Rosenzweig has. In the final analysis, the fact is that many of us do feel that we have the right as individuals to determine how to express our Jewish commitment, to choose those forms of expression that are "meaningful" to us.

Rosenzweig may or may not accept "meaningfulness" as an appropriate criterion for the sense of being commanded. He would probably prefer the sense of "fear and trembling" in the presence of God (Psalm 55:6), or the intimacy and yearning of "Like a hind crying for water, my soul cries for You, O God" (Psalm 42:2). But it must be emphasized that Rosenzweig has hardly done away with the sense of Jewish behavioral obligation. What he has done is addressed our modern wish to assume at least a share of the authority for determining what we are obligated to do and when.

The second of our nontraditionalist options, the position of Abraham Joshua Heschel, poses a different set of problems. Heschel was probably the least systematic of contemporary Jewish thinkers. His thought calls to mind the aggadic, or homiletical material scattered throughout talmudic literature in the richness of its insight and the poetic quality of its expression, as well as in its rapidly shifting perspectives, its delight in paradox, and its reluctance to tie together various strands of an inquiry into one coherent, systematic statement.

Heschel also delights in presenting us with religious polarities, all the while insisting that authentic Judaism is located precisely within the ensuing tension. On the role of *mitzvot,* he begins by emphasizing the centrality of deeds for authentic religious living. Inwardness, faith, devotion of the heart, and piety are not enough. At the same time, he rails against what he so felicitously dubs "religious behaviorism," the purely mechanical, routinized performance of the *mitzvot.* God demands both the deed and the devotion. The demands are in tension, but that tension is precisely what we must affirm.

But then we meet another set of polarities, this time the methodological tension between anthropology and theology. Sometimes Heschel speaks as a religious anthropologist. In this vein, human beings need *mitzvot,* a discipline of sacred deeds, because we are driven by the conflict between conscience and ego, because life is complex and serious, because interpersonal relationships are morally ambiguous, because deeds are the expression of our power to build or to destroy, because the world demands redemption, and that is our ultimate responsibility. Note that in these moments the issue of God's will remains in the background.

But then, almost in alternating paragraphs, Heschel assumes a theological voice. The world is imbued with the presence of God. Jews respond to this presence through their every deed. Through *mitzvot,* we articulate God's concern for the world and for civilization, we adopt His perspective on the way life is to be lived, we become His partner in the work of creation, we walk in His ways.

Ultimately, and not unexpectedly, these two perspectives become one, for it is God who created us as we are: free, impulse-ridden, mortal, of unparalleled dignity and value, yet capable of unimagined depths of evil. Heschel's anthropology and his theology are two sides of the same coin; they complement each other. But Heschel insists on retaining the two voices and the tension between them remains palpable.

Heschel's anthropology and theology form one global metaphor, a *midrash*. In yet a third of his voices, that of philosopher of religion, Heschel insists that human beings can not speak of God in literal terms. Torah, then, is Israel's understanding of God's revelation, not God's explicit communication. The authority intrinsic to the anthropology/theology picture is then itself midrashic, not literal. In contrast to Rosenzweig, Heschel insists that God's revelation has specific content. But only God knows that content in its pure form; only God knows what He wills of humanity. What we have is our best understanding of what God wills.

What are the concrete implications of that distinction? Clearly a difference in feeling about the claim of the body of *mitzvot* on us. It emerges subtly in Heschel's attack on "religious behaviorism," in his insistence that many of the *mitzvot* were originally conceived as "hedges" around the Torah and that the hedges have inherently less authority than what lies within. It emerges in the hierarchy that Heschel establishes between the ethical and the ritual *mitzvot*. From Lamm's point of view, even the ethical *mitzvot* should be performed as arbitrary rituals, purely as obedience to God's explicit command and not because of their inherent value or meaning. Such a claim is inconceivable in Heschel's framework.

Heschel was not a systematic thinker. He seems to have been torn between the implications of his theological position on revelation on one hand, and his impulse to maximalize Jewish observance on the other. His audience was American Jewry in the middle decades of this century, hardly one of the most committed Jewish communities in our history. That may explain why he writes so forcefully on the indispensability of the *mitzvot* to any authentic reading of Jewish religion. But at the same time, if the Torah is a *midrash*, if it is Israel's understanding of God's will, then its authority has shifted perceptibly from God to the living community of Israel, whose authentic and legitimate task it is to discern what God asks of us in each generation. In asserting the authority of the community over that of the individual, Heschel is much closer, paradoxically, to Kaplan than to Rosenzweig. But in contrast to Kaplan, both Heschel and Rosenzweig insist that the implicit and explicit authority for the *mitzvot* is the supernatural, personal God immediately present in the world and to the believer who is open to His presence. Their stance is elusive and precarious, but it represents a significant and influential option for contemporary Jews.

Mitzvot and the Jewish Myth

The third version of the middle option on revelation, the version that sees Torah as the classic embodiment of the Jewish religious myth, claims that covenant and *mitzvah* are the two complementary cornerstones of the structure of meaning through which our ancestors organized their experience of the world and of history. This myth was their attempt to discern specific patterns in their experience, and to shape these patterns into a meaningful whole that gave order to their world. In turn, the myth lent integrity and identity to its community, generated loyalty to its unique destiny, motivated behavior, and established deep and lasting affective impulses.

Myths, or portions of complex myths, can "live" or "die," and they can be "broken"—these are commonly accepted terms in the language of the philosophy of religion. A live myth is a myth that continues to work; a dead myth is one that has ceased to function. A broken myth is one that is acknowledged as myth. When a myth is broken one is tempted to respond in either of two ways: to proclaim it as dead or to deny its brokenness and retreat to literalism. But neither response is necessary; a myth can be broken and still live.

A myth can be broken and still live because there is simply no alternative to myth making. The issue is never myth or no myth but which myth, for myths are the only means available to us for comprehending complex and elusive dimensions of our experience. Astronomers and psychoanalysts know this very well. If we abandon one myth, it can only be in favor of another. What we can not endure, simply because we are human beings, is the utter confusion or chaos that results from the absence of a structure of meaning by which to read our experience.

Even more important, once we have accepted the inevitability of myth making, we begin to welcome the uncanny power that myths exercise over us. This post-literal or post-critical phase of the inquiry has been dubbed, by the French philosopher Paul Ricoeur, a state of "second" or "willed na-ïveté." We willfully accept the mythic structure precisely as myth and allow it to work for us as the poetic, dramatic, and imaginative creation that it is.

The mythic definition of Jewish identity as formed out of a covenant with God and concretized in a series of behavioral obligations remains alive, however broken it may be for many of us. Its vitality emerges in the palpable sense of a shared history and destiny that binds Jews everywhere, even those who are not formally "religious" or observant. See how quickly Jews mobilize their energies to support the State of Israel or persecuted Jews wherever they may be. The very sense that their fate is our fate can only be accounted for by the sense of covenantedness.

That sense of covenantedness invariably gets expressed in some type of behavior or activity—not necessarily the ritual activity of the observant Orthodox Jew. It may be expressed in some form of social action on behalf of Jewish causes, whether local or international, such as the State of Israel or Soviet Jewry. But it continues to manifest the sense of Jewish covenantedness and it is frequently performed with the same strong sense of obligation that accompanies traditional Jewish observance.

Finally, note the very distinctive mood that accompanies the performance of the ritual of circumcision whereby the male child enters into the covenantal community. There is joy but it is mingled with a sense of awe, a palpable tension that is felt by all, participants and onlookers alike. This is the most ancient ritual we have, dating back to Abraham and our very beginnings as a people. It is also a blood ritual and the sign of the covenant imparted on the male child is indelible. Most of all it expresses the sheer fact of continuity, of another link in the chain of the generations.

At this moment, all of the features of Jewish identity come together: a shared destiny, an indelible bond, a commitment that defies historical forces, and a clear statement that that commitment has to be expressed behaviorally in the performance of a ritual that will forever transform the very body of the male Jew. There is no greater testimony to the power and efficacy of this ritual than the demand by many of our contemporaries for a parallel ritual celebrating the birth of a female child. In fact, many such rituals have emerged out of the community itself, frequently without official rabbinic sanction, simply as an expression of our impulse to celebrate another link in the chain of Jewish continuity.

Just as the sense of covenantedness is very much alive, so is the commitment to the fact of *mitzvot,* or more precisely, to the fact of *mitzvah.* For if God did not dictate the content of Torah, then He did not dictate the specific *mitzvot.* The immediate corollary of this conclusion is that it is not possible for us to speak of *the* body of *mitzvot* or of *the halakhah* as if it formed one clearly circumscribed, monolithic, internally consistent system. There never was such a system and there surely can not be one in our day.

We should, instead, view the community of caring, committed Jews as a series of overlapping mini-communities, each of which centers itself about a body of *mitzvot* that it accepts as binding. Institutionally, these mini-communities organize themselves into three major coalition movements, Orthodox, Conservative, and Reform, with right-wing Orthodoxy (or the Hasidic communities) and left-wing Reform forming the boundary positions. Reconstructionism, representing one modern attempt to reconceptualize the relationship between the Jewish religion and the sense of Jewish peoplehood, sharpens the Conservative and Reform thrust. It might even be arguable, as noted above, that Jews who do not formally affiliate with a synagogue or observe the rituals of Judaism, but work actively within the framework of what we call Jewish "civil religion," also belong in the picture, for they too feel a sense of coercion about their Jewish activity. It is not always clear, then, who is the "observant" Jew and who is not; the dividing line is not sharp and clean.

This view denies neither the existence of parameters for what constitutes authentic Jewish behavior nor the fact of authority.

It does insist, however, that both the parameters and the authority emerge out of the community. But once we deny verbal or propositional revelation, there is simply no escaping that conclusion. It is the community that decides for itself what will be considered *mitzvah* and it does so on its own authority. The assumption, of course, is that this process is taken seriously, not casually. It is clearly not taken this way by the entire community; substantial numbers of Jews have no interest in any of it. But many Jews do. In the final analysis, all we can do is speak to and for them.

The position also makes two assumptions about the nature of Judaism that are very much part of the modern consciousness: pluralism and historical development. Much has been made of the diversity and divisiveness that characterize Jewish life today. But never in the long course of Jewish history did all Jews agree on what they should do as Jews. That diversity—even in the content of the body of *mitzvot*—was always understood as both inevitable and a mark of vitality. It is all the more so today. One of the reasons for pluralism is that various segments of the community differ on which of the *mitzvot* are still binding, which are no longer binding, which new ones should be adopted, on whose authority, and when.

One example will lend concreteness to this discussion. The most divisive issue in the Jewish community over the past decade has clearly been the role of women in Jewish religious life. The range of options is very wide, from right-wing Orthodoxy, which continues to consign women behind a synagogue partition, to contemporary Reform, which offers full and equal participation in all ritual and liturgical roles. In the middle lie different versions of the Conservative position: Some allow a woman to be called to the Torah on notable occasions, others on any occasion; some allow her to go up to the Torah but do not count her in the *minyan* of ten Jews necessary for a formal service of worship, others do; and, more recently some accept the fact that she can lead the congregation in worship and serve as rabbi or *hazzan* if she wears a *tallit* and *tefillin* and obligates herself to perform all of the *mitzvot* that are binding on a Jewish male. In yet other Conservative circles, women are denied all of the above but are permitted to sit with the male members of the family in the synagogue sanctuary.

Each of these options constitutes a different response to the conflicting claims of tradition and modernity, or of theonomy and autonomy. Each represents a different consensus arrived at by a mini-community on what constitutes the legitimate parameters within the body of *mitzvot*. Each can be buttressed with precedents from the Jewish past, some emphasizing the traditional role of the Jewish woman, and others the prophetic call for justice and equality. Each assigns a different weight to factors that are not explicitly legal. There is inevitably a subjective dimension to the way all of these issues come together in the final decision. But all of the positions take very seriously the fact of obligation, all struggle with the issue of authority, and all claim to be authentic. The ensemble is clear testimony to the vitality and seriousness of the community as a whole.

The Limits of Legalism

From the outside looking in, the insistence on prescribed behaviors as the test of authentic Jewish expression is vulnerable to two charges. The first is that it inevitably breeds a routinized, mechanical form of religious life that tends to stifle inwardness and genuine emotion. The second is that the sheer omnipresence of the law can only loom as a burden to anyone who takes it seriously. Taken together, they draw attention to what has frequently been called, pejoratively, the "legalism" of Judaism, presumably as opposed to the spontaneity of other religious traditions that place greater, or even exclusive, emphasis on inwardness.

Both charges are serious; both point to real dangers that have to be recognized and opposed. It is true, for example, that prayer can easily become a matter of racing through paragraph after paragraph of prescribed words while our minds and hearts are elsewhere. And there are moments in the day-to-day life experience of the Jew where the sense of obligation seems unbearably weighty. We yearn to break free and express ourselves in a spontaneous way, to pray, for example, only when we are moved to do so and to say only the words that come to mind at that moment.

There are, of course, numerous biblical and rabbinic texts that teach explicitly that the *mitzvot* are the means, not the end of Jewish religion; that they are God's gift to us, designed to bring us closer to Him, not a barrier to His fellowship; that a *mitzvah* performed without emotion is religiously sterile. But it is also clear that religious devotion is singularly difficult to achieve, especially under the stresses and tensions of our day-to-day responsibilities. A case can be made that precisely in our day it is even more important than ever that a structure be available—moments designated for prayer, the Sabbath for rest, the Festivals for celebration—that impels us out of the everyday and creates windows of opportunity for religious feelings to emerge. Most of us need structures of this kind; few of us can generate spontaneity in a vacuum. There is always the danger that the structure will take on a life of its own. But usually we are aware of those moments, guard against them, and try to rekindle our inner life. Some of us are more successful than others, but at least we try.

Obligations can become burdensome but they can also generate genuine pleasure and a sense of privilege. At such moments, the rabbinic tradition of *simkhah shel mitzvah,* the joy that emerges in fulfilling a *mitzvah,* becomes palpable. But such moments can only be felt from the inside; their test is experiential, not intellectual or theological. In the final analysis, after all of the theology has been spelled out, the Sabbath has to be lived to be understood and appreciated.

There is simply no religious authenticity in Judaism outside of a halakhic system—not necessarily *the* halakhic system that the traditionalists exalt, but *a* halakhic system that concretizes our sense of covenantedness as a community to God. For all of its inherent dangers, this commitment is axiomatic to Jewish religion. It stems from our earliest attempts at religious and communal self-definition. The challenge is to view *halakhah* as the means, not the end of Jewish piety, to welcome the opportunities it provides for worship and celebration, and then to strive for that elusive blend of structure and spontaneity that has been the hallmark of Jewish religious living from time immemorial.

FOR FURTHER STUDY

The major covenant texts in the Bible can be found in Exodus 19–24, Joshua 24, 2 Kings 22–23, and Nehemiah 8–10. On the first, and clearly the most important of these, see Nahum M. Sarna, EXPLORING EXODUS *(Schocken, 1986), particularly, chs. 7–8. The parallels between the biblical covenant form and Hittite treaties are studied by George Mendenhall in his "Covenant Forms in Israelite Tradition," reprinted in* THE BIBLICAL ARCHAEOLOGIST READER, *Vol. III (pb Doubleday Anchor, 1970). A fruitful elaboration of the implications of this material for biblical religion is in G. Ernest Wright,* THE OLD TESTAMENT AGAINST ITS ENVIRONMENT *(pb SCM Press, 1950), particularly, ch. 3. A classic statement on the assumptions of biblical law is Moshe Greenberg, "Some Postulates of Biblical Criminal Law," reprinted in* THE JEWISH EXPRESSION, *edited by Judah Goldin (pb Bantam, 1970; pb Yale University Press, 1976). This anthology is a remarkable collection of scholarly articles on all areas of Jewish studies by some of the giants of Jewish scholarship in this century. On the "faith vs. works" issue, and, more generally on the emergence of Christianity out of its original Jewish setting, see Morton Scott Enslin's* CHRISTIAN BEGINNINGS, *Parts I and II (pb Harper Torchbooks, 1956). W. D. Davies'* PAUL AND RABBINIC JUDAISM *(pb Fourth Edition, Fortress Press, 1980) and E. P. Sanders,* PAUL AND PALESTINIAN JUDAISM *(Fortress Press, 1977) locate Paul's teachings within the context of Rabbinic Judaism.*

For contemporary views on the place of law in Judaism, Norman Lamm's version of the traditionalist position is in his contribution to THE CONDITION OF JEWISH BELIEF *(see ch. 1). Mordecai Kaplan's struggle with the term is in ch. 19 of* THE FUTURE OF THE AMERICAN JEW *(see ch. 1). Abraham Heschel's position is spelled out in Part III of* GOD IN SEARCH OF MAN, *and Franz Rosenzweig's, in* ON JEWISH LEARNING *(see ch. 1). A fruitful comparison of these varying approaches is in Louis Jacobs,* A JEWISH THEOLOGY *(pb Behrman, 1973) chs. 14–15. This volume is a superb general introduction to the field*

of Jewish theology. See also Elliot N. Dorff's CONSERVATIVE JUDA-
ISM: OUR ANCESTORS TO OUR DESCENDANTS *(pb United Synagogue
of America, 1977) for a clear analysis of the implications of these varying
positions for Jewish practice today.*

On *"living," "dead," and "broken" myths and the possible responses to the breaking of our myths, see pp. 48–54 of Tillich's* DY-
NAMICS OF FAITH *(see ch. 1).*

The *notion of a "willed" or "second naïveté" is discussed in James
W. Fowler's* STAGES OF FAITH *(Harper & Row, 1981), pp. 187–188.
Fowler's work is an imaginative attempt to integrate faith development
in the human personality with cognitive and psychological development
(à la Piaget and Erikson).*

The *rabbinic notion of "the joy of the law" is elaborated in
Solomon Schechter's* ASPECTS OF RABBINIC THEOLOGY *(pb Schocken,
1961), ch. 11. This volume, originally published in 1909, remains the
best one-volume summary of rabbinic theology available. Schechter's
introduction is a classic statement on the perils involved in studying
rabbinic theology, and chs. 8–11 are required reading for anyone who
wishes to understand the place of law in rabbinic Judaism.*

III

Knowing God:
How and What?

THE CENTRAL QUESTIONS OF THEOLOGY PERTAIN TO THE EXIS-
tence and nature of God. Etymologically, the very word
"theology" means "thinking" or "talking about God" (from
the Greek: *theos,* God; *logos,* reason or discourse). In fact, thinking and talking about God are part of one process.

As we open this complex issue, two distinct questions separate
themselves out: *How* do we know anything about God? And *what*
is it that we know about God? The two questions are inextricably
intertwined. The "how" question clearly implies a prior agreement on "what" it is we are talking about in the first place: An
old man with a white beard sitting in the sky? A natural process?
A distinct if immaterial being? But at the same time, each of these
concepts of God forces us to ask: How do we know? How do
we know anything about this God? How do we know that He
exists in the first place?

But all issues can not be discussed simultaneously; certain ones
have to be temporarily bracketed, even if somewhat arbitrarily.
We begin, then, with the "how" question and turn to the "what"
question below.

The Existence of God: A Persistent Issue
The most striking fact about the issue of the existence or nonexistence of God is its sheer persistence over centuries, not only as

a technical philosophical problem but in the popular imagination as well. From the earliest records of humanity's attempts to understand itself and its world to our own day, people have had recourse to the notion of an ultimate Being or Power, both as a way of explaining why things are the way they are and, more existentially, as a help in coping with the problems of living. There is hardly a human being who, at one point or another in the course of his or her lifetime, did not feel the need at least to struggle with the problem.

It is commonly held that the classic text of our tradition, the Bible, takes the existence of God for granted. This is not completely accurate. It may well be the official or editorial position of the Bible, the perspective from which the Author—or authors—of the biblical narratives wrote, but it is far from true of the biblical communities. In fact, what is most striking about the biblical record is the repeated refusal of Israel to accept the reality of the biblical God despite what would seem to be the very convincing displays of His presence and power. It is precisely the generation who personally experienced the Exodus from Egypt and the revelation at Sinai—of whom it is said ". . . when they saw the wondrous power which the Lord had wielded against the Egyptians, . . . they had faith in the Lord and in his servant Moses" (Exodus 14:30–31)—who shortly thereafter persuaded Aaron to build a golden calf and danced about it while exclaiming "This is your God, O Israel, Who brought you out of the land of Egypt!" (32:4).

This is only one of a long series of rebellions against God that the Bible records with painful candor. Even the remarkable narrative of Elijah on the Carmel (1 Kings 18), which records what we might take to be a decisive experiment to prove the reality of God, proved to be utterly inadequate, even in the short run. In fact, believers among us today see equally dramatic or "miraculous" divine interventions everywhere—for example, the State of Israel's military victory in the Six-Day War, the sudden reversal of a seemingly terminal illness, or the birth of a perfectly normal baby. But the skeptics among us remain unconvinced.

Is the issue, then, intrinsically unresolvable? Part of the problem, at least in the two biblical narratives referred to above, is not so much the existence of a supreme Being but, rather, the nature or the identification of that Being: the biblical God or a golden calf; God or Baal. The traditional theistic God—infinite, transcendent, disembodied, omnipotent, omniscient, omnipresent, personal—is unique among beings. He does not enter into our normal or natural experience in the way that flowers, or even blood cells, atoms, or galaxies do. The Bible is extremely reticent about suggesting that He can be perceived by human beings, as in the cautious language of passages such as Exodus 24:17, Exodus 33:20–23, Deuteronomy 34:10, Isaiah 6:1, and Ezekiel 1:28 (though the Bible is considerably less reticent about claiming that human beings can hear His voice). The literature of the mystics, both Jewish and otherwise, who claim to experience God at the climax of their mystical quests, confirms the highly ambiguous nature of what in fact they do experience. There seems to be an intrinsic incompatibility between the content of the experience and our human powers to conceptualize or express it.

Typically, in the Bible at least, the revelation is not of God Himself but rather of a second-level manifestation of His presence; not His being, but events that He brought about. What the biblical community was asked to perceive was a complex pattern of events in nature and history—sunrise and sunset, the cycle of the seasons, the workings of the human body, the Exodus from Egypt, the splitting of the sea, the covenant at Sinai, mannah in the wilderness, the victory over Amalek. Later generations added the Maccabean victory, the establishment of the State of Israel, and the Six-Day War to this list. The editorial perspective of the Bible knits these events into a pattern that "reveals" God's intervention into nature and history on behalf of His people. But a skeptic can always refuse to acknowledge the pattern, or choose to see a different pattern, or attribute the pattern to some other power—be it Baal, self-sufficient nature, intrinsic human resourcefulness, or even a series of coincidences. If anything, that kind of skepticism comes more easily to us than it did to the biblical community, for we have a far more sophisticated understanding of natural and historical processes than our ancestors did.

A closer look at the first of the biblical passages cited above—
Exodus 14:30–31—provides a vivid example of our problem
here. The two verses make five distinct claims:

1. Thus the Lord delivered Israel that day from the Egyptians
2. Israel saw the Egyptians dead on the shore of the sea
3. When Israel saw the wondrous power which the Lord had
   wielded
4. The people feared the Lord
5. They had faith in the Lord and in His servant Moses

The first claim is really the conclusion of the narrative. Note
the word "thus." It represents the editorial perspective from
which the narrative is written. Even more, we may surmise that
it represents the prior belief structure through which the event
was perceived in the first place. It is the perspective, then, of the
believer, the already convinced. The remaining four claims then
proceed to trace the process of inference through which, the
editor claims, the rest of the community reached the same conclusion and attained faith in the Lord.

Note, however, the implicit argumentation of claims two
through five, in particular the movement from claim two to
claim three. The second reports a natural sense experience: Israel
saw—*literally* saw—dead Egyptians on the shore of the sea. The
third reports that they also "saw" something else: God's wondrous power. But this second seeing is clearly not a literal seeing
but, rather, a seeing that is fraught with interpretation, a highly
metaphorical kind of seeing. It is one thing to see dead Egyptians,
quite another thing to "see" God's "wondrous power." What the
community "sees" is the dead Egyptians as the manifestation of
an invisible and omnipotent God's intervention into history. In
fact, however, there is an enormous leap from claim two to claim
three, a leap that the editor has made and that he claims the
community was also able to make.

But one can easily imagine the skeptic, standing on the
sidelines observing the event, concluding that God had nothing

to do with it at all; that Israel was the beneficiary and the Egyptians the victims of a fortuitous wind storm that stirred up the waters. In fact, the biblical narrative of the golden calf episode, which, according to biblical chronology, occurred just a few weeks later, confirms that there must have been a sizable number of skeptics on the shores of the sea that day. They may not have attributed the event to natural forces, but they clearly did not believe that the biblical God had anything to do with it.

Contrary to the popular adage, then, seeing is not necessarily believing. In fact, we could easily claim the contrary: We see what we already believe, what we are prepared to see, what we are convinced we are going to see—especially when *what* we "see" is something as elusive as an invisible God's "wondrous power."

God's Manifestation and Human Perception

These conclusions, taken together, suggest that if human beings are to achieve an "awareness" (a much weaker or more neutral term than "knowledge" or "experience") of God's reality, two complementary kinds of activity must take place. In one, God is active—by creating the natural order, by intervening in human events, by rewarding or punishing His people. In the other, people are active as well—by seeing the world as created by God, by acknowledging the Exodus as His intervention in history, by accepting His revealed Torah and obeying His will.

That God's self-manifestation is an "activity" is clear. That our recognition of His manifestation demands an equally active role on our part is more problematic. We intuitively view our role in experience as passive; somehow, objects or events "out there" impinge themselves on our perceiving apparatus and we simply absorb or record these images. In reality, however, all of our human experience is a highly complex transaction involving both the "out there" and our sensory, intellectual, and even linguistic skills. The simple act of perceiving and identifying a red patch involves an aggressive set of human activities that becomes even more complex as the object of our perception changes from a red patch to a red sweater or a rare flower; or to a pattern such as the structure of a Bartók sonata, a basketball team's passing game, the cycles of nature, or, at the extreme, the history of a community over centuries.

To identify an active human role in experience is, at the same time, to acknowledge its inexorably subjective character as well. My "red" patch may be Picasso's "fuscia" patch. An amateur's characterization of the basketball team's "skilled" passing game may appear to its coach as an off-night. A trained musician will perceive the structure of a Bartók sonata but the ordinary listener will hear only cacophony. A blind person can skim a page of Braille with his fingers and read the text; for someone who can not read Braille, all the patterns seem identical. We put a good deal of ourselves, then, into every piece of our experience. Our inherent genetic make-up, our education, our total experience to date, our innate or acquired perceiving skills—all of these and more affect how and what we are prepared to see in the world outside us.

This subjective dimension of human experience constitutes what might be called an "escape clause," for it permits us to "escape" or to avoid seeing what to others is palpably obvious. This "escape" is not necessarily conscious or deliberate. In fact, it is most frequently not at all deliberate. We simply may not be prepared, educated, attuned, or endowed with the ability to see what others see and want us to see. At other times, however, we will not want to see, or make the effort to see, or even remember what we see, or integrate this piece of seeing into the rest of our experience. Philosophers have written at length about the "will to believe." But if we have to will belief, we can also refuse to believe.

One further complication. This discussion seems to assume that the God-pattern is simply"out there," waiting to be acknowledged by human beings. In fact, however, there are many possible patterns out there. Even more troublesome, it is entirely possible to construct a pattern that "reveals" a capricious or malevolent God, a God who deliberately absents Himself at moments when we cry for His presence, or in the extreme, a pattern with no God at all. In other words, the task of pattern creating also involves deciding what we do with the contrary evidence. Do we simply ignore it, explain it away, or do we try to integrate it into the pattern that we want to see? This last strategy, the need to integrate apparently contradictory evidence into our larger pattern, serves as the impulse for "theodicy" (from the Greek: *theos,* God; *dike,* order, right, just), the part of theology that aims to "justify" or vindicate God despite the evidence that seems to contradict His justice or even His existence.

Our task may be compared to that of the child who is playing connect-the-dots. In our book, however, the dots are not numbered. We can trace a bunny rabbit but we can also trace a tiger. Or, no matter how many different attempts we make, we simply can't produce a pattern at all. We always end up with total chaos. To continue the analogy, the function of the Bible and of post-biblical Jewish religious literature is precisely to assign a number to the dots of our communal experience so that Jews will continue to trace the predetermined pattern of God's power and love for Israel. The entire purpose of Jewish religious education throughout the centuries can be summed up in one mandate: to teach each successive generation of Jews to see the classical Jewish pattern, to "see" God's power and love in the events of nature and history, to "read" nature and history as "revealing" God's presence, and then to live in response to that presence.

Both partners in this complex transactional experience—the divine and the human—are active in this transaction but the extent and/or the quality of their activity can be understood in varying ways. God can reveal Himself in a strikingly aggressive way as He did to Elijah and his contemporaries at the Carmel, or in a more natural or restrained way as, for example, in the everyday cycles of nature or in the normal functioning of the human body.

To a degree, God's activity and ours vary in an inverse proportion. God's aggressive revelation demands less from us; His restrained revelation demands a much more aggressive act of seeing on our part. Of course, the more that is demanded from us, the more likely we will invoke the "escape clause" of subjectivity and remain "blind" to the revelation. The distinction is clearly not absolute. One believer's aggressiveness may be another's credulity or naïveté, and what appears to some of us as God's restrained revelation may appear infinitely compelling to others. The liturgical passage in the closing benedictions of the *Amidah* that begins, "We give thanks unto you, Lord our God . . ." and refers to God's "miracles that are daily with us" might seem incongruous; how can a "miracle" occur "daily"? They clearly do, however, to this liturgist and to other believers.

Both dimensions of the experience are indispensable. A totally "hidden" or "hiding" God is irrelevent to human concerns. But His revelation is for naught if people are "blind" to His presence, refuse to see it, or focus instead on the contrary evidence. It is easier for us to accept the fact that our ambivalence about whether God exists stems from His hiddenness. We look back at the experience of the biblical community and long for equally dramatic manifestations of God in our own experience. But it is not at all clear that the fault is with God alone. It may also lie in the differing sensibilities or perceptual sets with which we read our experience. A believing Jew and a secular military analyst will "read" the dramatic rescue of the Israeli hostages at the Entebbe airport either as "revealing" God's dramatic intervention on behalf of His beloved Jews or as the superior military intelligence and skills of the Israeli armed forces. The dispute between the believer and the atheist, then, is only partially related to what God does or does not do in our day. It is as much a matter of what we are or are not prepared to see Him as doing.

Of course, what we are intuitively prepared to see can also be changed, sometimes dramatically, sometimes more slowly, through education and life experience. The literature of religion is filled with narratives of this kind of turn-about. Our tradition calls it *teshuvah*. We usually take this term to mean "repentance," but "repentance" is much too narrow a term. *Teshuvah,* more accurately, refers to a total reorientation of one's perspective on the world, a transformation in how one confronts one's life experience, a fundamental change of character. Our tradition is absolutely on target in comparing the *ba'al teshuvah,* or "repentant Jew," to a new-born child, and in insisting that though this kind of transformation is monumentally difficult, it is not at all impossible to achieve. The move from nonbelief to belief involves this kind of reeducation.

Facts and Illusions

Another dimension to this general problem of subjectivity is even more subtle and troublesome. The adherents of one of the youngest and most rapidly growing religious communities in the world today, the Mormons, believe that God and Jesus of Nazareth revealed themselves to a young man named Joseph Smith, in the year 1820 in upstate New York. That revelation and the subsequent revelations of the angel Moroni, which led Smith to the discovery of a book written on golden plates, constitute the founding revelations of Mormonism. Those of us who are not Mormons contemplate the account of these events with a sense of incredulity—we have enough trouble with God's revelation to our ancestors in Egypt and at Sinai. But those events are buried in early antiquity and we don't even know precisely which of the mountains in the Negev is really Sinai. We can, then, more easily blur the historicity of the events. But that God should reveal Himself in 1820, and in New York State—that is simply too much for us to believe.

The subjectivity issue, then, raises a multitude of problems beyond our simple inability or refusal to discern the patterns that others see. People see many things that are extraordinarily vivid and compelling—dreams, illusions, hallucinations, or visions— but which are the totally subjective product of the believers' own minds. When we know that the individual is an alcoholic, or under the influence of drugs, or mentally ill, we feel that we can screen out his visions and brand them as the illusions that they are. Those are the easy cases.

But in the case of Joseph Smith, the private vision of an individual is accepted by millions of people as absolutely factual. In fact, not only Smith himself but many of his followers underwent bitter persecution for their beliefs, were prepared to endure martyrdom, and in fact did die because of their conviction that what Smith saw was not an illusion.

If we can legitimately wonder about the veracity of such

experiences, how much easier is it to question the factual nature of those complex patterns in nature and history that the believer claims to "see" and that serve as the basis for his religious commitment. Our liturgy, the *Amidah* for Festivals for example, has us recite "You have chosen us from among all peoples, You have loved us and favored us." The liturgist clearly believed that this was a factual claim, supported by overwhelming evidence and absolutely verifiable. Many Jews, over the centuries, clearly agreed.

But the skeptic would question the claim. He would wonder: First, how can such a claim be verified? How can we prove it to be true? We know how to verify a scientific claim such as what happens when we combine sulfuric acid and zinc in a test tube; we simply do the experiment, repeat it again and again and look at the results. But theological or religious claims do not lend themselves to controlled experimentation, so they can not be verified in that way. But in what way are they verifiable? What makes them true? What happens if they are not verifiable or true? More generally, what does "truth" mean in a theological system?

In fact, the skeptic may go even further and insist that the claim that God loves the Jewish people is not only not *provable,* it is not even *disprovable.* He would guess that no matter what contrary evidence he would bring to bear, the believer would continue to insist that God really does love the Jewish people— but He has to punish them for their sins, but He has to test their loyalty to Him, but we don't understand His ways, but . . . but . . . but. . . . Eventually, then, both the believer and the skeptic realize that neither can convince the other, that the claim that God loves the Jewish people is neither provable nor disprovable in any conclusive way. It becomes clear that, in a very real sense, the evidence pro and con is almost irrelevant to the belief structures of either of the disputants.

But if the evidence is almost irrelevant, then in what sense is God's love for the Jewish people in any way factual or real, let alone true? Could we not conclude that it is more the believer's wish projection, an expression of his most profound hope, a covert way of enabling him to feel better about himself and his community, a poetic way of saying that Jews are pretty special, a device to get Jews to be loyal to their Jewish heritage? In short, is it not a totally subjective expression of how the believer feels about himself and his Jewishness? It might seem to parade as an objective statement about God and His feelings about Jews, but it is in fact very far from that.

It is small wonder, then, that on the issue of God, every generation finds itself back at square one. There is no escaping the inherently subjective character of this entire inquiry. The only question is: What do we do with this subjective dimension? Do we try to cancel it out? Minimize its impact? Or accept it, even flaunt it, and go on from there? Different theologians and philosophers of religion, at different times, have adopted all of these strategies.

Three Pathways to God

Over the centuries, Jewish thinkers have used three separate approaches to deal with the question of how we attain an awareness of God's existence: the path of reason, or the rational approach; the path of experience, or the experiential (or empirical) approach; and the path of interpersonal encounter, or the existential approach.

The rational approach claims that God's existence can be demonstrated through a series of deductive arguments or proofs—the familiar "proofs for the existence of God" that philosophers have been debating since antiquity. Religious rationalism enjoyed its heyday in the Middle Ages when believers of all traditions felt compelled to counter a pervasive atheistic rationalism with their own brand of believing rationalism. Its most notable Jewish proponents were Saadia Gaon (892–942) and, of course, Moses Maimonides (1135–1204). The approach itself, in its purity, is somewhat in disrepute today since each of the proofs has been demolished at one time or another—though there are respectable contemporary rationalists who would disagree. Either way, the issues that religious rationalism tried to solve remain genuinely significant and must be answered by any believer, whatever his approach.

The experiential approach claims that God's presence can be experienced—that is, "seen" or felt in the world—either through a distinctive "religious" experience or as an equally distinctive dimension to all of our natural experience. It is the pervasive approach of biblical and rabbinic Judaism, of Yehuda Halevi (ca. 1080–1140) in the Middle Ages, of the mystics and of Abraham Joshua Heschel and Mordecai Kaplan in our day. Our preliminary discussion of the issues involved in dealing with the "how" question earlier in this chapter was couched in terms of the experiential approach, and both rationalism and existentialism can be understood as reactions to the problems that this approach raises.

Finally, the existentialist approach disclaims the effectiveness of either reason or experience as a pathway to God. It insists, instead, that God can be "encountered" in an intense personal relationship, much like an interpersonal relationship, though greatly intensified, and with the additional difference that though God may not be "physically" present to the believer in the way that the believer's spouse may be, His presence is yet infinitely more real than that of any mere human being.

Existentialism is one of the youngest philosophical movements. As an approach to religion, it is commonly traced to the Danish Christian thinker Sören Kierkegaard (1813–1855). It served as the impulse for equally powerful theistic and atheistic philosophical schools that flourished in Europe during the first half of our century. Martin Buber and Franz Rosenzweig are acknowledged to be the fathers of a modern existentialist reading of Judaism; their students include such notable thinkers as the late Will Herberg and our contemporaries Eugene Borowitz and Emil Fackenheim. Not unexpectedly, however, most Jewish existentialists find anticipations of this approach in biblical passages such as the story of the binding of Isaac (Genesis 22), the Book of Job, in numerous talmudic homilies, and preeminently in the teachings of some of the Hasidic masters.

It is rare for any one of these approaches to appear in all of its purity. Some of the so-called rational demonstrations of God's existence invoke our sense experience of the natural world as their point of departure. The experiential and existential approaches are easily confused with one another, depending on how one uses the term "experience." We should not be surprised, then, if we see traces of different approaches in any one theological statement, or even if we ourselves find different approaches more congenial to us at different points in our lives.

These approaches, however, do serve to clarify three principle thrusts in the ways in which thinkers have tried to reach God throughout the centuries. If for no other reason, there is a pedagogical value in trying to isolate and capture the distinctive logic that each one employs, its appeal, and its weaknesses.

All three approaches will have to deal with the same set of questions. First, why this approach and not the others? Is its appeal intrinsic? Are there other, broader cultural factors that render it more attractive at a particular time or to a particular personality type?

Second, how does it deal with the issue of subjectivity raised above? How does its specific form of what we have called the "escape clause" function? How does it understand and address the nonbeliever?

Third, since religion is littered with claims that strike us as patently illusory, how does each approach deal with separating out what it understands as "truth" from fiction? How does it verify its own claims? What are its criteria for theological "truth"? Even beyond this, does the approach claim that its "truths" are in principle provable or disprovable? What happens if they are not? What then is the status of its claims? If they don't reflect objective reality "out there," then what purpose do they serve?

Fourth, how does it understand faith or belief in religion? Is it a kind of knowledge, similar to other forms of knowledge, a cerebral achievement? Or is it more an act of the will, a form of trust, loyalty, or commitment, shot through with emotion? To use a common distinction, is religious faith "belief *that* . . ." or "belief *in* . . ."?

Finally, what are the implications of each of these approaches for the second of the broad questions with which we began our discussion: What kind of God does it inevitably seem to lead us to? What is the nature of this God?

To get us started, a preliminary look at the issue of subjectivity will show us that whereas the experiential approach acknowledges the inevitability of a subjective dimension to all theological claims and devises strategies to cope with it, religious rationalism is embarrassed by subjectivity and tries to eliminate it as much as possible. In contrast, existentialism flaunts subjectivity and insists that this is what makes religious faith unique and particularly significant in the life of the believer.

We will begin our more detailed analysis with the experientialist approach, not only because it is the pervasive approach of the classical texts of the Jewish tradition, but because it also serves as the point of reference for the two alternatives.

One final note of caution before we turn to the "what" question. We began by noting that the issue of the existence or nonexistence of God has persisted, unresolved, since the beginning of human experience. Our emphasis on the inherent subjectivity of all theological claims is an attempt to account for this enigmatic quality of the inquiry. But the sheer persistence of the issue—the fact that for all of our failures, we human beings return to the issue again and again—is all the encouragement we need to jump in. The issue will not go away, simply because it is at the very heart of our attempt to make sense of our human situation.

FOR FURTHER STUDY
The literature on the existence and nature of God is voluminous, but one inexpensive anthology, THE EXISTENCE OF GOD, *edited with an introduction by John Hick (pb Macmillan, 1964), covers most of the classical discussion from antiquity to our day. Hick's introduction is a superb summary of the issues. Extracts from the writings of philosophers from Plato through Thomas Aquinas, René Descartes, David Hume, and John Stuart Mill to Sören Kierkegaard, Bertrand Russell, and other contemporary scholars, represent the main approaches to the problem. The debate between the atheist, Bertrand Russell, and the*

believer, Father F. C. Copleston is a sparkling confrontation. Finally, the concluding material on the falsification and verification of religious claims brings the debate up to the present. In preparation for this last issue, you might want to read John Wisdom's seminal paper, "Gods," anthologized in RELIGIOUS LANGUAGE AND THE PROBLEM OF RELI-GIOUS KNOWLEDGE, *edited by Ronald E. Santoni (pb Indiana University Press, 1968), pp. 295–314.*

Beyond this, since this issue is part of the broad, traditional agenda of the discipline of philosophy, you should consult all the relevant entries in THE ENCYCLOPEDIA OF PHILOSOPHY, *edited by Paul G. Edwards (Collier-Macmillan, 1967, 8 vols. bound as 4). This relatively inexpensive and accessible work is indispensable for the serious student of philosophy in general, and since Jewish philosophy almost always nurses from the broader field of Western philosophy, it provides a fundamental background for the Jewish material as well.*

An excellent, more technical study of the specific problems entailed by religious epistemology is by William T. Blackstone, THE PROBLEM OF RELIGIOUS KNOWLEDGE *(pb Prentice-Hall, 1963).*

Studies focusing on the Jewish discussion of the issue are Julius Guttmann's PHILOSOPHIES OF JUDAISM *(Holt, Rinehart, and Winston, 1964; pb Schocken 1973), which remains the best one-volume study of Jewish philosophy from the Bible to the early moderns, and Louis Jacobs'* FAITH *(Vallentine, Mitchell, 1968) and his* A JEWISH THEOL-OGY *(see ch. 1). Rifat Sonsino and Daniel B. Syme's* FINDING GOD: TEN JEWISH RESPONSES *(pb Union of American Hebrew Congregations, 1986) is a clear and concise study of classical Jewish approaches to God in nontechnical language.*

IV

Talking About God:
Symbolic Language

The Language of God-Talk

THE TWO QUESTIONS THAT WE CAN ASK ABOUT GOD ARE: HOW? and What? *How* do we know or say anything about God? And *What* can we know or say about God? Jewish thinkers have answered the latter question in diverse ways. We will see that Jewish rationalists talk of God as pure thought and the efficient cause of the natural order. Experientialists, such as Abraham Joshua Heschel tell us of a God who is all pathos—a caring, reaching out, emotion-ridden God who is omnipresent in nature and history. For existentialists, such as Martin Buber, He is the supreme and eternal Thou, the preeminently personal God who enters into relationship with those who seek to encounter Him. We also know that because God creates and reveals, He is not at all self-sufficient. The biblical God needs a world, needs people—specifically *a* people—to help accomplish His purposes on earth.

More important, we have emphasized the problem of knowing, thinking, or saying *anything* about God. This is the ultimate paradox that pervades all of theological inquiry. Precisely because God is *the* supremely transcendent reality, neither the human mind nor human language is equipped to characterize Him in any objectively accurate way. We know how to describe those dimensions of the world that are accessible through sensation—colors, chemical reactions, the anatomy of the human body. But the more reality escapes direct sense experience—the internal make-up of the atom or of galaxies beyond ours, for example—the more we must mistrust the literalness of our thinking and speaking. If God is intrinsically other than anything human or natural, then how can we say anything that is literally true about Him—unless, of course, we believe, as the traditionalist believes, that God Himself spoke at Sinai and instructed us regarding what to believe about Him.

The dilemma is that we want to say a great deal about God. At the same time, we want to preserve that transcendent quality that makes Him inaccessible to ordinary language. The alternatives are to remain silent or to reduce God to merely human or natural terms, which is idolatry, the cardinal theological sin.

Theological literal-mindedness is idolatrous, not because it claims to describe the transcendent God in human and natural terms—what other terms can we use?—but, rather, because it insists that these descriptions are literally accurate and true. Exodus 20:4–5 forbids us from making and worshiping any "sculpted image, or any likeness of what is in the heavens above, or on the earth below, or in the waters under the earth," and the biblical community was justifiably punished for worshiping the golden calf. The problem is not sculpted images, however, but rather conceptual and linguistic images. We are haunted by Isaiah's warning (40:25), "To whom, then, can you liken Me, to whom can I be compared?", and later (55:8–9), "For My plans are not your plans, nor are My ways your ways. . . . But as the heavens are high above the earth, so are My ways high above your ways and My plans above your plans." The assumption that God's nature can be conveyed *in a literal way* by our natural language is as idolatrous as building a golden calf.

We must speak about God, *and* we must also recognize that all of our God-talk is built on a skeleton of metaphors, constructs, models, paradigms, or, more technically, "symbols." These symbols are then grouped together to form "myths."

Symbols and Signs

We drive along a street, encounter a red light, and we stop. The red light is a "sign." It "stands for," "represents," or "points to" something else: namely, the command that vehicles and pedestrians must stop until the light changes. But there is no inherent connection between the red light and the order to stop. It is just as conceivable that red might stand for "Walk" and green for "Stop"; or that the colors might be blue and yellow; or that the order to stop might be represented by a picture of an upraised hand, a policeman, or a tiger. Signs are conventions, and conventions of this kind can easily be changed.

But now look at the American flag. Here again, the flag "stands for," "represents," or "points to" something else: the United States of America. But the relationship between the flag and the country "for which it stands" is much tighter. A visitor in a foreign land sees the flag flying over an embassy building and feels an onrush of emotion—pride, security, and dignity—that comes with being a citizen of this country. Or conversely, when the American flag is defaced, it is not only the cloth that is being mistreated but the country itself; its dignity and integrity are being attacked. In fact, the critics of the Vietnam War in the 1960s who urinated on the American flag were using this singularly effective method to express the contempt they felt for America and its foreign policy.

A flag, then, is more than a sign; it is a powerful visual symbol. It inspires emotion, awakens a web of associations, and mobilizes loyalty because in some way, it "participates in"—or "shares" or "is nourished by"—that reality which it represents. Symbols have a much greater density than signs. They are hardly conventions. The history of the flag goes back to the bitterly fought founding moments of the nation and its display calls forth that history. It is only with great difficulty that Congress would create a new flag.

Flags are visual symbols and religion is constructed out of conceptual symbols, but apart from this difference, these two symbolic languages work in much the same way. In each case, we borrow aspects of familiar human experience to express a complex set of truths about a reality that transcends everyday experience. Religious symbols, too, emerge out of a profound, communal experience and become concretized in the patterns of thought and life experience of a community. They too are hardly conventions. They draw their power from or participate in that community's ongoing experience—in this case, the experience of some transcendent reality that brought the community into being and remains responsible for its ultimate destiny.

When the Jew addresses God as *Avinu Malkenu,* "our Father, our King," he is invoking symbols that have a powerful resonance among human beings. These terms have symbolic power precisely because they are fashioned out of the community's experience of God. That's what makes them more than conventions, more than signs. The symbol "Father" captures a mix of affection, expectation, security, and anger that quickly becomes compassion—qualities that Jews saw in God. The symbol "King" captures His majesty, otherness, sublimity, and the absolute sovereignty of His will. God also has a "mighty hand"; He "speaks" to Moses; He "listens" to prayer; He "redeems" from slavery; He "punishes" and He "forgives." God becomes humanized. This transcendent being becomes a vital center in the life experience of the community.

Symbols of God can function either theologically or religiously. Theological symbols have a primarily intellectual valence; they appeal to the mind, to the need to ground belief in the understanding. The Aristotelian "Unmoved Mover" or Kaplan's "power that makes for salvation" are theological symbols. But when we turn to God in prayer and address Him as *"Avinu Malkenu,"* we appeal not to the mind but to the heart, to God as He is felt and experienced in life situations. These symbols are more broadly religious than theological. The distinction is more one of function than of essence; the same symbolic system can be used in either context.

Finally, though symbols can not be easily changed, they do have a life of their own; they are born, they flourish, and sometimes, when they simply lose their effectiveness, they die. Aristotle's "Unmoved Mover" was intimately tied to a certain cultural setting; when that setting vanished, the symbol died with it. Today, many feminists have questioned the masculine quality of traditional Jewish symbols for God, and are trying to create a more feminine, or at least gender-neutral language to characterize God. After all, if we can not know God, how can we know that God is male? In fact, "He" is literally or objectively neither male nor female. The masculine characterization is part of our human, symbolic system. But at the same time, note how difficult it is for some of us to abandon our traditional characterizations of God, even for those of us who are basically sympathetic to the feminist agenda. Religious symbols are deeply entrenched in our personal and communal psyches.

Symbols can live and die, and they can be "broken." A "broken symbol" is one that is recognized as a symbol and not as a literal description of God. When our symbolic language is "broken," or exposed as symbolic, we can react in various ways. Some of us will reject the entire notion that our images of God are symbols and retreat to a precritical literalism: God really speaks and really listens. Others will treat a broken symbol as a dead symbol: If God doesn't really speak and listen, then who needs religion? But neither of these reactions is inevitable. A third possibility is not only to accept the inevitability of symbolism but even to revel in the power that genuinely living symbols can exercise.

When Jeremiah has God lamenting, "Truly, Ephraim is a dear son to Me, a child that is dandled! Whenever I have turned against him, my thoughts would dwell on him still; I will receive him back in love" (31:20), he is invoking the image of God as a father, torn by conflicting emotions—justified anger, compassion, yearning, rejection—all at once. The image is a complex of symbols which, for most of us, is clearly broken. Yet when this passage is chanted in the context of the *Zikhronot* (literally "remembering") passages of the High Holiday liturgy, within the pervasive High Holiday mood of repentance, rebirth, and renewal, no one can deny its uncanny power to touch and move us in a genuine and even profound way. Such is the power of a living religious symbol.

Myths

Symbols of God are usually embedded in complex myths. Sometimes myths appear in a narrative form, such as the Creation story in Genesis 1 or the Exodus saga in Exodus 1–14. Sometimes they assume a more discursive form, as in Maimonides' *Guide* or Buber's *I and Thou.* Like symbols, myths can have a primarily theological or religious function. Theological myths serve to create conceptual patterns of meaning; religious myths serve to animate the life experience of the believing community.

No term in the study of religions has suffered more from confusion and misunderstanding than the term "myth." The confusion stems primarily from two factors. First, in popular parlance, the term "myth" is usually used as a synonym for "fiction," in contradistinction to "reality," or the "facts." A magazine article dealing with the 1987 congressional "Iran-gate" hearings, entitled "The Myth of the Reagan Debacle," listed ten "myths" as to the effect of the episode on Ronald Reagan's presidency, and in each case contrasted the "myth" with the author's perception of the corresponding "reality." The unambiguous message was that each of the "myths" was false or fictitious, sometimes even deliberately so. In other words, a myth is a lie.

This popular distortion is compounded by a generalized scholarly disagreement on the precise, technical definition of the term "myth." It is used in a wide variety of scholarly disciplines—the social sciences, literary criticism, the study of religions, and the philosophy of science, for example—and each of these disciplines imposes its own constrictions on the use of the term. We are left, then, with a bewildering variety of interpretations, and it is frequently not at all clear which ones apply to our issues. In fact, in the course of teaching this material, this author has isolated some fifteen possible scholarly definitions of the term "myth." Some of these apply specifically to our discussion here.

First, myths deal with beginnings. They tell the story of how

something—either a community, a nation, or a people, or frequently, the world as a whole—came to be. In this role, myths
assume a narrative form. They relate what might be called a
"master story," a story on a grand scale, which explains why
things are distinctively as they are, for me, my people, humanity,
and the cosmos as a whole. The Jewish "master story" begins with
the creation of the world, by a free, omnipotent God, out of
primitive chaos (Genesis 1), continues by accounting for the basic
facts of human existence as we know them—sexuality, death,
labor, the tension between man and woman and between humanity and nature—(Genesis 3), and then moves on to narrate the
beginnings of this particular community (the Patriarchal narratives in Genesis), culminating with the story of the community's
redemption from slavery and its embracing a unique destiny at
Sinai. I recite or retell that latter piece of my master story on
Passover—the Festival that celebrates the birth of my community, because that story is also *my* story. It tells me who I am.
It establishes my identity.

Myths of this kind, especially in their cosmological form,
frequently invoke the activity of supernatural beings and their
encounters with human beings. When they do, they acquire a
religious or theological function. Things are the way they are in
the world because of the activity of God or the gods, either on
His or their own initiative, or in reaction to the behavior of some
primordial human beings.

Sometimes myths are elaborated in a more discursive form.
Rather than narrating *how* things came to be as they are, they
simply articulate or describe the underlying structure or order
that pervades all things. They then become ways of structuring
our experience of the world. Scientific theories are frequently
mythic in this sense. Freudian psychoanalytic theory, for example, structures human behavior so that we can discriminate between the normal and the pathological, and within the latter,
between various forms of pathology. Quantum mechanics does
the same for the behavior of matter on the subatomic level, and
astronomy, for that of the galaxies. Myths of this kind function
like a pair of spectacles; they enable us to see the patterns and

structures that might otherwise escape us. They organize our experience into meaningful wholes.

In order to accomplish this explanatory work, myths of this type frequently invoke realities that are not accessible to direct human experience, such as an id, ego, or superego, a neutron, electron, or quark, or a black hole. They explain the visible world by conjuring up a second, more elusive or hidden dimension of the world. These inaccessible realities can be viewed as constructs, imaginative projections, or, to use our earlier language, symbols. We acknowledge, thereby, that however inaccessible these realities may be to direct perception, our theories can not do their explanatory work without recourse to them. But this does not, for a moment, imply that these realities are fictitious or invented. They are, rather, very much discovered in the world outside us, even though they are not as clearly or obviously "there" as those dimensions of reality that can be sensed.

Theology takes on a mythic character when it describes the structures that underlie reality as a whole, using the symbols of religion. When Jews describe the ultimate structure of reality—as opposed to *how* it came to be that way—they are invoking this discursive function of myths. In this sense, myths can be viewed as "revelatory." They "reveal" dimensions of reality that would otherwise be closed off to us. Because we are part of that total reality, they can also be said to "reveal" dimensions of our own selves. What theological myths "reveal" are precisely those realities that are inaccessible to direct perception, such as God, but without which our explanations would simply not work.

Both scientific and theological myths share an explanatory function. But they differ in scope. Scientific myths are content to explain a corner of our experience: human behavior, the structure of matter, the behavior of the planets. Theological myths aim to explain everything, namely, how the grand panorama of nature and history comes together to form one structured whole. They differ also in substance, in the kind of explanations they adduce. The Jewish myth, for example, explains everything that happens in nature and history as the work of an omnipotent God. Because of their grander scope, theological myths will also distance themselves more from common experience than will scientific myths.

Finally, theological myths, when embedded in complex religious traditions, have a much sharper existential focus than scientific myths. They address the broad range of questions posed by the human condition: Why are we here? Where do we come from? What is our ultimate destiny? How are we to live? What ultimate meaning does our existence have? How do we handle guilt, suffering, sickness, and death? They provide patterns and justifications for certain forms of human behavior and serve as an impetus for morality. They also have a powerful affective thrust; they touch us at the most primitive layers of our being.

Myths, then, are tied to communities; they emerge out of a community's struggle to understand the world and to define its intrinsic character. Second, myths are designed to explain, to answer the ultimate questions posed by human experience. Third, myths explain by referring to a realm that is "beyond," either to events that happened "beyond" or at the beginning of history, or to realities that are beyond everyday experience. Finally, these explanations are artistic creations, dramatic and poetic visions, not factual or scientific accounts, for these transcendent events and realities simply can never be captured in literal form.

Thus the aesthetic and affective character of a great myth, and its capacity to generate sensory symbols and ritual dramas that bring the myth into individual and communal experience. The American myth is evoked by the flag, the national hymn, the Statue of Liberty, and the Lincoln Memorial; it is dramatized in the Pledge of Allegiance, the celebration of the Fourth of July, the Thanksgiving Day meal, and the rituals surrounding the Presidency, the Congress, and the Supreme Court. The mark of circumcision, the *tallit* and *tefillin,* the wine, spices, and candle for *havdalah,* the *sukkah, matzah,* and bitter herbs lend a sensory dimension to the Jewish myth, and the ritual dramas of Jewish life—the Sabbath and Festivals, the rituals surrounding birth, marriage, and death and mourning, and the dietary laws—articulate the structures of the myth in experiential form.

Finally, myths are embodied in canonical documents such as

the Declaration of Independence, the Constitution, and the Hebrew (or Christian or Muslim) Scriptures, and in liturgies, such as the American Pledge of Allegiance or the Oath of Office, and the daily, Sabbath, and Festival liturgies of the Jewish year. Frequently ritual dramas are accompanied by liturgical restatements of the myth. The Passover *seder* is a vivid example of an elaborate pageant that combines historical narrative, theology, liturgy, and ritual in order to communicate our people's myth from one generation to another. The process of canonization accomplishes two purposes: It confirms the authority of the myth, and it effectively limits its further development. Not only the myth itself but also its literary formulation, the very text itself, becomes sacred. Neither can be changed.

But like the symbols out of which it is fashioned, a myth can live and die, flourish or simply cease to function effectively. But here the similarity ends. Precisely because a myth is a complex of many symbols, it can usually survive the death of any one or even of a group of its symbols. Beyond this, a living community will strive valiantly to preserve the vitality of its communal myth; nothing less than its own *raison d'etre* as a community is at stake.

Midrash

When a portion of its myth dies, the community will be impelled to replace it through a process that we call "remythologizing" or, in Jewish sources, *midrash*. The assumption that underlies all of *midrash* is that although the text itself may be closed, it still remains open to infinite layers of reinterpretation. In effect, the text can come to mean whatever the community wants it to mean—often in open defiance of its obvious grammatical and syntactical structure. The community can thus have it both ways: It can preserve both the sanctity of its sacred text and the plasticity of its myth. In fact, we can even suggest that it is the power of *midrash*, or the plasticity of the myth, that makes the canonical text possible in the first place. We will retain the text, unaltered, precisely because we can interpret it in an infinite number of ways.

We can see the process of midrash at work both within Scripture itself—corresponding to the progressive canonization of the various layers of the scriptural text—and beyond. The author of the Book of Jonah, for example, reinterpreted Exodus 34:6–7 (in Jonah 4:2) because he no longer accepted the notion that God must eventually punish the sinner, come what may. That portion of the pentateuchal myth had died for the prophet. In its place, he drew on the prophetic notion of repentance as preempting punishment, and of a God who pleads for this repentance—both radically new symbolizations and departures from the earlier version of the myth. Note also how the author of Jonah inserts his new theology into the very text of the Exodus passage itself. He could not change the Exodus text; in his day it had long been accepted as canonical. But what he could do was make the Exodus passage yield an entirely new meaning. Such is the power of *midrash.*

In our own day, the impulse behind the enterprise of Holocaust theology is the nearly universal acknowledgment that the Holocaust can not be understood as God's punishment for the sins of the Jewish people. For most of us, the Jewish myth that interprets historical trauma as divine punishment has died. If our own midrashic activity has not as yet yielded a widely accepted, new set of symbols, it is probably because the Holocaust itself is only decades old. *Midrash* takes time. Note that in this context the *midrash* is based not on a text, but rather on a historical event which we "read" or interpret much as we do a text.

What, then, does Judaism say about God? The answer to that question is the organic pattern of images that Jews have used in the course of their centuries of thinking and talking about God. We can only speak in images, symbols, or myths. But these images form a pattern and the pattern is "organic" because it is constantly in motion, constantly evolving in line with the changing historical experience of the community. True, some images are more pervasive than others and the pattern as a whole shows remarkable continuity. A community is inherently conservative about its myth because the process of abandoning and recreating mythic structures is long and painful. But sometimes change is necessary. We will have to focus, then, both on the pervasive Jewish image of God and on some of the more recent reformulations of that image as well.

The Pervasive Image of God

HE ALONE IS GOD: "Hear, O Israel! The Lord is our God, the Lord alone" (not "the Lord is One"), is probably the most accurate translation of Deuteronomy 6:4, the *Shema*, which Jews are commanded to recite twice daily and in the final moments of life. What is being rejected here is not polytheism but idolatry. The issue is not one God or many but, rather, who is truly God. Only the God of Israel is God; He alone is God. The other gods are no gods at all.

We tend to take God's "*ehad*-ness" for granted, so much is it ingrained into the classical Jewish image of God. But in fact, when we pause to think about it, biblical monotheism represents a startling claim. When our ancestors attempted to wrest meaning out of the broadest possible canvas, nothing less than the panorama of nature and history as a whole, they "saw" it all as reflecting a single all-powerful, dominant impulse, one guiding hand. In fact, when we consider the data, it would be not at all farfetched to conclude that such a diversified experience could lead people to conclude that the world is governed by two dominant, warring impulses—an impulse for harmony and order and an impulse for chaos and anarchy—as dualism propounded, or by multiple impulses as the polytheists insisted. Our ancestors rejected these alternatives. They saw the world as ultimately unified, and hence as ruled by one God. True, they then had to account for the contrary data, for the mysterious presence of evil and suffering, but they preferred to handle this problem than to deal with the ambiguity and irresolution implied by the alternatives.

HIS WILL IS SOVEREIGN: This is the immediate corollary of His uniqueness. If He alone is God, then His will is absolutely supreme, unchallenged, and unchallengeable. In the later literature, this quality came to be known as God's "omnipotence." The

Bible itself avoids this kind of abstraction and simply portrays God at work. There is absolutely no question that God is fully capable of doing whatever He wishes in order to fulfill His plan for creation. The biblical account of creation shades imperceptibly into the story of civilizations, and ultimately into the story of one people. All of it forms one integrated panorama under one guiding hand. The biblical juxtaposition of Genesis and Exodus teaches that this mythic structure makes no distinction between natural and historical processes; there is only one panorama, under one guiding hand.

It is precisely this sovereignty of the biblical God that the late Israeli scholar Yehezkel Kaufmann singled out as the most revolutionary teaching of biblical religion. In his multivolume *History of Israelite Religion* (published in Hebrew, with only selected portions available in an English translation), Kaufmann studied the image of the biblical God against the backdrop of the pagan culture within which it emerged. The distinguishing character of the pagan god, whatever form he may take, Kaufmann notes, is that his will is not sovereign. Pagan gods and goddesses evolve from and remain dependent on some preexistent realm that is itself governed by an impersonal set of laws or forces that determine the course of events. They are as much at the mercy of the forces that rule the world as are human beings.

The contrast with the biblical image of God could not be more striking. The Bible tells us nothing about the personal biography of God. He simply appears in the first verse of Genesis and remains throughout the Bible. He alone is God and His will is sovereign. He is not subject to any other force or law beyond Himself. His uniqueness is unchallenged; His freedom is absolute. In fact, God's freedom becomes the paradigm for human freedom. The pagan is in league with his god because together they are dependent on forces that transcend them both. In biblical religion, both God and the human being are free. Paradoxically, this sets the stage for the only challenge that the biblical God does have to face: the confrontation with human beings.

When the later philosophical literature speaks of God's "supernatural" character, it is again using an abstraction to capture this quality of absolute sovereignty. He is "super" nature in the sense that He is totally other than anything natural, independent of natural processes, "eternal," or unaffected by time as well as space. It is difficult for we who live, think, and talk in spatial and temporal dimensions to capture this image of God. That's why our theological language is symbolic. We struggle, for example, to unravel the dilemma of how we can be truly free if God knows all that will be in the future. But what creates the dilemma in the first place is the very assumption that our theological language is literal and objective. For God Himself, there is no past or future; He inhabits an eternal present.

God's sovereignty also means that He is the source and authority for all value. His will determines what is good—not the other way around. When Abraham challenges God in that memorable confrontation before God's destruction of Sodom (Genesis 18:17–32), he does not invoke an independent, humanistic value but rather God's own commitment to justice. In the prelude to that debate, God Himself says that "doing what is just and right" is *His* way, "the way of the Lord"; that's why Abraham can then challenge: "Shall not the Judge of all the earth deal justly?"

Our own struggle with the morality of a host of biblical narratives stems precisely from this encounter between a humanist ethic and the biblical ethic rooted in God's will. We are appalled at God's command to exterminate the Midianites (Numbers 31) or the Amalekites (Deuteronomy 25:17–19). When later in the Bible, Saul spares the Amalekite sheep and oxen, God is furious and wrests the kingship from him (1 Samuel 15). Where is God's compassion, we ask. But the biblical narrator focuses purely on Saul's defiance of God's explicit command (vv. 22–23). It is God, not we, who defines what is good and evil, what is compassion, and when we are to be compassionate. Moral values are rooted in a power that transcends the merely human. The tension that later generations felt about some of these biblical narratives was precisely the kind of stimulus that led to theological reinterpretation through *midrash*.

HE HAS A STAKE IN HUMAN CIVILIZATION: He cares passionately for what transpires on earth. That's why He reveals His will, enters into covenants, sends prophets, constantly intercedes in the drama of history to try to get people to achieve His purposes, by and large ineffectively. It is this symbolic pattern that Abraham Joshua Heschel characterizes as the "divine pathos."

Thus the tragic paradox at the heart of the biblical image of God. Sovereign of nature and history though He may be, He emerges as frustrated and disappointed. His power is largely *de jure,* not *de facto,* more often blunted than actual. And the source of this tragic paradox is that He created human beings free—free even to flout His will. Only we human beings have that freedom and power, and only because that's how God created us.

It is hard to believe that this sovereign God is unwilling to restrain our human tendency to rebel. He rails against it. He punishes. He just about exterminates civilization as a whole, but then regrets His action (Genesis 8:21–22) and promises never to do it again. Later, He is ready to exterminate the Israelite people. This time He is stopped by Moses' threat that the Egyptians might read God's extermination of Israel as a sign that He never intended to fulfill His promises to bring them into their own land, and by Moses' reminder that God Himself had promised Abraham, Isaac, and Jacob to make their offspring as numerous as the stars of the heaven (Exodus 32:11–14). So God mitigates His punishment. This supremely free and powerful God is, in actuality, very much not free and hardly all-powerful.

It is clear that these limitations on God's freedom and power stem from His own, freely willed commitments, not from His essential character. The pagan god was limited because of his inherent nature. The biblical God limits Himself, primarily by creating human beings free to challenge Him, and then by committing Himself to a unique relationship with Israel. To put the issue sharply, God could have created a perfect world and a perfectly obedient people at the outset, but He chose not to do so. Instead, He staked His fate on the loyalty of His people. The relationship brings Him great frustration, yet He persists in hoping that His dream for Israel and humanity will be fulfilled.

HE IS A PERSONAL GOD: His interactions with human beings are deliberate and intentional, not blind and mechanical. He shapes historical events with conscious purpose. He reacts and responds to human beings in a direct and highly emotional way. Read the Abraham narratives in Genesis 12–25, for example, concentrating not on the events themselves but on the texture of the relationship between God and Abraham, and the range and intensity of the feelings that flow back and forth. The broader canvas of prophetic literature captures that same richness in portraying God's relationship with Israel—from the passionate rage of Isaiah 1 and the bleak despair of Isaiah 5, to the wistful nostalgia of Jeremiah 2:1–3, the tenderness of Jeremiah 31:20, and the hopeful expectation of Hosea 2:16–25. Or note the explicit lesson of Jeremiah's visit to the house of the potter (Jeremiah 18:1–12). This sovereign, all-powerful God waits for a human initiative before determining how He will act.

Buber's notion of God's I-Thou relationship with Israel is a modern formulation of that personal quality of the biblical God. The I-Thou relationship personalizes in both directions; we referred to the "mutuality" of the relationship. A particularly striking, if subtle, expression of that quality is in the daily morning liturgy, in the passage immediately prior to the recitation of the *Shema.*

The *Shema* itself is a series of three biblical passages (Deuteronomy 6:4–9 and 11:13–21, followed by Numbers 15:37–41) but the preceding passage is rabbinic. It serves, together with the passages that follow the recitation of the *Shema,* as a frame for the biblical passages themselves.

Here are the concluding lines of the liturgical passage and the opening lines of the *Shema:*

You have singled us out from all peoples and nations and brought us near to your glorious name in order that we may praise you and proclaim your uniqueness. Praised are you, O Lord, Who, in love, has singled out His people Israel.

Hear, O Israel! The Lord is our God, the Lord alone.

You shall love the Lord your God with all your heart and with all your soul and with all your might. . . .

The passage as a whole makes an intricate theological statement. By reciting the *Shema,* we proclaim that God is singled
out, unique, that He alone is God. In the same breath, we proclaim our love for Him, which is the same theological claim, this
time expressed affectively. But we can do all of this because, in
the liturgical passage that leads into the *Shema,* we recall that
He has singled *us* out (more accurate than the popular "chosen
us") from among the nations, and proclaimed *our* uniqueness,
again "in love." What is love if not the mutual "singling out"
of two persons—or beings—in an intimate relationship!

The apparent simplicity and straightforwardness of this passage is highly deceptive. Theologically, it is incredibly complex.
God's uniqueness, His personal reaching out to Israel in love, His
intervention into history, the reciprocal nature of Israel's relation
to God, the very fact that God's uniqueness has to be affirmed by
human beings in the first place, that God should *need* this affirmation—all of these images come together in a few spare liturgical sentences, and all are shown to be interrelated.

Parenthetically, this is a superb object lesson in the way the
classical liturgy captures the central motifs of the Jewish myth.
Because the liturgy is recited daily, and because its recitation is
a *mitzvah,* it becomes a textbook for educating the community
in its myth. In fact, it is precisely in the liturgy, not in the
theological homilies scattered throughout talmudic literature,
that we find the extension of the canonical version of the Jewish
myth beyond the Bible. The liturgical text itself is codified, and
hence represents the consensus of rabbinic authorities on matters
of belief. It is the closest Jews come to reciting a form of the
Credo as Roman Catholic Christians do in their Mass.

This "pervasive" image of God is as close as we can come to
a normative Jewish position. It forms the grid or skeleton on
which Jewish theologians have proceeded to graft a wide range
of more idiosyncratic images in line with the demands of their
own intellectual milieu. Some of these have had a wide influence,
not only on Jewish thought but on the course of Western intellectual history as well.

Note that in each of these instances, what we call the "idiosyncratic" image is clearly in tension with the "pervasive." This

tension has impelled more traditionalist Jewish thinkers to brand these further images heretical. In fact, however, the tension reflects the vitality of our religious symbols and myths. Religious symbols live and die, and when they die, a living community will create their replacements. Each of these further statements, then, must be viewed as the thinker's acknowledgment that the normative Jewish image of God has in some way become inadequate. That's why he has to go beyond it—even if, in the process, he offends the sensibility of his coreligionists. His ultimate purpose is to save God for the believing community.

Maimonides' "Negative" Image of God

No Jewish thinker worked more passionately than Maimonides to disabuse Jews of the assumption that human beings can capture the essence of God in literal terms. His overriding purpose was to harmonize Torah and Greek philosophy. The only way to accomplish that was by a radical reinterpretation of Torah and the key to that reinterpretation is to view the language of Torah—particularly as it applies to the nature of God—as allegorical.

Maimonides was simply appalled at the fact that Jews believed that God was corporeal, that He really saw, spoke, listened, felt anger or pleasure, stretched out His arm over Egypt, and the like. But then how can we speak of God? And this linguistic problem masks a conceptual or philosophical problem, namely, what then *is* God? What is His essence?

The answer to that question is an elaborate theory of "divine attributes," which is one of Maimonides' most important contributions to the history of Western philosophy. Maimonides divides all of God's characteristics into two broad classes, those that define God in Himself, in His essence, and those that describe the effects of His activity. That God is wise refers to His essence; that He is compassionate refers to the way He acts in the world. Note that these latter attributes tell us nothing about God Himself, only about how we humans experience the effects of His behavior toward us. We tend to infer that because He has acted compassionately, therefore He *is* compassionate. This inference is illegitimate. The attributes of action tell us nothing about God's inherent nature.

Nor, for that matter, do the attributes of essence, for humans simply can know nothing about God's essential nature. Here is Maimonides' most radical thesis: The attributes of essence must be understood as covert negations. They tell us what God is *not,* not what He *is*—for any statement about what God *is* would limit Him. If we say that God is wise, then, what we are really saying is that He is not not-wise, for to say that He *is* wise would constitute a limitation on God. But God can have no limitation and remain God.

All of our conceptualizations of God's essence are negations. He is "living" means He is not dead; He is "eternal" means He is not created; He is "wise" means He is not ignorant. The effect of this accumulation of negatives is to eliminate any limitation on God. But by implication, then, it also becomes an extraordinarily positive statement about God's transcendence. By a strange, conceptual twist, God as the wholly Nothing becomes God as the totally Everything. As we strip away all the limitations on God, we are left with the image of God as the sum total of all attributes, as absolute perfection.

Having solved his philosophical problem about the nature of God, Maimonides now has to deal with the more religious problem of bringing this completely transcendent, essentially unknowable God into relation with the world and with human beings. The key to this step is Maimonides' proof that God created the world in time—the issue on which he disagrees with Aristotle. Since God created the world and since He is absolute perfection, God acts freely and purposefully to achieve His predetermined goals. The attributes of action now come into play, and the familiar personal God of the Bible is restored. God does answer prayer; God does love Israel; His providence does rule over all things. But what God is in Himself we can not know. Maimonides' agnosticism on this issue is absolute.

There is no denying the inherent tension between Maimonides' God and the God of the biblical and rabbinic traditions. Maimonides himself was convinced that his philosophical work was indispensable to preserving the God of Jewish religion. The real issue here is the tension between two symbolic systems: the theological/philosophical and the religious. Maimonides was primarily concerned with the former. First and foremost, our *thinking* about God had to be subjected to the most sophisticated and critical analysis. That inquiry would then dictate the way we deal with the remaining issues, among them, how this philosophically refined God enters into the religious life of the community.

But it is clear that Maimonides' resolution of the tension between the two symbolic languages is awkward at best. His audience was primarily those members of the community who shared his agenda, who could not get on with the business of religious living without attending to the issues posed by the intellect. There will always be Jews of this kind and Maimonides remains the champion of that constituency.

Images of God in Jewish Mysticism

The tension between intellectual and religious symbolic systems pervades the literature of Jewish mysticism as well, but here it is resolved in a very different way. This rich and diverse material has had much more influence on the popular Jewish imagination than the better-known Jewish philosophical tradition.

Like Maimonides, Jewish mystics insist that no human being can know God as He is in Himself, in His essence. They characterize this dimension of God as *Ein-Sof,* literally "Without End" or "Infinite." Note the absence of a pronoun—not "He That Is Without End" but simply "Without End." Even the use of a personal pronoun would constitute a limitation on Him. Again we have God in Himself defined in negative terms. But again the accumulation of negatives is the only way to capture the all-encompassing totality and perfection of the divine.

Thus far we are on familiar ground. In fact, there is a clear congruence between the God of the rationalist Maimonides and the God of the mystics. Although their points of departure are widely divergent, their conclusions coincide.

When the mystics deal with God as Creator of the world, they break sharply with the rationalist tradition and, in fact, with most traditional readings of Genesis. The plain sense of Genesis 1 seems to suggest that first there was God alone and nothing else. Medieval philosophers read the Genesis account of creation as teaching that out of this realm of nothingness (or *ex nihilo*), God created the world by His word alone. But God and the world are separate from each other.

The mystics disagree. They understand creation as a process of emanation that takes place within God Himself, within the *Ein-Sof.* The world flowed out of God in such a way that God pervades all of creation. There is no separation between God and the world; they form one interconnected whole. Creation is thus an unfolding, an externalization of the *Ein-Sof.* They even proceed to label that dimension of God that forms the created world with one of the traditional Jewish synonyms for God, the *Shekhinah.* God then has two dimensions, two faces: God in Himself, the hidden, unknown, and unknowable God, or the *Ein-Sof;* and God as the created world, the externalized, revealed God, or the *Shekhinah.*

This is *midrash* with a vengeance, for God still creates the world "out of nothing" only now the "nothing" is not outside of God but is precisely God Himself, the *Ein-Sof,* infinite and freed of all limitations. We are remarkably close to the Maimonidean God who is both the wholly Nothing and the sum total of all perfections.

In the most influential book of Jewish mysticism, the thirteenth-century *Zohar* (literally, the "Book of Splendor") and in the sixteenth-century mysticism of Rabbi Isaac Luria, this notion of the dual faces of God was taken to even more radical extremes. *Ein-Sof* and *Shekhinah* are viewed as split apart, or, to use the actual language of the mystics, the *Shekhinah* is "in exile." This exile is not simply a historical fact but a profound symbol for the state of disharmony that exists throughout creation, even up to and including God Himself since creation is pervaded by Him. Not only Israel, but the world and even God Himself is in exile. This cosmic exile will end with the coming of the Messiah. At that point, Israel will return to its land, the *Ein-Sof* and the *Shekhinah* will be reunited, and the harmony that existed at the moment of Creation will be restored.

The scandalous implications of this position are clear. It skirts two classical Jewish heresies: dualism (for God is both the *Ein-Sof* and the *Shekhinah*) and pantheism (for God and the created world are one and the same). But the mystics counter by noting that these two heresies are contradictory, that one can not be both a dualist and a pantheist at the same time. In effect, then, the two heresies cancel each other out. To the charge that the view is dualistic, the mystics insist that of course God is one, that the *Ein-Sof* and the *Shekhinah* are but two aspects of the one God, that the *Shekhinah* is not inherently separate or distinct from the *Ein-Sof*. To the charge of pantheism, the mystics respond that God as *Shekhinah,* God as the created world, does not exhaust the nature of God. There is always God as the *Ein-Sof,* God in Himself, hidden and inaccessible to human beings.

But look at the way this theology resolves the tension between the two symbolic systems, the intellectual and the religious: the *Ein-Sof* is the intellectual symbol; the *Shekhinah,* the religious. One attends to God's philosophical purity; the other to His religious relevance. God is both very much transcendent and also very close to us, present in creation, in us, in all we do.

For all of its heretical implications, the doctrine of creation as emanation is a brilliant solution to Maimonides' problem of bringing the transcendent God into relation with the created world. The relation could not be tighter. God *is* the created world, at least to the mystic who knows how to "see through" the material world and perceives God's presence throughout. In the teachings of Rabbi Isaac Luria, this image of God as the *Shekhinah* is the basis for the notion that every *mitzvah* performed by a Jew with the proper mystical intent has a direct, redemptive effect on God Himself. Since the material world is an extension of God's very own being, everything that takes place here and now also takes place within God. The *mitzvot* become the means of reuniting God as the *Ein-Sof* with God as the *Shekhinah* again. The original harmony within creation and within God is restored through the performance of the *mitzvot*. The *mitzvot,* then, become the tools of redemption. Can there be a more powerful motivation for observing the *mitzvot* than this?

Jewish mystics had a very different agenda than Maimonides.

He was primarily concerned with the cerebral dimension of religion; the mystics, with its affective, living texture. Jewish mysticism never shunned speculation; in fact, the speculative chapters in Jewish mystical writings are among the most intricate in all of Jewish literature. But this enterprise invariably has a self-consciously practical focus: to enable the Jew to live his Judaism to the fullest—to pray, to observe the *mitzvot,* to endure the exile, to deal with guilt, suffering, and death, and ultimately, to enjoy that intimate communion with God which is the goal of all mystical teachings.

The mystical tradition in Judaism stretches from the Bible through to contemporary Hasidism. One of the pervasive characteristics of this tradition, throughout Jewish intellectual history, is its tendency to embrace the language of symbol and myth. This readiness gives it its compelling emotional power and vitality. How much the mystics themselves are aware that they have departed from the literal meaning of the Torah is open to question; it undoubtedly varied from writer to writer. We today, however, are free to appreciate the power of this mythic system, and to appropriate it for our own more normative theological reformulations.

Kaplan's God as a Power Within Nature

Of all contemporary reformulations of the Jewish image of God, none is more radical than Mordecai Kaplan's. In retrospect, Kaplan's most "heretical" claim was not so much his new image of God as his naturalist version of the emergence of Jewish religion in the first place. Kaplan is a "religious naturalist" because he understands religion as emerging out of the natural functioning of a community of human beings. Communities create religions in as natural a way as apple trees produce apples. This is simply the way people are, the way they intuitively behave. The traditional notion that religion stems from the revelation of an active, supernatural, revealing God who addresses a passive, accepting community, struck Kaplan as preposterous.

Of course, Kaplan did not do away with the notion of revelation, but he understood it in a very different way. Revelation is human discovery. The Kaplanian God does not thunder from a mountaintop. He works in and through human beings. Torah, then, may have been formulated and written by the Jewish people, but it remains revealed because it was God, working within the human community, who stimulated the discovery of its contents.

Kaplan's naturalist account of the emergence of Jewish religion enables him to locate the center of authority for what constitutes Torah in the living community. What the Jewish people originally create, they can recreate from generation to generation. The teachings of Jewish religion then become subordinate to the sense of Jewish peoplehood. Our identification as Jews is predominantly through this sense of belonging to a vital community. Jewish belief and practice are designed to make that identification possible. Hence Kaplan's readiness to reinterpret the contents of both theology and practice to make that identification possible in a new cultural setting.

It is this original departure from classical Jewish thinking that made all of Kaplan's further departures possible—including his reformulation of the concept of God as that power within nature that "makes for salvation." God is a "power"—not a Being, certainly not a personal Being, but a force or a process. We commonly assume that a noun in our language refers to some entity. But there are nouns that refer not to entities but to activities or behaviors. These nouns are really adverbs in disguise; they describe an activity.

The noun "God" is really an adverb parading as a noun. Like the noun "mind," for example, it describes a certain manner of activity, this time an activity within nature. The distinctive character of this divine power is its focus on salvation. By "salvation" Kaplan means nothing more than the sum total of perfections that Jews have used to describe the world at its best: universal peace, human fulfillment, social justice, and the rest. He discerns that salvational impulse in every human being. Kaplan's "leap of faith" is that if there is a salvational impulse within us, it is but one dimension of an impulse that pervades all of reality, for we are part of the natural order. It is simply inconceivable to Kaplan that the world would be so structured as to frustrate the most intuitive dimension of our human nature. Kaplan's faith commitment as a Jew is that all of reality complements our internal impulse for redemption. God, then, is precisely that power within the natural order that impels a salvational outcome. He is the "power that makes for salvation." He doesn't cause that power from the outside. He literally *is* that power itself.

In illustrating his concept of God, Kaplan uses the analogy of iron filings placed above an electromagnet. The electromagnetic current itself is not visible, but sprinkle the iron filings on a piece of paper, place the paper over a magnet, and the filings will form patterns representing the current. God is the current and the iron filings are the visible signs of that salvational power that courses within nature.

God is a "power" within nature. Nature, here, is simply all there is. There is nothing "beyond" nature; the notion of any "supernatural" reality struck Kaplan as silly. There is simply no "beyond" to nature.

Kaplan departs from the more traditional Jewish images of God, first in his methodological claim that Jewish theology, like the rest of Torah, was not dictated by God but rather emerged out of the needs of the Jewish people; and second, in his insistence that what is important about God is not what God *is* but rather what God *does*. While Jews have always disagreed about the "nature" of God, there has been significant agreement about how He functions in the world. The Kaplanian God does everything that the traditional God does: reveals, creates, redeems, rewards, and punishes.

Of course, Kaplan's understanding of all of these divine activities is highly idiosyncratic. For example, God rewards and punishes in the sense that if we behave "salvationally," if we strive to make the world a better place, we will be rewarded because we will be inhabiting a better world. Conversely, when we behave in a countersalvational way, we will suffer from living in a less-than-perfect world. That is our punishment. God's reward and punishment take place not through His direct intervention but rather through the natural process that, according to

Kaplan, is God's presence in the world. That's why one of the functions that Kaplan's God does not exercise is to "elect" Israel from among the nations. A choosing God is a God who functions with purpose and intention, a personal God, and Kaplan's "power that makes for salvation" can not be personal in that way.

Like the traditional image of God, Kaplan's God is limited in His power. The salvational impulse has not conquered nature. But in Kaplan's theology, God's limitation is inherent, not deliberate and self-willed as in the Bible. Evil has not been eliminated from the world, not because God does not will to do so but because as yet He simply can not. The salvational impulse is but one of many at work within nature. The impulse toward chaos and anarchy is also at work in us and in the world—and we are free to ally ourselves with either one.

Kaplan's writings provide a classic example of the process of theological resymbolization. The traditional Jewish symbols for God—God as a sovereign, personal, and supernatural Being—had died for Kaplan and, he claimed, for his generation. He proceeded to create their replacements—God as power or process, as within nature, and as limited. His locating the impulse for the process of symbolization within the living community is completely on target. Religious symbols and the myths in which they are embedded grow out of a community. Kaplan's naturalist account of the emergence of religion illuminates the origins of that process. His own work illustrates the way in which symbolic and mythic systems live, die, and can then be restored.

The Tensions in Jewish God-Talk

This tension between what we have called the "pervasive" Jewish image of God and its more idiosyncratic reformulations runs through all of Jewish theology. In fact, it provides an extraordinarily important perspective on the way Jewish thinkers have pursued their theological inquiry.

It is entirely understandable that the more traditionalist of Jewish thinkers should be offended by what Maimonides in his day, or Mordecai Kaplan in ours, does with the classical, or normative, Jewish concept of God. The traditionalist is perfectly satisfied with that traditional image—both intellectually and religiously. Maimonides and Kaplan were not. It seemed to them to be intellectually primitive and religiously ineffective. That dissatisfaction impelled them to rethink the basic premises of Judaism.

Tension is almost always a sign of concern and vitality. The alternative is to acknowledge that the entire enterprise is irrelevant, and of course, to Maimonides and Kaplan, that outcome would have been disastrous. The sense of alienation that emerges when a received tradition is perceived to be anachronistic then becomes the stimulus for a new *midrash*.

The process of creating a new *midrash* almost invariably causes anxiety. First, it takes time. Second, it shakes up our familiar world of discourse and points to a new, as-yet-unknown religious idiom. If we are intuitively apprehensive about the ensuing commotion—in Maimonides' case, it lasted for close to two centuries—we can be reassured that Judaism survived not only despite the tensions but possibly also because of them.

But the tension that pervades all of our God-talk has another, more troublesome dimension. It stems not only from the conflict between old, dying symbols and new, unfamiliar ones, but it is also endemic to the view that all of our concepts of God are symbolic or mythical in the first place. First, we are being asked to get rid of the notion that God is literally as we describe Him. That goes against some of our most primitive, deep-seated impulses. How can we pray if we no longer believe that God really hears our prayers?

Second, by its very nature, every religious symbol exists in a state of tension. It straddles two worlds, the familiar world of concrete human experience and the world that lies "beyond" nature and history. These two demands inevitably work against each other. To be effective, our symbols for God have to be concrete and familiar—God is our Father—but this impulse toward concreteness always threatens to rob Him of His otherness and transcendence, and then we fall into idolatry. The symbol takes the place of God. We have molded a conceptual golden calf.

We began by noting that the Bible warns us against the sin of creating plastic images of God, but that our problem has less to do with plastic images and more with conceptual ones. These images are both indispensable and yet perilous. In fact, we have no alternative. We must both speak symbolically and know that we are speaking symbolically. We must create symbols and yet remain perpetually suspicious and critical of them. That is our uniquely modern dilemma.

FOR FURTHER STUDY
Most important for this chapter, read the Bible closely and carefully. Watch how it characterizes or images God and how that characterization evolves before our eyes as we move from the Genesis narratives, through the Exodus and desert wanderings, and into the writings of the prophets, the Psalms, and Job.

The premier Jewish scholarly authority on biblical religion was Yehezkel Kaufmann. Unfortunately, only a small portion of his monumental and multivolumed TOLEDOT HA-EMUNAH HA-YISRAELIT *is available in English translation. Most notable is the selection collected under the title,* THE RELIGION OF ISRAEL, *translated and abridged by Moshe Greenberg (University of Chicago Press, 1960; pb 1972). A more concise overview of Kaufmann's conclusions is in his essay, "The Biblical Age," included in* GREAT AGES AND IDEAS OF THE JEWISH PEOPLE, *edited by Leo W. Schwarz (Random House, 1956.) Equally important is Abraham Joshua Heschel's discussion of the divine pathos in his* THE PROPHETS *(see ch. 1).*

Specifically on the issue of biblical monotheism, see chs. 2 and 3 of THE RELIGION OF ISRAEL, *and also E. A. Speiser's Introduction to his translation of* **Genesis** *in The Anchor Bible series, in particular, pp. xliii–lii. The earlier pages of Speiser's introduction are a concise summary of the major conclusions of biblical criticism.*

On the distinction between symbol and sign, and on the distinctive role of symbols in religion and theology, begin with Tillich's DYNAMICS OF FAITH *(see ch. 1) and also John Herman Randall, Jr.'s* THE ROLE OF KNOWLEDGE IN WESTERN RELIGION *(pb University Press of America, 1986), particularly, ch. 4. Tillich and Randall jointly conducted seminars in the philosophy of religion at Columbia University and these two volumes represent the conclusions of their inquiry.*

The literature on the nature and function of myths in religion and elsewhere can be confusing in the diversity of its conclusions. Begin, again, with Tillich's DYNAMICS OF FAITH *(see ch. 1)*, and Ian Barbour's MYTHS, MODELS AND PARADIGMS *(see ch. 1)*. Will Herberg's "Some Variant Meanings of the Word 'Myth'," in his ESSAYS IN BIBLICAL THEOLOGY, edited with an introduction by Bernhard W. Anderson *(Westminster, 1976)*, is an excellent illustration of the difficulties involved in using the term "myth" even in a technical discussion. Mircea Eliade wrote extensively on religious myths; his MYTH AND REALITY *(pb Harper & Row, 1975)* is a good summary of his conclusions. An excellent collection of material can also be found in the anthology, SACRED NARRATIVE, edited by Alan Dundes *(pb University of California Press, 1984)*. Finally, Thomas S. Kuhn's THE STRUCTURE OF SCIENTIFIC REVOLUTIONS *(2nd edition, enlarged, pb University of Chicago Press, 1970)*, a classic in the philosophy of science, can also be read as a suggestive study of how religious myths evolve, or of what we call midrash.

An influential study of biblical religion as exemplifying a myth-opoetic approach to the world is in BEFORE PHILOSOPHY, *by Henri Frankfort and others (pb Penguin, 1949)*.

Finally, particularly striking and illuminating is THE POWER OF MYTH *by Joseph Campbell with Bill Moyers (pb Doubleday, 1988)*. Campbell wrote extensively on myth and myth making and these conversations with Moyers bring together the conclusions of his lifelong study of the topic.

On the Jewish material, apart from Kaufmann, and chs. 2–7 of Schechter's ASPECTS OF RABBINIC THEOLOGY *(see ch. 2)*, Maimonides' doctrine of divine attributes is discussed in Part 1 of his GUIDE OF THE PERPLEXED, *chs. 51–60*. The authoritative English version of the GUIDE is by S. Pines *(University of Chicago Press, 1963; pb 2 vols. 1974)*. Pines' own introduction and the accompanying essay by Leo Strauss are indispensable. Isaac Husik's A HISTORY OF MEDIEVAL JEWISH PHILOSOPHY *(Jewish Publication Society, 1948; pb Meridian, 1958)* paraphrases the argumentation in the original texts, often in less technical language. See also the relevant chapters in Guttman's PHILOSOPHIES OF JUDAISM *(see ch. 3)* for a more scholarly discussion. Lectures 6 and 7 of Gershom Scholem's MAJOR TRENDS IN JEWISH

MYSTICISM *(Schocken, 1941; pb 1961), the first major work by the scholar who created the field of Jewish mysticism as a scholarly discipline, will do the same for the material on the image of God in the writings of Jewish mystics.*

Finally, the clearest and most concise exposition of Mordecai Kaplan's naturalist concept of God is in a brief reply (pp. 80–89) included in his QUESTIONS JEWS ASK: RECONSTRUCTIONIST ANSWERS *(pb Reconstructionist Press, 1956). A more elaborate discussion is the central theme of his* THE MEANING OF GOD IN MODERN JEWISH RELIGION *(The Jewish Reconstructionist Foundation, 1947; pb 1975).*

V

Sensing God's Presence:
Empiricism

MOST OF OUR KNOWLEDGE OF THE WORLD OUTSIDE OF US ORIGI-
nates through sense experience. From the most common
kind of everyday knowledge to the most refined type of
scientific knowledge, what we know about the world originates
in the use of our senses. Of course, we usually go well beyond
these simple sense perceptions and shape the data into increasingly complex patterns. We interpret and reflect on what we
sense, and we deduce even more complex conclusions from
these reflections. The acts of seeing and hearing are by no means
as simple and uncomplicated as they might appear. But it is
indisputable that without sense experience we would know
very little about our world.

Can our knowledge of the existence and nature of God
originate in the same way? If the testimony of many believers
over the centuries and in varied cultural settings is to be taken
seriously, the answer would be an unequivocal yes. Experientialism, or empiricism, is the single most pervasive and persistent of
the methods used by human beings to attain religious faith.

The very term "experience" is highly ambiguous. We use it
to refer to what happens when we see a red patch or a blood cell,
hear an infant cry, or taste a hot fudge sundae. Or we speak of
seeing more complex patterns such as the motion of subatomic
particles, or the cycles in a nation's economy, where our sensory

perception is accompanied by highly refined interpretation. We also talk of an "experience" of love or guilt, of awe in the midst of a thunderstorm, or of terror when our lives are in danger. Here the act of sensing is shot through with the most powerful of emotions so that the experience as a whole is compelling and transformatory. In still another vein, we speak of some people as having accumulated a rich "life experience," of having negotiated multiple complex or difficult life situations and emerged with a perspective that gives their lives a certain unity, integrity, and fulfillment. This experience seems to yield a global vision of life as a whole, of how all things come together in some meaning-filled way.

What Makes an Experience "Religious"?

Believers who talk of their own "religious" experience may be using the term in all of these ways. At one extreme, every religious tradition has its visionaries who claim to have had a direct sense experience of some divine being—God Himself, an angel, or a divine messenger. Exodus 24:9 and Isaiah 6:1 allude, however cautiously, to visions of this kind. Many believing Christians, from the apostles in antiquity to the "born again" in our own day, claim to have had visions of Jesus of Nazareth. Joseph Smith, the founder of Mormonism, had visions of God, Jesus, and later, an angel. But in Judaism at least, it is much more common to find reports of "hearing" the voice of God than of "seeing" Him. The Pentateuch and prophetic literature provide numerous examples of the former, but when biblical figures claim to have seen God, it is usually the blurred "appearance of the semblance of the Presence of the Lord," as Ezekiel 1:28 describes it, rather than something as direct and clear as Isaiah's "my Lord."

More common in Jewish religious sources is a highly interpretive kind of seeing, frequently an interpretive seeing that is shot through with emotion. Our analysis of Exodus 14:30–31 in Chapter 3 is a vivid example of this kind of religious experience. The Israelites saw dead Egyptians on the shores of the Sea, but they also "saw" God's wondrous power and feared Him. The psalmist claims that "the heavens declare the glory of God, the sky proclaims His handiwork" (Psalm 19). The psalmist sees the heavens but he also "sees" God's glory in the heavens, and, as the psalm continues, this experience inspires him to intuit certain things about God's teachings, decrees, precepts, and instruction.

More frequently, the biblical community is asked to direct its interpretive seeing to its history. Deuteronomy 26:5–10, Joshua 24:1–13, Psalm 105, and Nehemiah 9:6–37 are examples of brief surveys of paradigmatic events in the experience of the community, knitted together to reveal God's presence in its history. The tone of these passages is didactic; they teach the community how to understand its historical experience.

Deuteronomy 4:1–40 provides a particularly vivid case study in how the Bible uses the experiential pathway to God. The passage is studded with various references to seeing (vv. 3,9,12, 15,19, and 35) and hearing (vv. 1,6,12, and 36). The community is instructed in what it saw and heard, how it should understand what it saw and heard, and what conclusion it should draw from this evidence: "It has been clearly demonstrated to you that the Lord alone is God; there is none beside Him" (v. 35). Note that the community is also instructed in what it did *not* see: "You saw no shape when the Lord your God spoke to you at Horeb" (v. 15). It is also warned against the danger that it may then see something else: "The moon and the stars, the whole heavenly host" (v. 19) and conclude that it should worship these in place of God. The passage is also sadly aware of the possibility that people easily "forget the things that you saw with your own eyes" (v. 9). That's why they have to "make them known to your children and to your children's children," precisely through narratives such as this one, which teach succeeding generations how and what to see, and how to interpret what they see. There is no better one-sentence summary of the function of the Bible in the life of the community. It is precisely a manual in how to see God in nature and history.

The Mystical Experience

What is striking about this passage from Deuteronomy is the absence of any powerful emotional coloration to the religious experience. One senses the narrator's passion and conviction about his interpretation of what he sees and about the conclusions he draws from his seeing, but the seeing itself is dry and factual. The pattern is laid out before the community; one simply has to look.

The literature of mysticism presents a very different account of the religious experience. Mysticism is one of the most complex and subtle forms of religious expression, and we will study specifically Jewish mystical doctrines as we proceed. But in this context, when the mystic describes what he achieves at the climax of his experience—and to the extent that he can describe it at all—his testimony will be both highly metaphorical and transfigured with emotion.

Mystics, for example, will typically quote verses such as Psalm 34:9—"Taste and see how good the Lord is"—to capture the quality of their experience. Note the appeal to the sense of taste, however metaphorical its use here. Tasting is very different from seeing or hearing. The connection between the taster and what he tastes is far more intimate than that between the seer and what he sees or the hearer and what he hears. The mystic strives to achieve this same kind of intimacy or union with God. Thus the sensual, and frequently even sexual imagery that is pervasive in mystical literature.

The mystic can not achieve this intimacy and remain detached or cerebral about his experience. Ezekiel (1:28) beholds the semblance of the Presence of the Lord, and, overwhelmed, he flings himself down on his face. In a different mode, the psalmist captures the feeling of being encircled, embraced, guided, and possibly judged by God—all at the same time:

> Where can I escape from your spirit?
> Where can I flee from your presence?
> If I ascend to heaven, You are there;
> if I descend to Sheol, You are there too.
> If I take wing with the dawn
> to come to rest on the western horizon,
> even there Your hand will be guiding me,

Your right hand will be holding me fast.
If I say, "Surely darkness will conceal me,
night will provide me with cover,"
darkness is not dark for You;
night is as light as day;
darkness and light are the same.
(Psalm 139:7–12)

Or catch the yearning in the poem *Yedid Nefesh* by the sixteenth-century mystic Eliezer Azikri:

Soul mate, loving God, compassion's gentle source,
Take my disposition and shape it to your Will.
Like a darting deer will I rush to you.
Before Your glorious Presence humbly will I bow.
Let your sweet love delight me with its thrill.
Because no other dainty will my hunger fill.

We have clearly moved far away from the view of experience as primarily sensory. In fact, in *Yedid Nefesh,* there is not the slightest allusion to any sense datum. The experience is vivid, intense, compelling, and transformatory, but it is totally inward and hence intrinsically private, personal, and subjective. Azikri's God is very real and present to him, very much "out there," but He is to be reached by a yearning of the whole person, primarily of the will and the heart, to a far lesser degree of the mind and the senses, but all of these working together.

The Experience of the Numinous

The notion that every religious experience has a mystical quality was proposed by the German Christian scholar of the history and phenomenology of religions, Rudolf Otto (1869–1937), in his seminal work, *The Idea of the Holy* (an unfortunate translation from the German *Das Heilige*). Otto insisted that there is a unique, distinctive dimension to the religious experience which he designated the sense of the *numinous* (Latin: *numen*, spirit): the utterly nonrational, hence mysterious but compelling, sense of a transcendent Presence, both beyond and also very close to me. This Presence generates a powerful and complex emotion that Otto describes as a mixture of fear and fascination, terror and bliss—in sum, a sense of my "creatureliness" and of the abyss that separates a person, as merely human, from the transcendent Presence, but that can also be bridged by God's compelling power and by my acts of worship.

Read the accounts of the call to prophecy, for example, in Isaiah 6, Jeremiah 1, and Ezekiel 1, and Otto's description becomes compellingly clear. We can see it strikingly in Jeremiah's ineffectual struggle to avoid God's call (20:7–18), beginning with his pathetic cry, "You enticed me, O Lord, and I was enticed; You overpowered me and You prevailed." It pervades the passages in Psalm 139, in *Yedid Nefesh,* and in the *Unetaneh Tokef* poem that is the centerpiece of the High Holiday liturgy. Otto has also captured the transforming quality of the experience, the way in which the worshiper emerges from the experience with a sense of having been "born again."

Otto insists that the religious experience must never be reduced to a mere psychological, subjective phenomenon alone. The worshiper, in the throes of the experience, senses the unquestioned reality of the transcendent Presence. Nothing is seen, but something is very clearly sensed or felt, encircling and overwhelming me. There is also no interpretation here; that would be much too cerebral. The experience has a quasi-physical quality to it; we can understand why Ezekiel would fling himself down on his face in the presence of the Lord. Otto warns against the tendency of the outsider to dismiss the experience through a facile psychological interpretation. In effect, it is impossible for the outsider to appreciate the power or the significance of the experience; it is absolutely personal and private and must be accepted as such, just as is the mystical experience.

The Experience of Cosmic Order

Finally, in its most extended sense, a religious experience can be understood as emerging out of a broad, unified perspective on the world as a whole. Here, the distinguishing factor is an intuitive, almost primitive sense of cosmos, of an order and harmony that pervades all of reality, and of my place in this ultimate order of things. Through this awareness of place, of where and how I belong, my life acquires meaning.

The clearest biblical reference to this kind of experience comes at the climax of The Book of Job. From almost any perspective—linguistic, literary, theological, and exegetical—Job is one of the most difficult books of the Bible. It is the story of a saintly man whom God tests by the most crushing of disasters simply because Satan has questioned the disinterested quality of his piety. Yet Job never renounces God, nor does he accept his friends' consolation or their attempts at theodicy. Finally, God speaks to Job out of the whirlwind and Job emerges from his experience with a measure of serenity. He is recompensed by God for all his losses, becomes the father of still more children, and lives to old age.

God's answer to Job in chapters 38–41 of the book serves neither to explain Job's suffering nor to vindicate God's justice. It is, rather, a paean to God's majesty, His power, the complexity of His creation, and His presence throughout the natural order. It is also an affirmation of the intrinsic inadequacy of human reason and human moral categories when applied to God and His dealings with His creation. "I am God," God says to Job, "and you are a human being. Don't try to comprehend Me or my relation to the created world. Don't try to subject Me to your judgment. Your perspective is not Mine. What seems to you to be unreasonable, unfair, or unjust reflects your limited point of view. I am infinitely more complex than you can possibly fathom. You must simply accept Me as I am."

Leaving aside the theological problems this answer raises, what is stunning is that Job accepts it in a brief, six-verse response that reaches its climax in this memorable acknowledgment:

I had heard You with my ears,
But now I see You with my eyes;
(42:5)

Job acknowledges that his experience has given him a new and different perspective. But the change is not simply from one perspective to another. His earlier perspective was "hearing"; the new one is "seeing"—clearly broader, more comprehensive, more adequate to the totality of things. Note that God never tells Job why he suffered, never actually describes how all things cohere, only that they do. That is the most that a human being can have and that is all that Job needs to know. What appeared to him to be contradictory can now be integrated. What was out of joint, now belongs. Order, a sense of rightness is reestablished. Chaos has been replaced by cosmos. And with this awareness of a transcendent order comes inner peace and harmony—a sense of closure.

When a believer speaks of experiencing the world religiously, he may well be echoing the kind of "seeing" that Job achieved. What makes this experience "religious" is first its global quality and then its integrating capacity, its reach for a pervasive sense of order and harmony throughout, and the sense of belonging that this conveys. My life acquires meaning when the world as a whole has meaning. Ultimately it is God who is either the source of this cosmic order or, in a more pantheistic framework, is Himself that order.

An experience, then, can be "religious" in four possible ways: either because of the object of the experience, "what" is actually experienced—God, Jesus of Nazareth, angels, or the saints; or because of the interpretation that is given to the experience—the patterns of nature and history are interpreted as revealing God's presence; or because of the emotion that the experience and/or its interpretation inspires—typically a feeling of awe, dependency, guilt, or salvation; or because of the global, perspective-yielding quality of the experience, the sense of a cosmic order through which my life acquires meaning. Most frequently, two or three of these components will come together. In Jewish sources, for example, the last three factors usually coincide. But, invariably, one will be dominant. As we shall soon see, that dominant factor will determine how the experience is to be understood and what theological significance it will assume.

The Problem of Subjectivity

Our definition of religious experience shifted from pure sense experience; to a more interpretive kind of sense experience; to interpretive sense experience transfigured with emotion; to a more inward, intense, personal, and mystical experience; and, finally, to experience as yielding a global, integrated perspective on the world as a whole. It is clear that in the process the subjective character of the experience increased steadily. Most of us would agree that the patch out there is red. The members of a jury will frequently agree to interpret the pattern of evidence in a complex business case as revealing fraud rather than legal business practices. But when the emotional dimension of the experience becomes dominant, we are being asked to accept an experience that is ineluctably personal as legitimate and valid for all. And when the yield of the religious experience is the perception of an order that pervades all things, we sense that we are dealing with a vision that can neither be proven nor disproven, but represents an individual's or a community's most intuitive stance toward the world as a whole.

In all of our three approaches to God, certain basic questions must be asked: First, how does the approach deal with what we called "the escape clause" of the experience, the factor that enables someone to refuse to see, or not to be able to see, to forget what has been seen, or to be unwilling or incapable of interpreting what has been seen as the believer does? Second, how does the approach deal with the problem of illusory or hallucinatory seeing? Third, how does it prove, verify, or establish the truth of its claims while at the same time disproving or falsifying contrary claims? Finally, how does it handle the charge that the claims are mere wish-fulfillments, far from objective reports of anything out there but, rather, statements about the state of mind and soul of the believer himself?

If there is one characteristic stance of the religious experientialist on the issue of subjectivity, it is this: Subjectivity is an inevitable component of all religious experience; but religious communities, especially those with a long and continuing historical experience, have worked out ways of minimizing its impact.

The most fruitful analogy for the approach of the experientialist is that of the jury in a complex business case. The evidence is provided by the records of the corporation over a decade. The task of the prosecuting attorney is to review the records, highlight the instances of apparently fraudulent activity, connect these instances into a pattern, draw that pattern to the attention of the jury, and convince it that this pattern is sufficiently dominant to constitute grounds for conviction. The defense attorney will seek to highlight the evidence of acceptable and legal business practice, connect that into a pattern, draw that pattern to the attention of the jury, and try to persuade it that this pattern is sufficiently convincing to warrant acquittal. Each of the attorneys will simultaneously do some disconnecting or try to unravel the pattern that the other has shaped. The jury will weigh the conflicting patterns and, in most instances, reach a decision.

Of course, the process is more complicated than we have described. The attorneys will pay careful attention to jury selection, trying to anticipate what factors may predispose one juror to see the evidence in one way over the other. Sometimes these factors may not even be conscious to the juror; they may be issues of innate disposition, education, or personal style. Witnesses will be chosen with an eye to their general credibility and persuasiveness. In their summations, the two attorneys will use rhetorical devices that will appeal to the emotions of the jurors and influence how they read the evidence.

But the core of the process is the presentation and sharing of complex patterns in time and space. This is essentially a social or communal experience; it takes place in the context of a group. In the privacy of the jury room, members of the jury will share their reading of the data with each other and try to convince each other of the persuasiveness of one or the other outcome. They will retrace the connections made by each of the attorneys and weigh the strength of the emerging patterns. They will also retrace the attempts of each attorney to disconnect or destroy the opposing patterns. They will examine the conflicting readings of the evidence. They will attempt to explain or integrate apparently discordant data. Eventually, in most instances, the process works—a consensual reading emerges and a verdict is reached. Sometimes the process is inconclusive. In American law, with its presumption of innocence, the burden is on the prosecutor to prove the dominance of his pattern. If he fails to do this, or if the defense is successful in unraveling the pattern, the jury will acquit. If the patterns seem to have equal weight, the jury will be "hung" and the defendant remain innocent.

The process of evolving a religious reading of experience is similar to that used in a court of law, but the evidence is infinitely more complex, the jury is much larger, the time required for the process stretches over centuries, and the record of the deliberations is rarely available to us. It is very much a social process; it takes place in the context of a community of believers. But a good part of the process is completed before it emerges into the light of history. We become aware of it, for example, when we have a Bible, or even one of the documents or books that became part of the biblical canon. But the very fact that a biblical document exists indicates that the process has been largely completed and that it has worked successfully. The Bible represents the verdict, the consensual decision of a centuries-old community to choose one specific reading of the pattern over another. From that point on, the Bible becomes the textbook through which each successive generation within the community is instructed in the community's reading of its experience.

That function is shared with the later texts that the community accepts as canonical—preeminently in the case of Judaism, talmudic literature and the daily, Sabbath, and Festival liturgies. That there is a post-biblical, canonical literature in the first place—indeed that the Bible itself includes earlier and later strata—indicates that the community's reading of its experience has a certain plasticity, that it is never entirely closed.

Jews use the term *midrash* to denote the process of modifying, expanding, or, at times, deleting and recreating portions of their consensual pattern. For example, the Bible says almost nothing about the afterlife of the individual, while postbiblical literature is positively voluble about the immortality of the soul and the resurrection of the body. Another example is suffering. The dominant biblical explanation for suffering is that it is God's punishment for sin, but Job repudiates that explanation. In a striking piece of intrabiblical *midrash*, Jonah 4:2 rewrites Exodus 34:6–7 because the author of Jonah no longer believes that God must inevitably punish us for our sinfulness; the possibility of repentance is now introduced into the pattern.

Then there are those instances when the community refused to accept a proposed extension of their consensual pattern. Most first-century C.E. Jews refused to go along with Paul's proposal that Jewish messianic expectations had now been fulfilled in the life and career of Jesus of Nazareth. They would not, or could not, interpret and integrate that series of events into their consensual pattern.

The analogy of the jury's decision-making process works well when the religious experience is directed to patterns in nature and history. In these instances, there is clearly something out there that can be "seen," however much interpretation the seeing requires. The social context works to direct the seeing and its interpretation, to screen out idiosyncratic (i.e., illusory or hallucinatory) interpretations, to achieve consensus. What is gained through the experience can be accepted as "true," where truth is understood to mean that which corresponds to reality. Because the data is so infinitely more complex, we do not hold religious truths to as high a standard as we do most scientific truths. They can not be verified by repeatable experiments. But they are roughly comparable to the scientific truth of the more global and abstract of scientific theories, those that deal not with the immediate data of scientific experiments but more with the underlying nature of reality, such as in quantum mechanics or astronomy.

The less the religious experience is directed to something that is even vaguely identifiable as "out there," the more the experience is inner-directed, the greater the emotional dimension of the experience, or the greater the very personal nature of the experience (as in mysticism), the analogy of the jury becomes progressively less helpful. In fact, this is the point where experientialism shades into existentialism and the subjective quality of the experience is not only accepted but even extolled.

Typically, at this point the believer will refer to his experience as "self-verifying." This is simply a polite way of dismissing the subjectivity questions as irrelevant. The believer knows beyond question that the experience is true because it is true *for him,* and this personal conviction is the single most important condition of the truth of the experience. But then we have redefined what we mean by truth in religion. We no longer even aim for objectivity. "True" means "true for me" and the experience carries its own warranty. Just about any religious claim based on a personal experience of this kind is implicitly acceptable as legitimate. However, if the preeminent religious experience is only personal, then the very possibility of a religious community is called into question. Small wonder, then, that most religious traditions have been wary of relying on experiences of this kind.

Actually, most religious communities have been able to make room for and even to welcome their mystics, and that for two reasons. First, the community exercises powerful control over the shape of its mystics' experiences, accepting those that reflect the specific religious tradition. Jewish mystics will never have mystical experiences of Jesus of Nazareth or of his mother Mary, or of the Christian saints; they will, instead, invoke themes and symbols that emerge out of the classical texts of the Jewish tradition, such as Ezekiel's vision of the divine chariot (Ezekiel 1), or Isaiah's vision of the heavenly host praising God (Isaiah 6). Or a classical Jewish institution such as the Sabbath becomes personified as a bride or a queen, and then becomes the channel for a mystical experience. Though a Jewish mystical experience may strain the parameters of the *halakhah,* it will never deliberately seek to undermine its authority. Effectively, then, the mystical experience, however idiosyncratic and personal it may be, can enrich the emotional coloration of the traditional pattern and thereby strengthen its appeal.

It can do even more. It can infuse the everyday experience of the community with a mystical dimension. The late Max

Kadushin's study of rabbinic Judaism, *The Rabbinic Mind,* employs the felicitous term "normal mysticism" to capture what Kadushin considers to be the normative way in which the rabbinic Jew experiences the world. It is "mysticism" because God's presence in the world is experienced directly. But it is "normal" because this experience is never private, esoteric, ecstatic, or incommunicable. It is, rather, very much a communal experience and an experience of ordinary, everyday things and events. The food that we consume, the normal functions of our bodies, sunrise and sunset, the cycles of the seasons—all of these become infused with a sense of the mystical that makes us aware of God's immediate presence in the world. The *halakhah* serves to structure and communalize the experience, and the liturgy, specifically the *berakhot* (the benedictions that we recite, e.g., before and after we eat), directs our attention to God's presence in the experience.

Finally, what of those religious experiences that perceive a cosmic order pervading all things? Here, if anywhere, the questions that the subjectivity issue poses appear irrelevant. These cosmic configurations are neither provable nor disprovable. They emerge in the earliest stages of a community's awareness and are solidly in place long before they assume literary form. Genesis 1–3 records the classic Jewish description of that order, describes how it came to be, and, subsequently, how it was disrupted by the behavior of primordial and paradigmatic human beings— Adam and Eve, and Cain. Essentially, these chapters provide the Jewish account of why things are as they are in nature and in human life. The Exodus/Sinai narrative explains why the Jewish people is the way it is. Not unexpectedly, these accounts are couched in metaphorical terms; how else can human beings portray events and realities that lie beyond human perception? But once in place, the metaphor determines everything else about the community's experience. Cosmic metaphors of this kind effectively define the community. They shape the community's most primitive or intuitive sense of its role and destiny, and they are well nigh invulnerable.

Cosmic metaphors of this kind share many of the qualities we earlier ascribed to a community's myth. In fact, a myth should be understood as a literary rendition of the community's metaphor. The metaphor itself has a more pictorial quality; it is more the result of "seeing." It is a visual prefiguration of the myth, the source of the dramatic and poetic quality that is characteristic of a great myth. To put this another way, the myth is a discursive rendering of the community's metaphor. The metaphor is also the source of the inherent subjectivity that is characteristic of myths, the quality that makes them easily identified as fictions. But as we have seen, neither myths nor their underlying metaphors are fictions. They emerge out of a community's most primitive confrontation with the world. They carry their own distinctive kind of truth, for they have been verified many times over, as witnessed by the community's continued vitality through centuries. They are "true" because they have enabled the community to maintain its integrity and its members to live satisfying and fulfilling lives; thus, what we have called the singular "invulnerability" of these structures. The community will cling to its picture of the world, come what may, for what is at stake is the community's very existence.

Note also the emotional component of these cosmic metaphors, or, indeed, of any religious experientialist reading of events. Some forms of the religious experience have a direct emotional component. But even the more low-key perception of those patterns in nature and history carry an emotional charge. This is what distinguishes them from more scientific readings of experience. Religion is expected to engender pervasive moods in the community of believers. The moods are not always congruent. One believer may feel a sense of "all's right with the world"; another, a sense of guilt or imminent disaster; a third, a sense of authenticity, of having been "saved" for all time. A religious reading of the world should also motivate behavior, engender a sense of loyalty to the community, and enable its members to cope with the normal stresses of everyday life.

What emerges from the religious experience? A certain body of knowledge about the world, an awareness that certain patterns prevail. To a significant degree, it understands religious faith as "belief that . . ."—belief that the world out there reflects these patterns. In this mode, it tends to view the atheist as "blind," incapable of seeing the patterns or of understanding them as the community does. Here, the believer and the atheist can still speak to each other and examine the evidence or lack thereof.

But when experientialism begins to emphasize the highly personal and self-verifying nature of the experience, religious faith tends to become "belief in . . ."—an instinctual, emotional, gut conviction that the believer's experience is veridical. In this mode, atheism represents more a failure of will than of vision, for now the evidence is irrelevant, for or against. The atheist refuses to take the step that the believer has taken. At this point, the atheist and the believer speak past each other.

A Medieval Experientialist: Yehudah Halevi

Experientialism constitutes the pervasive approach to God in the Bible and in later rabbinic sources. But in this literature, the resort to experience is totally instinctive. There is little awareness of other possibilities, little attempt to justify the approach, and no systematic effort to study its strengths or the problems it raises.

The first systematic reading of Judaism on experiential grounds is in the *Book of the Kuzari* by the medieval Spanish poet-philosopher Yehudah Halevi (ca. 1085–1141). *The Kuzari* is one of the most remarkable creations of medieval Spanish Jewry, totally unique in its cultural context and remarkably contemporary in its thrust. Halevi's philosophical contemporaries were largely religious rationalists. They sought to demonstrate the inherent rationality of Jewish theology, to harmonize the revealed truths of Torah with the rational truths of Aristotelian philosophy, and thereby to eliminate the apparent subjectivity of religion. Halevi, in contrast, wanted to separate Torah from philosophy, revelation from reason, and to highlight the superiority of the former as the source of truth. His purpose is disclosed in his subtitle: *The Book of Argument and Proof in Defense of the Despised Faith.* He tries to demonstrate that of all the conflicting faiths and philosophies, the most despised—Judaism—is alone the bearer of ultimate truth, and, furthermore, that because Judaism is the purest embodiment of religious experientialism, it is the bearer of the superior revelation.

The book itself is loosely based on a historical event. Rumors had reached Spain that the Khazars, a people who inhabited an area near the Crimean Sea, had converted to Judaism after their king examined the conflicting claims of Judaism, Christianity, Islam, and Aristotelian philosophy. Halevi recreates the story of this conversion and uses it as the framework for his defense of Judaism. Hence the dialogical format of the book, which begins with a debate among a rabbi, a philosopher, a Christian, and a Muslim in the presence of the king of the Khazars. The king decides to accept Judaism over the alternatives and then enters into an extended dialogue with the rabbi in which, through the device of the rabbi's instructing the king, Halevi spells out his understanding of Judaism. The book provides a striking example of the wedding of substance and form to defend a religious position.

Halevi does not disparage reason *per se,* but he declares it sterile as an approach to God. Philosophy has to resort to reason because it does not have a revealed tradition. But Jews do. The revelation at Sinai was witnessed by 600,000 people and the report of that experience was handed down from generation to generation in an unbroken chain. Since the original experience and the subsequent tradition are beyond question, Halevi makes two claims: First, *in principle* revelation is inherently superior to reason as a source of religious truth; for all of their appeal to reason, philosophers have yet to agree on anything. Second, the public nature of the revelation at Sinai establishes that this revelation did *in fact* take place. No other religious community can match that experience.

Thus the striking character of the rabbi's opening words. When asked by the king to describe his beliefs, he responds: "I believe in the God of Abraham, Isaac and Israel, who led the Israelites out of Egypt with signs and miracles; who fed them in the desert and gave them the (Holy) Land, after having made them traverse the sea and the Jordan in a miraculous way; who sent Moses with His Law, and subsequently thousands of prophets. . . ." In other words, he begins with nothing less than a lesson in Jewish history. When the king challenges the rabbi and suggests that he should have responded in a more universal way—for example by demonstrating the existence of God from Creation—he responds: "I made mention to you of what is convincing for me and for the whole of Israel, who knew these things, first through personal experience, and afterward through an uninterrupted tradition, which is equal to experience." The basis for religious faith, then, is a community's personal experience of events in history, not the universal truths of reason.

Why should Israel merit this distinction? Because Israel alone, among all the nations, possesses a unique "religious" (or "prophetic") faculty (or sensitivity) that enables it to experience revelation. Israel alone is innately attuned to experience God. Halevi accounts for this unique sensitivity through a complex—and to modern ears somewhat shocking—theory of biological conditioning in which Abraham's ancestry, the Holy Land, the Hebrew language, and the ceremonial law all play an interlocking role. However he accounts for it, this faculty predisposes Israel to receive revelation. Thus Israel is "elected" from among the nations, singled out by its ability to experience God. Sinai is the paradigmatic revelation, the exemplar of the religious experience, and the entire structure of Jewish religion is designed to promote that supreme communion with God that is uniquely in the reach of all Jews.

Halevi defends a series of explicit priorities: religion and history over philosophy, the particular over the universal, the fact of religion over the idea of religion, experience over reason or logic, the religious experience over other experiences, the God of Abraham, Isaac, and Jacob over the God of the philosophers, the Holy Land over other lands, the Hebrew language over other languages, the Torah over other revealed traditions. All of these priorities establish the supremacy of Judaism. The most despised religion is the most true.

Halevi characterizes the religious experience as an emotion-laden, worshipful love of, or communion with God. God initiates the relationship through revelation, which alone creates genuine religion. Human beings—and Jews especially—have an innate yearning to reach God and the revealed religion that provides the structure to fulfill this yearning, through its distinctive language, liturgies, and ceremonial laws. But what we achieve is nothing intellectual or cerebral—certainly not the knowledge of God, for God can never be an object of human knowledge. What the believer desires above all is something far more intimate and emotional: to live with God, to be close to Him, to be bound to Him in intimacy.

The prophets achieved this intuitive communion with the living God, who revealed Himself to them through sensory images that they understood as manifestations of His presence. These images inspired emotions of love and awe. But there is no intrinsic difference between the prophetic experience and that of the ordinary mortal, just differences of intensity. Every pious Jew, by living his religion, can attain this supreme form of religious devotion.

But if religious experience is the unique source of truth, how does Halevi deal with the issue of subjectivity? Simply by appealing to the fact that all the prophets agree in their descriptions of their experience, and to the public nature of the revelation at Sinai and its transmission through an uninterrupted tradition. The genetically based prophetic faculty was shared by all the Israelites at Sinai and, albeit in an attenuated form because of the conditions of the exile, by all Jews to this day.

But herein lies the problem with Halevi's argument: Our sole evidence for Sinai is the very book whose veracity as the bearer of revelation is precisely in question. The skeptic who questions the truth of Torah will not be convinced by an appeal to the Torah's account of revelation. The argument is simply circular; it begs the question. It may work for the already convinced, but it will hardly convince the nonbeliever.

Despite this flaw at the heart of Halevi's argument, *The Kuzari*—largely because of its experiential perspective—remains the most classically Jewish and, at the same time, the most contemporary product of medieval Jewish thought. Its basic theological thrust is that of the Bible and rabbinic literature. Halevi's religious experientialism enables him to paint a remarkably sensitive portrait of Judaism as it is lived through the Sabbath, the Festivals, prayer, the liturgy, the Hebrew language, and the Jew's love for the Holy Land—all of which work together to engender, confirm, and support the religious experience. We emerge with a fully integrated reading of Judaism on its own terms. Judaism provides its own validation; there is no need to appeal to any extrinsic criterion, certainly not to reason.

Halevi is the theological father of contemporary Jewish experientialists, certainly of Abraham Joshua Heschel. Jewish philosophy's flirtation with rationalism was intense but short lived. It was narrowly tied to the distinctive temper of the Middle Ages. Our contemporaries have returned to experientialism, and with it, to Halevi's emphasis on religion's independence from philosophy, on the *sui generis* quality of the religious experience, and on Jewish living as providing a supportive context for the experience of God. In all of this, they are the legitimate heirs of Halevi and *The Kuzari*.

A Modern Experientialist: Abraham Joshua Heschel

The most thoroughgoing, contemporary reading of Judaism from an experientialist perspective was developed by Abraham Joshua Heschel (1907–1972) in his two companion volumes, *Man Is Not Alone: A Philosophy of Religion* and *God In Search Of Man: A Philosophy of Judaism*.

Heschel's theological and spiritual roots lay in the Polish Hasidic world of his childhood with its devotion to intense Jewish learning and traditional Jewish living, infused with the mystical yearnings of his forbears, who were among the earliest disciples of Israel Ba'al Shem Tov, the eighteenth-century founder of Hasidism. Heschel's personal religious and intellectual quest later took him into the world of Western scholarship in Berlin. He left Europe shortly before the outbreak of World War II and eventually reached America, where his mature years were devoted to the development of his singular theological perspective, to scholarly work in Jewish thought, and to intense involvement in a wide range of social and political causes, such as the struggle for racial equality in the United States and opposition to the Vietnam War.

Heschel's output was prodigious, illuminating just about every significant issue in Jewish philosophy. But the heart of his work lies in his phenomenological description of the religious experience. With fine-tuned acuity he traces the contours of the experience, the wrestling that takes place as God and the human being struggle to overcome the barriers that stand in the way of their engagement with each other. As in Halevi, the experience is very much a mutual engagement; it involves both God and the human being actively, even aggressively—not at all one of a human subject experiencing an object-God, for how can God be an object for me? If anything, to experience God is to experience myself as being engaged by God. But I cannot be engaged by God unless I too seek Him, respond to His call, actively open myself to His presence all around me.

Heschel characterizes God's aggressive cries for acknowledgment as manifestations of His "pathos." This image of God that Heschel delineated in one of his earliest works, *The Prophets,* (originally written in German in the early 1930s and later extensively revised and translated into English), quickly emerges as the cornerstone of his personal theology as well.

Heschel asks us to read the Bible carefully and accept it as a serious intellectual document, as serious as the writings of the great philosophers. In *The Prophets* he asks: Why is it that at a certain moment in history, a group of men claimed to be conveying the word of God? What made it possible for them to make this claim? They were not all psychotic, not dishonest. In fact, most of them bitterly resented their calling; they fought God desperately. Yet they were compelled to speak by a force that was infinitely more powerful than their will. Heschel asks: What kind of a God is this who creates prophets?

Obviously it is not the God of the philosophers, not the self-sufficient, ultimate abstraction, not at all a God who is the embodiment of ultimate perfection. Such a God would simply not care about the spiritual and moral state of society. But the

God of the prophets is supremely concerned, intimately and personally involved with the world, moved and affected by what happens in society, reaching out and calling for a certain kind of social order. It is the biblical God's reaching-out-of-Himself that Heschel characterizes as His "pathos." Heschel finds its imprint on every page of the Bible.

Heschel acknowledges that we are embarrassed by this image of God; we label it as primitive in contrast to the presumably more sophisticated, "apathetic," or emotionless, self-sufficient God of the philosophers. Why should the Master of the Universe concern Himself with the fate of widows and orphans? But that prejudgment is more a function of our cultural and educational milieu than a deliberate theological option; we are all products of Western culture, shaped more by Greek philosophical modes of thought than by the Bible. Heschel devotes four chapters of *The Prophets* to a close study of how and why, in the history of religions, the apathetic God of the philosophers came to over-shadow the caring God of the Bible. He exposes the assumptions behind this prejudgment and he concludes that the biblical image of God as caring, as "in search" of human beings, stems from the intuitive conviction that if God doesn't care about the world, then the human enterprise is irrelevant and even absurd.

God's pathos forms the ground-tone of His engagement with the world. The three preeminent moments in which God turns to the world—creation, revelation, and redemption—are con-crete manifestations of His pathos. God's presence, then, is re-vealed in nature, in the Torah, in sacred deeds, and in history.

I look at an anemone. The artist in me sees the play of line and color, shape and form. The botanist in me sees a field of research, an opportunity to acquire knowledge of how this flower came to be what it is. The merchant in me sees a way of market-ing it. The aesthete in me sees it as matching the color scheme of my living room. But the believer in me sees an infinitely more primitive dimension of the anemone. What cries for recognition here is the simple anemone itself, the fact that it is there in the first place, the inherent mystery of its very being, and my intrinsic inability to account for the fact that there are facts in the first place. I am then thrown back to a much more primitive level of awareness, a level that is "preconceptual," that precedes my ability to think or say anything else about the flower or about any aspect of my experience.

What I see remains the anemone, but I "see" it as transfigured, as calling attention to a dimension of reality beyond itself. That transcendent dimension is the world as infused with God's presence, one manifestation of the divine pathos. It is the world as embodying God's cry for attention.

But that distinctive quality of the anemone requires an equally distinctive perceiving faculty on the human side of the transaction. Heschel's most fruitful characterization of that distinctive religious sensibility is "radical amazement."

Radical amazement is, as its name indicates, a "root" or equally primitive way of looking at the world. It is the very opposite of a stance that takes the world for granted. It is also distinct from curiosity. Curiosity stimulates a search for knowledge. I am curious as to how the brain works. I ask a neurologist who explains its mechanism. With this acquired knowledge, my curiosity is dispelled. But on an entirely different level of awareness, the more my curiosity is dispelled, the greater my amazement at the fact that my body works the way it does. Radical amazement denotes a stance that sees everything in the world, constantly, as if for the first time. It is properly the attitude of the child, the poet, or the artist to whom the world is infinitely wondrous or mysterious. But then we grow up. We have to negotiate with the world. Slowly and systematically, our radical amazement is dulled and the world becomes commonplace, everyday, suffused with a pervasive grayness. One anemone is like every other anemone, one human body like every other human body.

But there are discrete moments in each of our lives when the commonplace is pierced with a fresh, new vision, when our ability to be radically amazed is revived, when the mystery that is at the heart of the familiar is encountered and acknowledged. That fresh perception is the religious experience. It is ephemeral or momentary, immediate, personal, and ineffable. It is momentary because God is not always equally accessible and we are usually not sensitive to His presence. It is ephemeral because we are all-too-soon pulled back into our constant need to negotiate with the world. It is personal because only the individual in the throes of the experience can testify to its presence. And it is ineffable because our ordinary language is simply incapable of capturing the rich texture of the experience.

But Heschel is convinced that we all have such experiences. And the central function of a religious tradition, its institutions, liturgies, sacred texts, rituals, and communal structures is to create settings that will stimulate the experience and preserve the memories it leaves behind. The Sabbath and Festivals, for example, and the rituals of daily prayer impel us out of our everyday living and create "sanctuaries in time" wherein we can look at ourselves and our world anew.

The parallels between Heschel's account of the religious experience and Halevi's are striking. First, neither writes in the straightforward expository style common to philosophical or theological discussion. Halevi adopts the dialogue form because it echoes the parry and thrust that forms the substance of *The Kuzari.* Heschel's evocative prose mirrors his purpose, which is not to expound a theological system but rather to awaken us to look at the world in a fresh and unanticipated way. In the first instance, theology becomes drama; in the second, it turns to poetry.

Note, second, their shared and pronounced antispeculative thrust. Religion and the religious experience are absolutely *sui generis.* The religious experience does not yield knowledge of any kind, certainly not knowledge of God. For Heschel, all conceptualizations in religion are afterthoughts, feeble accommodations of reality to the human mind and to human language. After all, what kind of God would He be if I can "comprehend" Him? The encounter with God takes place on a level of awareness that precedes conceptualization; theology, speculation—the entire cerebral side of religion—may clarify the experience but it can neither produce nor account for it. A discursive argument will never lead us to God. If He is not experienced preconceptually, He will never be experienced.

In short, what we may call the epistemological track that we use in our everyday dealings with the world is thoroughly inadequate for theology, simply because God is not a watch or a blood cell. In everyday life, and particularly in science, we move from ordinary sense experience to conceptualization, abstraction, experimentation, hypothesis building, and, ultimately, to a theory that accounts for our experience. That track will simply not work when we seek God. There are only two alternative possibilities. One is to sidetrack that method in its entirety, to adopt the primitive naïveté of the child as a fundamental stance toward the world, much as the artist or the poet does. The other is to pursue that knowledge-building track to its eventual goal and then, at its very climax, to be shocked into the realization that as much as we do know on a second, separate level of awareness, we know nothing at all. The more we know, the greater the mystery. We confront, we welcome the mystery, and then we sing, we worship, we dance, or, more characteristically, we fall silent in awe and wonder.

Much of Heschel's work is devoted to an extraordinarily sensitive description of the religious experience, that moment when our capacity for radical amazement responds to the inherently mysterious dimension of reality. He is a master religious phenomenologist. With a finely tuned and acute perception, he traces the wrestling that takes place as we turn away from and then back to God's presence all about us. But what we do not find in Heschel's writings is a systematic discussion of the more strictly philosophical problems that inevitably accompany this approach—particularly the issue of subjectivity. He is palpably aware of the problems, and he is certainly fully capable of dealing with them, but he seems to view them as intrusive. They come from a perspective that is external to the experience itself and they are thus simply illegitimate. Heschel writes from within the experience. The skeptic, who asks for verification and proof, stands on the outside looking in. Almost by definition, then, he has disqualified himself from questioning what the believer experiences.

At those moments when Heschel does confront the skeptic, he speaks in a classic experientialist voice. The evidence for the reality of God is all about us. We can learn to see it in nature and in history. The resources of our tradition serve as a pair of spectacles that enable us to read our experience as our ancestors did. The panoply of rituals, liturgies, and institutions of Jewish religion create multiple opportunities for us to look at our experience in a fresh and new way. And that tradition is very much the creation of a community, shaped at the outset by the community's reading of its experience and deliberately geared to promulgating that reading in the generations to follow. The religious community serves as a quasi jury. The subjectivity issues are dealt with and the emerging reading of the evidence is consensual.

But frequently Heschel's impatience with these questions breaks through. At these moments, he insists that God's presence in nature and history is an "ontological presupposition." What is absolutely primary is the overwhelming reality of God's presence. We praise, worship, and respond before we question, speculate, and prove. Our awareness of God is "preconceptual." The enterprise of reflecting about the experience is invariably anticlimactic, an "after-belief." What we might gain in clarity and distinctness, we lose in immediacy and genuineness. In this mode, to ask whether the experience is genuine or illusory, objective or subjective, is simply illegitimate. If anything, it testifies to the skeptic's refusal to open himself to the experience of God. It would never occur to someone within the experience to question its veracity. In other words, the experience is self-authenticating —and then, all of the problems associated with that stance inevitably reassert themselves. We have crossed the line that separates religious empiricism from religious existentialism.

We should not underestimate the full impact of this antispeculative thrust in Heschel's thinking. He is in effect calling into question the significance of a good deal of the classical agenda of the philosophy of religion. For Heschel, the entire range of questions that philosophers have addressed to theologians in an attempt to establish how they validate their theological claims have at best a subsidiary role. They may systematize and clarify these claims, but they can never call their basic veracity into question. The living quality of the immediate experience carries its own warranty of truth; it can never be undermined by rational speculation.

Faith for Heschel, then, is clearly not "belief that . . ."—not a matter of knowledge, not cerebral, not an act of the mind. It is very much "belief in . . ."—trust, loyalty, commitment, or, as Heschel identifies it, "faithfulness to the moment of insight." It is hardly a permanent acquisition, something we "have" and hold on to. It is rather an achievement won after a long and painful struggle, easily dispelled, yet still reattainable. It is also very personal and intrinsically subjective.

In this view, atheism represents either a failure of perception, an inability to see the world in the proper way, or a deliberate act of refusal—in which case it is sheer arrogance. Heschel has little tolerance for any form of systematic atheism. In the long run, we are either compelled to affirm God or to live with the absurdity of the alternative.

For all of our frustration at Heschel's elusiveness, his work can serve to warn us against viewing our three approaches to God as clear and distinct from one another. They do represent basic theological impulses and each does have its own distinctive logic. But in practice, we are dealing with a spectrum of tendencies that tend to shade into one another. If we begin with the experiential approach, it is not simply because it represents the classical thrust of Judaism. More important, as the middle position, it has served as the common point of reference for the other tendencies. They can be viewed as reactions to the problems raised by experientialism: rationalism in one direction and existentialism in another.

FOR FURTHER STUDY
Consult the material on religious experience in the volumes listed after ch. 3 above. The classic study of the religious experience in all its

possible permutations remains William James' VARIETIES OF RELI-
GIOUS EXPERIENCE *(pb Collier, 1961).*

The best introduction to Jewish mysticism is Gershom Scholem's
MAJOR TRENDS IN JEWISH MYSTICISM *(see ch. 4). See, in particular,
the "First Lecture" in this volume, outlining the general characteristics
of Jewish mysticism. Louis Jacobs'* JEWISH MYSTICAL TESTIMONIES
*(pb Schocken, 1977) is a valuable anthology of original texts, in transla-
tion, from the Bible to our time, which try to capture precisely what
the Jewish mystic experiences.*

The translation of Yedid Nefesh *is adapted from that of Rabbi
Zalman Schachter-Shalomi and appears on p. 253 of* SIDDUR SIM
SHALOM *(The Rabbinical Assembly and The United Synagogue of
America, 1985).*

*On Job's religious experience, see Moshe Greenberg's "Reflections
on Job's Theology" in the one-volume translation,* THE BOOK OF JOB
(Jewish Publication Society, 1980).

*The problem of subjectivity in an experientialist framework is
explored in John Wisdom's "Gods" (see ch. 3). The analogy of the jury
deliberation is Wisdom's. See also the discussion of falsification and
verification in the Hick anthology and in Blackstone's* THE PROBLEM
OF RELIGIOUS KNOWLEDGE *(see ch. 3). Max Kadushin's notion of
"normal mysticism" is developed in* THE RABBINIC MIND *(Jewish
Theological Seminary, 1952; pb Bloch Publishing House, 1972).*

THE BOOK OF THE KUZARI *is one of three classic Jewish philosophical documents collected in* THREE JEWISH PHILOSOPHERS *(pb
Atheneum, 1982). Isaak Heinemann's introduction and commentaries
to the book are always illuminating, as is Julius Guttmann's discussion
of Halevi in his* PHILOSOPHIES OF JUDAISM *(see ch. 3).*

Heschel's experientialism emerges in MAN IS NOT ALONE *(Farrar, Straus and Giroux, 1951; pb Harper Torchbooks, 1966) and in Part
I of his* GOD IN SEARCH OF MAN *(see ch. 1). The clearest exposition
of Heschel's thought is Fritz A. Rothschild's introduction to the anthology,* BETWEEN GOD AND MAN: FROM THE WRITINGS OF ABRAHAM
J. HESCHEL *(pb The Free Press, 1959). This anthology also includes
a bibliography of books and studies by, and on, Heschel. See also John
C. Merkle's* THE GENESIS OF FAITH: THE DEPTH THEOLOGY OF
ABRAHAM JOSHUA HESCHEL *(Macmillan, 1985), the first book-length*

study of Heschel's thought in its entirety. Lawrence Perlman's ABRA- HAM HESCHEL'S IDEA OF REVELATION *(see ch. 1) is a more technical and systematic study of Heschel's thought. Rudolf Otto's* THE IDEA OF THE HOLY *(pb Oxford University Press, 1958) is a classic study of the phenomenology of the religious experience which obviously influenced Heschel's thought.*

VI

Proving God's Existence:
Rationalism

The Cultural Setting

THE NOTION THAT IT IS A *MITZVAH* TO DEMONSTRATE THAT THE teachings of Torah are rationally true would have appeared ludicrous to any Jew prior to the ninth century of our era. By the end of the tenth century, that mandate was taken for granted. This transformation in both the style and substance of Jewish religious expression became the hallmark of medieval Judaism. It was part of a much broader cultural upheaval in Jewish life that followed upon the Muslim conquest of the Mediterranean world in the century after the death of Mohammed in 632 C.E.

Because Islam recognized the authenticity of God's revelation to the Jewish people at Sinai, the Jews who inhabited the Islamic world (together with the Christians) were not confronted with the choice of conversion to Islam or death. In return for a head tax, Jews were given the rights of domicile and of personal safety and the opportunity to earn a livelihood. Jewish religious life was governed by the Jewish community itself. Through the tenth century, it was administered by the Jewish self-government in Baghdad, and later by the new and emerging centers of Jewish learning in North Africa and Spain.

Effectively, then, Islam lent the Jewish community a singular cohesion. Jewish self-government served as the supreme authority on internal affairs. The Babylonian Talmud achieved canonical status as the authentic interpretation of Scripture in matters of belief and practice. And the Arabic language became the *lingua franca* for all Jews from India in the east through North Africa to Spain and southern France in the west.

Islam gave the Jewish world much more than cohesion. The Arabs may have achieved military domination over a vast empire, but they remained uncommonly open to the cultural riches of the civilizations they conquered. A vast body of non-Islamic learning in medicine, physics, astronomy, mathematics, and belles lettres was translated into Arabic and thereby mediated to the entire Arabic-speaking world. The scholarly ferment that followed created a new intellectual elite. Because of the openness of the social setting, Jews were quick to take part.

The centerpiece of the new learning was Greek philosophy. Jews had encountered Greek culture much earlier in their history, in the wake of Alexander the Great's conquest of the Middle East in the fourth century B.C.E. But that encounter was perceived as profoundly threatening to the integrity of Judaism and, despite multiple traces of Hellenistic influence in the literature of the Talmudic era, Jewish religious life was largely unaffected. The one early attempt to integrate the teachings of Torah with Greek philosophy was by Philo of Alexandria (ca. 25 B.C.E.–50 C.E.), but Jews did not discover Philo until the sixteenth century; he exercised no influence on medieval Jewish thinking.

However, in the medieval setting, the philosophical literature that Jews began to read had already been translated into the idiom of religion, first by Christian and later by Muslim philosophers. Its impact on Judaism, then, was somewhat cushioned; other religious communities, with a belief structure similar to Judaism, had already begun the process of accommodation. From the ninth through the fifteenth centuries, then, the primary task of Jewish thought, a task shared with both Christianity and Islam, was the harmonization of the teachings of Torah with those of Platonic and Aristotelian philosophy.

The authority of Torah was grounded in divine revelation. The authority of philosophy was grounded in rational inquiry. Aristotle begins his *Metaphysics* with the claim that "all men possess by nature the desire to know." His aim was precisely to know—to understand everything about the world in which he found himself in a systematic, integrated way through the application of reason on the data of sense experience. Reason is the paradigmatic human faculty, the faculty that distinguishes human beings from all other creatures. Our ultimate fulfillment as human beings lies in the perfection of our power of reason.

Since there can only be one truth, the religious dilemma is clear: If revelation and rational inquiry are both sources of truth, how is it possible for their conclusions to be contradictory? And if reason can yield all possible knowledge, why then do we need revelation in the first place? These two questions haunt all of medieval thinking. They form the agenda of medieval religious philosophy in Judaism, Christianity, and Islam. The common task was to rethink and rewrite the substance of their teachings in the style and idiom of rational philosophy.

A second, subsidiary task was to deal with the existence of three worldwide religious communities, each claiming exclusive truth, each claiming to represent the final will of the one God for humanity. The very fact of religious pluralism made religion a subject of investigation. But since each of the competing communities based its claim to exclusive truth on its own revelatory event, their polemic could never be settled by an appeal to revelation itself. What was required was some external criterion that each community accepted as legitimate. What better criterion than reason! Thus, still another stimulus for the transformation of each of the religions into a rational belief structure.

The Allure of Rationalism

Jews may have required an external stimulus to get into philosophy, but once they were involved there was no questioning its intrinsic attractions. Foremost among these was the promise of eliminating the subjective factor in religious belief. The faculty of reason is the universal heritage of all human beings. Its laws apply to all people at all times and in every culture. Revelation, in contrast, is addressed to a particular community or individual, at a particular time. It appeals to experience, to a community's or an individual's ability and willingness to see the revelation. But from the Bible on, believers were painfully aware that others frequently did not see, or did not want to see God's revelation, or forgot what they had seen. If the existence of God could be demonstrated rationally, that truth would win universal assent. The issue would be settled for everyone and for all time.

The second intrinsic problem with revelation is that a later revelatory event can always claim to have superseded an earlier one, as the existence of Christianity and Islam all too painfully demonstrated. But, again, what is rationally demonstrated to be true can never be superseded.

Third, the reliance on experience as the main pathway to God raises the troublesome problem of illusory or hallucinatory experiences, or erroneous interpretations of genuine revelations. The truths of reason, on the other hand, carry their own warranty of absolute certainty. The truths they yield are not only universal, but also conclusive.

Finally, if reason is *the* distinctive human faculty, then the exaltation of reason is at the same time the exaltation of God, for it is God who has created us with our power of reason. The application of reason to the claims of religion is, then, far from a rebellion against God. It is instead a genuine act of worship, a *mitzvah*.

This final consideration exercised a powerful impact on thinking Jews. Judaism was unique among world religions in its self-conscious intellectualism. Here was a religion that glorified the life of the mind, that saw the study of Torah as a preeminent *mitzvah*. Its daily liturgy praised God for favoring human beings with knowledge and teaching mortals understanding. Blind faith was never a Jewish virtue.

The growing attraction of religious rationalism can be traced through the career of medieval Jewish philosophy. Its first major spokesman, Saadia Gaon (892–942), whose landmark *Book of Doctrines and Beliefs* inaugurates the enterprise, feels compelled to demonstrate by appeal to biblical proof texts not only that it is not heretical to speculate on matters of religion, but that we are even commanded to do so. In his day, the case for rationalism still had to be argued. Over a century later, Bahya ibn Pakuda's *Duties of the Heart* (late eleventh century) is able to claim that one who believes simply because of tradition is like the blind following the blind; the person who believes because of reason has had his eyes opened.

Finally, at the climax of the period, the arch rationalist Moses Maimonides (1135–1206) insisted that when the Bible speaks of us as created in the image of God, it is referring to our faculty of reason. God is pure rationality and our faculty of reason is His image within us. In a striking allegory near the end of the *Guide of the Perplexed* (III:51), Maimonides paints his hierarchy of ideal human beings. At the very top of the hierarchy is the one "who has achieved demonstration, to the extent that this is possible, of everything that may be demonstrated." He is far ahead of those who have no doctrinal belief, or of "the ignoramuses who observe the commandments," or of those "who believe true opinions on the basis of traditional authority . . . but do not engage in speculation concerning the fundamental principles of religion."

As rationalism became increasingly attractive, the very need for revelation came to be questioned. At the outset, in Saadia, revelation and reason are portrayed as two parallel and necessary pathways to religious truth. We need revelation because rational inquiry is long and arduous, because it is strewn with potential pitfalls for mistakes in reasoning are prevalent, and because many human beings have not adequately developed their rational faculties. God, then, in His mercy, reveals the truth and then asks us to demonstrate it ourselves.

But in Maimonides, reason and revelation are essentially one path, differing only in the idiom that they use. There is no inherent difference between the prophet and the metaphysician, between the ultimate prophetic experience and the ultimate metaphysical act. What is different is the language they use to describe their respective paths. Maimonides then spends much of the first book of the *Guide* dealing with the problems raised by the language of Torah and translating it into the idiom of philosophy. But the very claim that Moses was a metaphysician, that his vision of God was reached through metaphysical speculation, and that metaphysics is, as Maimonides calls it, "the divine science," is eloquent testimony to the transformation in Judaism wrought by its philosophers. It is small comfort to realize that Aristotle would have been just as stunned were he to know how medieval thinkers transformed his own thinking. In reality, the philosophers' midrashic skills were applied to both texts: to the Bible and to Aristotle as well.

This idealization of reason did not go unchallenged. We saw earlier that Yehuda Halevi wrote *The Kuzari* in the period when religious rationalism was nearing its apogee, early in the twelfth century. Halevi deliberately dismissed the power of reason and philosophy in favor of revelation and tradition. He insisted that for all philosophy's claim to universal and conclusive certainty, it had hardly generated widespread agreement regarding its own conclusions. There were as many philosophical schools as there were religious traditions—a fact that the philosophers preferred to overlook.

In time, Yehuda Halevi's contentions emerged as amply justified. Most of the specific claims of medieval religious rationalism were refuted and abandoned. Indeed the entire enterprise was narrowly tied to its cultural setting. When that setting changed, the method itself lost its attraction. It enjoyed a brief revival at the beginning of the modern period in Jewish history, for example, in the writings of Moses Mendelssohn (1729–1786), the philosopher of the Jewish enlightenment. But by the dawn of our own century, religious philosophy began to move toward the opposite pole. Rationality came to be viewed as a blemish on the act of faith, as diminishing the radical freedom that faith demands. One should believe, not because it is reasonable, but simply because God demands it. The new thinking chose as its motto the claim of the second-century Church Father, Tertullian: "I believe because it is absurd." Faith is the subjective act *par excellence;* to rob it of its subjectivity is to destroy it.

Despite this, the hope that religion should at least aim for a degree of rationality persists as a powerful, almost inarticulate impulse among us. We are aware of the irrational within us but we are apologetic about it and try to diminish its hold. We may not want to erect a totally rational religious belief system but we will try to eliminate the patently superstitious, illusionary claims that are often pronounced in the name of religion. We will also try to integrate the knowledge that comes to us out of religion into the fabric of our common, everyday, or scientific knowledge of the world, much as Aristotle tried to do in his day.

The Problem of Subjectivity

If the ultimate goal of the religious rationalist is indeed to integrate religious and scientific knowledge, then the subjective character of many religious claims is a source of embarrassment. It must be eliminated, and it can be in much the same way that it is eliminated in science.

The thoroughgoing rationalist will insist that human beings are endowed with one basic way of attaining knowledge. The religious rationalist will insist that we know God as we know anything else. We call this a single-epistemology structure as opposed to the dual-epistemology structure that we encounter in some forms of religious experientialism, where God can not be known through the same processes by which we gain knowledge of watches and blood cells. Halevi and Heschel, as we saw above, espouse a dual epistemology; since God is distinct from any natural object, we need an equally distinct faculty to reach Him.

Some religious experientialists in fact say much more. They insist that religion does not yield knowledge in the common or even scientific sense of that term, certainly not knowledge of God. The emotion-filled, quasi-mystical communion with or worship of God that they achieve at the climax of their experience is very far from a cerebral achievement. They spend much time debunking the speculative side of theology. The rationalist challenges that posture. If religion does not yield knowledge, what purpose does it serve? What value does it have?

For a religious rationalist, then, faith is very much "belief that. . . ." It is a body of knowledge "that" we believe about God, the human being, creation, revelation, the afterlife, and the rest of the agenda of Torah. Hence the "I believe that . . ." structure of Maimonides' Thirteen Principles of Faith. Faith is attained much the same way our knowledge of the world is attained, by speculation on the data of ordinary experience. If we are rigorous about confirming our sense experience, if our argumentation is pursued with care, if errors in logic are avoided, then the results of our inquiry will be objectively true, as true as any other body of knowledge derived in the same way and true for everyone and for all time.

Of course, we can not compel everyone to be rigorous about sense experience, to pursue the argumentation without faulty reasoning, or to read the writings of the philosophers who have. There is an "escape clause" even at the heart of rationalism. But its power is miniscule in comparison with that afforded by experientialism. Atheism, then, is largely a failure of the intellect, or a failure of will to use the intellect as the philosopher does.

The Arguments for the Existence of God

The ultimate goal of religious rationalism, as Maimonides described it, was to achieve "demonstration, to the extent that that is possible, of everything that may be demonstrated." The goal of the enterprise as a whole was to demonstrate, by rational means, the truth of all of the teachings of Torah.

But the heart of the enterprise was to prove the existence of God. If reason failed us here, its remaining accomplishments would be irrelevant. Arguments for the existence of God become the focal point of all of medieval philosophical literature. They appear in Jewish, Christian, and Muslim writings with ample borrowings back and forth.

Typically, three broad arguments are used, albeit with many minor variations in style and substance. Two of these are *a posteriori,* namely, they are posterior to, or follow, and are based on, some form of ordinary sense experience—the *cosmological,* or causal argument and the *teleological,* or argument from design. These two arguments are omnipresent in Jewish sources—the cosmological argument in a central role, and the teleological usually in a supporting role. The third, the *ontological* argument, is *a priori,* or "prior" to sense experience, that is, entirely deductive, based on logic alone. The ontological argument does not appear in Jewish sources until after the Middle Ages, in the writings of Baruch Spinoza (1632–1677) or Moses Mendelssohn a century later. We may surmise that this purely deductive argument was less congenial to Jewish thinkers, who were able to find biblical and rabbinic prototypes for the cosmological and teleological arguments, but not for the ontological.

The later philosophical literature found all three of the arguments wanting; they were refuted and dismissed. But in their day, they were viewed as vitally important and convincing. Today, in more popular circles, some form of the cosmological and teleological arguments are frequently invoked by believers who are asked to justify their conviction that God does exist. They have played a central role in the intellectual history of the West, and so they merit individual consideration.

The Ontological Argument

First a brief word on the *a priori,* or ontological argument. It received its classical formulation in the *Proslogion* of St. Anselm, Archbishop of Canterbury (ca. 1033–1109), and though periodically dismissed as simple-minded wordplay, it has exercised a peculiar fascination on thinkers to our own day.

The argument is essentially an attempt to prove the existence of God from the idea or definition of God. Hence its purely deductive character; it requires no sense experience, only thought. Anselm defines God as "a being than which nothing greater can be thought." But then, he concludes, this being must exist because otherwise He would not be that being "than which nothing greater can be thought"; there would then be some other Being whose greatness exceeds that of the former, because this second, greater Being does exist. In either case, God exists. He exists by definition. The very idea of God implies His existence.

Note the purely deductive character of the argument. It moves by logic alone, by demonstrating that existence is to God as, for example, three-sidedness is to a triangle. As a triangle, by definition, has three sides, so God, by definition, exists.

But it is precisely the assumption that existence is to God as three-sidedness is to triangles that was challenged by the eighteenth-century German philosopher Immanuel Kant. In his classic refutation of the argument, Kant insists that existence is not a predicate like three-sidedness. We can deduce three-sidedness from the very idea of triangle by logic alone, but we can not deduce that God exists from the very idea of God.

What Kant is saying is that we can construct a composite portrait of a most perfect Being in our heads—that He is omnipotent, omniscient, eternal, immaterial, and the rest. But that this God exists can not be one of these predicates. To say that God exists is, rather, to claim that this figure which is now "in our heads" has a reality in the world outside of us as well. That further claim, Kant insists, can not be made on the basis of a pure logical deduction from the fact of His perfection. We can legitimately conclude that "a being than which nothing greater can be thought" is omnipotent or omniscient—*if He exists*. Omnipotence and omniscience are genuine predicates. But that He exists can not be demonstrated by a sheer deductive argument. To ascertain that, we have to turn outside the world of ideas to experience. We have to look and see if indeed there is such a Being in the world, if this Being has a reality outside the world of our ideas. But once we do this, we have abandoned the ontological argument.

This is not the place to enter into the later reformulations of the ontological argument. Suffice it to say that it has been a source of both frustration and fascination to generations of thinkers, dismissed as facile and circular or welcomed as profound and convincing. Its attraction rests on the fact that it reduces subjectivity to a zero-point, simply because it is entirely deductive. If it works—and as we have seen, that is a big "if"—it establishes the existence of God as a thoroughly logical conclusion which no thinking human being could possibly deny. There is no possible "escape clause" from the argument. The issue is settled forever and for everyone. But this air-tight quality is achieved at the expense of more than a suspicion of circularity. It seems that the argument assumes what it wishes to prove—which is why it has been rejected as often as it has been raised.

Jewish thinkers ignored the ontological argument until well after the Middle Ages, probably because its thrust is so foreign to the approach of Torah. The goal of medieval Jewish philosophers remained primarily to explicate and defend Torah in philosophical terms. These thinkers, however, were very much intrigued by the two *a posteriori* arguments.

The Cosmological Argument

This argument is pivotal in all medieval Jewish, Christian, and Muslim sources. It was attractive to medieval thinkers because it was clearly anticipated in numerous biblical passages, as in the Creation story in Genesis 1–2, in Isaiah 40:25–26, and in Psalms 19, 104, and 148. Like the teleological argument, it is *a posteriori,* not purely deductive but based on one aspect of our sense experience of the world. The thrust of the argument is to argue from the world to God, from the order of nature to God as the ultimate cause of that order.

As it appears in medieval literature, the argument is loosely based on passages in Plato's dialogue *The Laws* and more directly on passages from Aristotle. In Books 8 of his *Physics* and 12 of his *Metaphysics,* Aristotle inquires into the cause or causes of the finite instances of motion or change that we observe in the natural world. Every instance of change must be caused by some other, prior instance of change (as a moving billiard ball is set into motion by a moving billiard cue), which is itself caused by some other, prior instance of change and so on. But this process of tracing effect back to cause can not go on to infinity. Ultimately, then, we must posit some original cause of change, some mover that is itself not in motion, that is unmoved by any mover prior to it. Aristotle refers to this unmoved mover as God. In the writings of the medieval philosophers, this God was identified with the God of the monotheistic religions.

Some comments on the argument at this stage. First, when the Greeks talked of "motion," they meant much more than the kind of motion exhibited by a moving billiard ball. They understood motion as roughly equivalent to what we would call "change." When the air about me changes from hot to cold, it is in motion. The point of departure for the argument, then, is the panorama of change that we see all about us. The argument claims that one instance of change is always caused by a prior instance of change, that the billiard ball moves because it is touched by a moving cue, or that the air changes from hot to cold because it is moved by a wind, and so on, until we reach an ultimate cause of the panorama, some cause of change or motion that is itself not in motion or in the process of changing.

Second, this ultimate mover or cause does not generate motion in the same way that a physical body does, as a billiard cue moves the ball, through its own motion—simply because it itself is not in motion. To use Aristotle's technical language, it is not the "efficient cause" of motion but rather its "final cause." It serves as a cause in the sense that it is the ultimate goal, purpose, or function that the moving object strives to attain or become. It causes by attraction. Thus, though the wind may be the efficient cause of the changing temperature of the air in my room, its final cause is warmth. Warmth is a cause, Aristotle claims, just as the beloved functions as a cause for the activity of the lover who strives to attain or approach the beloved.

This is very far from the efficient-cause God of Genesis. The biblical God initiates the natural processes *ex nihilo,* out of nothing. But for the Greeks, motion, change, and nature are eternal. There never was an ultimate efficient cause for the panorama of nature. But just as there has to be a final cause for every finite instance of change, so there must be an ultimate final cause for the process as a whole. In this instance, the final cause functions as the efficient cause as well.

This Unmoved Mover is not a body, not material, for then it would itself be in motion. Anything material is involved in change. The unmoved mover is also itself changeless; it is what it is all the time. Since it is not matter, it must be thought, pure thinking—for there are only two ultimate substantive realities, matter and thought. Finally, the content or object of this thinking—that which is being thought—can not change. Therefore it too must be thought. In fact, it must be the ultimate object of thought, namely, thought itself. Hence the "nature" of this unmoved mover: thought thinking itself, eternal and unchanging.

Aristotelian scholars to this day disagree on the precise interpretation of the passages in his writings that deal with the Unmoved Mover. It is clear, however, that Aristotle himself would have been surprised at the way medieval thinkers used his argument. If he has a "theology" in the first place, it is intimately tied to his physics. His goal was to understand why the natural order is the way it is, why change is omnipresent. His God is very much tied to nature, very much a "natural" God, as opposed to the supernatural God of the Bible. The Aristotelian God does not create the world. He does not know the world, only himself. He has no concern for civilization. He does not enter into history. He does not take Jews out of Egypt, reveal His will at Sinai, worry about the fate of orphans and widows, resurrect the dead, or send the Messiah. He is simply the ultimate "reason why" things are the way they are. He is very much the God of the philosophers, not the God of Abraham, Isaac, and Jacob, not the living God of religion.

But none of this was the primary concern of the medievals. Their purpose was precisely to make God philosophically—that is, rationally—acceptable. There was no denying the attraction of Aristotle's argument, then, particularly because it was Aristotle's, the arch proponent of an apparently skeptical rationalism. The issues raised by God's "religious" character could be dealt with elsewhere and by other means.

But there is also no denying how far afield all of this argumentation has taken us. The entire tone of this discussion, the technical, philosophical details that are indispensable for understanding the argument, should serve to highlight the very idiosyncratic approach of medieval rationalism to the issue of God. It certainly seems to be very far removed from biblical and rabbinic thinking. But in the Middle Ages, it was an integral part of the vocabulary of every thinking person.

The most refined versions of the cosmological argument in Jewish sources are in Maimonides' *Guide* (II:1), and, in a much more succinct and accessible form, in the first chapter of the first book of his *Mishneh Torah.* In the *Guide,* Maimonides offers four arguments that prove the existence of God, of which the first and fourth are versions of the cosmological argument. They begin with observed, finite instances of motion or change, each of which is caused by a preceding instance of motion and change. They assert that the chain of cause and effect cannot continue to infinity but rather that it must end. We are left with the existence of an ultimate Uncaused Cause, which is God.

This formulation of the argument assumes that the cause and effect sequence is temporal, that we argue back in time from the present to an original creating act. But it might help to use a second version of the same argument that was developed by Thomas Aquinas (1225–1274), the authoritative medieval philosopher of the Roman Catholic Church who borrowed extensively from Maimonides. Aquinas sees the cause-and-effect sequence, not as temporal but as hierarchical. At any *one* moment in time, each finite case of activity presupposes another higher activity, and the whole presupposes an Ultimate Actor who keeps the entire process going. Without a supreme or "first" (not in time but in structure) cause or mover, there would be no change or motion here and now.

Maimonides uses this nontemporal form of the argument in the *Mishneh Torah*. Maimonides writes: "It is He who controls the sphere of the universe with a power that is without end or limit. . . . For the sphere is always revolving; and it is impossible for it to revolve without someone making it revolve. It is God, blessed be He, who causes it to revolve, without hand or body."

This reformulation of the cosmological argument also enables us to understand the doctrine of creation in a different way. When we speak of God as having created the world, we do not mean that He simply set the process into motion eons ago. We also mean that at any one moment in time, the world would not exist without His continuing activity. We are in effect echoing the words of our daily morning liturgy, which praises God for "renewing the work of creation, every day, constantly." The doctrine of creation is not only a chronological issue; it is also a statement about the contingency of the world, its ongoing dependence on God's presence and activity.

The cosmological argument rests on the assumption that it is impossible to explain the natural order without positing God as its ultimate cause or source of intelligibility. That of course assumes that we need or want to explain why things are the way they are. Herein lies the first glimmer of an "escape clause" from the argument. Someone who simply accepts the natural order as there, who does not see the cause and effect sequence or want to explain why it is such, will not be convinced by this argument alone.

The vulnerability of the cosmological argument, then, stems from its *a posteriori* character, a problem that is not shared by the *a priori* ontological argument. The argument itself proceeds through rational demonstration alone, but its point of departure is sense experience. The moment experience enters the picture, so does subjectivity. It is a much less striking form of subjectivity than the experientialist framework demands. There, we are asked to see God as present in the complex patterns of nature and history; here, simply cause and effect in the natural order. But a dimension of subjectivity remains even in a rationalist approach.

We alluded to a more serious problem with the cosmological argument above, namely, the kind of God whose existence it demonstrates. The medievalists radically transformed the Aristotelian argument but could still hardly avoid its inherent naturalist thrust. They may have saved God's philosophical respectability, but at the price of His religious significance. He remains a button-pushing God, a God who sets or keeps the natural order in motion. To transform this God into one who listens to the prayers of a community of Jews would be a formidable task.

The Teleological Argument
The teleological argument, or argument from design (Greek: *telos,* end, purpose, design), inherits some of the problems of the cosmological argument and avoids some, but is saddled with still others of its own making. It too is an *a posteriori* argument, based on our sense experience of the natural world. Here what we experience is not simply motion or change in nature but rather design—that is, complex and often intricate patterns that are structured so as to bring about a specific purpose, order, or value.

The human body, for example, exhibits that kind of design. From this point of departure, the teleological argument piggybacks onto the cosmological argument: We understand design as an effect for which we infer a cause. The cause is the Ultimate Designer—God.

The notion that nature exhibits design and purpose was central to Aristotle, but the use of design to prove the existence of a designing God emerges first in Philo, and later (twelfth century), in Bahya as a supplement to the cosmological argument. Halevi uses the fact of design not to demonstrate God's existence but rather His wisdom and concern for creation. Again, the attraction of the argument to Jewish thinkers stems from the fact that it seems to have been anticipated in biblical passages such as Genesis 1–2, Isaiah 40, Psalms 8 and 104, and in many rabbinic homilies as well—all of which are frequently quoted by the medievals.

But note that these very same biblical passages were used earlier as reflecting the predominant biblical approach to God, which is experientialist and not at all rationalist. In fact, the distinction between an experientialist and teleological approach to God is not as clear as we would like it to be. Both appeal to our experience of complex patterns in nature. The experientialist *sees* God *in* the patterns; the rationalist *infers* the existence of God as the *cause* of the pattern. The "differential diagnosis," as it were, is the rationalist's insertion of an act of inference. That inference, though, may well be implicit. Sometimes we can't really tell if it is there or not. But if it is, we are dealing with a rationalist structure. When Psalm 19:2 speaks of the heavens declaring the glory of God, the psalmist seems to be saying that he sees God's presence pervading the heavens; he is not inferring God's existence as the cause of the heavenly glory. That would be an unnecessarily complicated way of getting to God, at least for the biblical mind set. Therefore we interpret this passage in experientialist terms.

The classic refutations of the teleological argument were provided by two later English philosophers, David Hume (1711–1776) and John Stuart Mill (1806–1873). In his *Dialogues Concerning Natural Religion,* Hume begins with the premise that "like effects prove like causes." He then rigorously examines the effects that the teleological argument uses as a point of departure and inquires as to what kind of cause they imply. He concludes that if the instances of design in the world prove anything, they lead us to a God who is finite (for the effects are finite), imperfect (for the design is clearly imperfect), multiple in number (for there is no evidence that one designer is responsible for all the design), and even corporeal (for all the designers we know of are corporeal). In short, if we argue from the design that we perceive, then the evidence points to a finite, faulty, imperfect, corporeal God. Surely, no God at all is preferable to this one.

Mill's criticism, in his *Nature and Utility of Religion,* is based on the problem of evil or suffering. It is a passionate tract that concludes that nature manifests infinitely more disorder and destruction than it does design and purpose. In fact, nature is more destructive than human beings. "Everything . . . which the worst men commit either against life or property is perpetrated on a larger scale by natural agents. . . . Anarchy and the Reign of Terror are overmatched in injustice, ruin, and death by a hurricane and pestilence. . . ."

Nature in fact manifests both design and chaos. The teleological argument asks us to see the design and ignore the chaos. The skeptic asks us to see the chaos as well, or even predominantly. Hence the teleological argument's "escape clause" is clearly far broader than that of the cosmological argument. In the latter, we are only asked to see natural change; in the former, design—a far more interpretive piece of seeing. The resolution of the dispute between the skeptic and the believer would then hinge on the same kind of process that we described earlier through the analogy of the deliberations of a jury, in our discussion of experientialism. In the context of a community, patterns are shared and a consensual reading of the experience might be achieved.

But the teleological argument shares the cosmological argument's vulnerability for one who can not or does not want to see or account for the natural order. It also requires a readiness to eliminate alternative explanations for that order. It is susceptible to the criticism that it leads us to a finite, imperfect God.

On the other hand, the God of the teleological argument

functions in an infinitely more familiar and "religious" way than the button-pushing God of the cosmological argument. He is not simply the cause of motion or change. He is intelligent, purposive, intentional, even personal in His dealings with creation. The person who reads the evidence of nature as manifesting order and harmony, ignores the evidence of anarchy, and is prepared to make the inference to a designing God, will find this argument convincing. In fact, to this day, many believers who have no philosophical training will frequently use a form of the teleological argument to justify their belief in the existence of God.

The Impact of Maimonidean Rationalism

The attempt to prove the existence of God may have been the centerpiece of medieval Jewish rationalism, but the enterprise as a whole had a much broader scope. In the hands of a Maimonides, for example, it was nothing less than a total transformation of the basic assumptions of Jewish religion as it had been articulated in the Bible and in rabbinic literature.

The scope of that transformation may be captured in this figurative manner. Were one to look at the Bible or the Talmud for one sentence that sums up what God, ultimately, demands of the Jew, the answer would be to obey His will, to follow His ways, to observe His commands. Were we to direct that question to Maimonides, the answer would be to know God. According to the Bible or the Talmud, the model Jew would be the observant Jew; to Maimonides, the Jew who has achieved intellectual perfection.

Intellectual perfection was very much the Aristotelian ideal, of course, and Maimonides was prepared to follow Aristotle a good deal of the way. He broke with Aristotle on one significant issue, on creation in time, but only after having demonstrated to his own satisfaction that Aristotle himself did not believe that he had conclusively proved the eternity of the world. Apart from that one issue, Maimonides is convinced that the entire content of Torah in matters of both belief and practice can be shown to have a rational basis. He then makes the more extreme claim that the Torah actually commands us to *pursue* that rational demonstration ourselves, that this is the ultimate *mitzvah*, that therein lies our fulfillment as Jews and as human beings.

This idealization of the intellect is at the heart of Maimonidean *midrash*. It posits a new and necessarily elitist model of Jewish piety. It creates a new curriculum for Jewish education, in which the study of Torah is supplemented by mathematics, logic, the natural sciences, and, ultimately, "the divine science" or metaphysics. It leads him into stipulating thirteen dogmas that constitute the minimal set of demonstrable beliefs required of the authentic Jew.

This intellectualism also explains Maimonides' sharply dualistic view of the human being. We are composed of two distinct entities, a perishable body and an immortal soul. The two are in tension, but it is the latter that is the source of my true identity and real worth. Its perfection remains my ultimate responsibility.

Finally, it underlies Maimonides' insistence that bodily resurrection is not the ultimate reward reserved for the righteous, as rabbinic thinking claimed. He assigns it only an interim place in the eschatological scenario. Ultimately, the resurrected bodies will die once again. The final reward, reserved for those who have achieved the highest possible intellectual perfection in their lifetimes, will be totally spiritual. Only our souls will achieve immortality.

But in the world of ideas, it is not unusual for opposites to meet. Scientific or rational demonstration may be the path to intellectual perfection, but when Maimonides comes to describe the goal of the entire enterprise, the ultimate religious/philosophical/prophetic act, the knowledge of God, he sounds suspiciously like the religious mystic. It is not at all a detached piece of scientific thinking, but much more an emotion-filled, blissful contemplation of or communion with God.

It is this kind of experience that the righteous will enjoy for eternity after death. Their "souls enjoy blissful delight in their attainment of knowledge of the truly essential nature of God the Creator, a delight which is like that experienced by the holy angels who know God's existence first-hand. The ultimate good, the final end is to achieve this supernal fellowship, to participate in this high glory in which the soul is forever involved with the existence of God the Creator. . . . This is incomparably good, for how could that which is eternal and endless be compared with anything transient and terminable?" Indeed, how could it!

The legacy of Maimonides is nothing less than this thoroughgoing rewriting of Judaism in terms of a foreign idiom. He deserves our gratitude for at least two reasons. One, he provides a point of entry into Judaism for the Jew who intuitively identifies with Maimonides' rationalism and intellectualism. One of the strengths of a centuries-old religious tradition like Judaism is that it provides multiple points of identification for the many characterological types that make up a community. His specific rational demonstrations may or may not be convincing. What remains important is the method, the thrust behind the enterprise, the goal.

Second, Maimonides' achievement is of paramount importance because it demonstrates the plasticity of a living religious tradition, or in more traditional terms, the power of *midrash*. His thought was nothing if not controversial; the controversy generated by his teachings raged for over two centuries after his death, with multiple bans and excommunications invoked by both his supporters and his opponents. But after the dust cleared, Maimonides remained the undisputed giant of Jewish intellectual history and he holds that position to this day. It is no accident that his example was so often invoked by a contemporary Jewish "heretic," Mordecai Kaplan, who had to justify his equally radical rewriting of Judaism in another foreign idiom. Maimonides remains the champion of all Jewish thinkers who struggle with a tradition that appears to have become anachronistic, that demands rethinking and rewriting, in order to preserve its vitality for another generation of Jews whose Jewish identity is in tension with its cultural setting.

But it is also clear that beginning with the dawn of our own century, Maimonides' rational approach to religious faith became less and less attractive. What Franz Rosenzweig called "The New Thinking," his term for existentialism, became the hallmark of twentieth-century Christian and eventually Jewish theology as well. Universality, objectivity, demonstrability—supreme values for Maimonides and his generation—came to be disparaged. Subjectivity, individualism, and passion came to be esteemed above all. In the process, of course, the Torah had to be rethought and rewritten once again. The process of *midrash* continues—this time in a different direction.

The final verdict of philosophy on the arguments for the existence of God is that at best they play a supportive role in tandem with experientialism. Each of the arguments has been amply refuted. Paradoxically, they seem to work best when they are least needed, but are ineffective as conclusive demonstrations. They are indeed not at all conclusive. Each leaves room for a subjective judgment to intervene.

The arguments, then, can be said to provide not "reasons" for belief but rather "grounds" or justifications for belief. They are not strong enough to convince the skeptic, but they can be used to justify or defend beliefs arrived at in some other way. This may not have been the goal of medieval rationalism, but it remains no small achievement. We frequently find ourselves in a situation where, after the fact, we are asked to justify or defend positions that we have taken. In this defensive posture, we appeal to arguments that we believe will be acceptable to our challenger, however little they may have figured in our own thinking at the outset. Thus the distinction between "reasons" and "grounds" for belief. The arguments are frequently invoked in the latter capacity but rarely, today, in the former.

But from a broader perspective, the ideal of rationality continues to exercise a hold over us. We may not want, or feel that we need to demonstrate the existence of God on strictly rational grounds, but we continue to expect that our theological structure *as a whole* exhibit a certain rationality, that at least it should be free of patently irrational claims, that it exhibit a certain coherence and reasonableness. That expectation is not the least of the legacies of thinkers such as Maimonides and his fellow rationalists.

FOR FURTHER STUDY

Again, begin with the material, cited after ch. 3 above, from Hick's anthology, the ENCYCLOPEDIA OF PHILOSOPHY, *on the three classical arguments, Guttmann's* PHILOSOPHY OF JUDAISM *(particularly on all of the medieval Jewish thinkers), and Louis Jacobs'* FAITH. *Hick includes representative versions of the three classical arguments and samplings from the literature surrounding them. The second, nontemporal version of the cosmological argument is in the selection by F. C. Copleston, pp. 87–88. This volume also includes Kant's classic critique of the ontological argument, and Hume's and Mill's, of the teleological argument. Hick's introduction is particularly strong on the rationalist approach as a whole.*

On the broad, medieval cultural milieu within which Jewish philosophy developed, see Abraham Halkin's "The Judeo-Islamic Age" in GREAT AGES AND IDEAS OF THE JEWISH PEOPLE, *edited by Leo W. Schwarz (see ch. 4). Isaac Husik's* A HISTORY OF MEDIEVAL JEWISH PHILOSOPHY *(see ch. 4), particularly the Introduction, clarifies the impact of Aristotelian thought on medieval Jewish philosophy.*

Specifically on the ontological argument, see the anthology, THE MANY-FACED ARGUMENT, *edited by John H. Hick and Arthur C. McGill (pb Macmillan 1967) for various statements of the argument from antiquity to the present. An excellent study of Aristotle's thought is John Herman Randall, Jr.'s* ARISTOTLE *(pb Columbia University Press, 1960), particularly ch. 6, with the material on the unmoved mover.*

For Jewish versions of the rationalist approach, see Saadia's BOOK OF DOCTRINES AND BELIEFS *included in* THREE JEWISH PHILOSOPHERS *(see ch. 5), along with Alexander Altmann's introduction and notes and Maimonides'* GUIDE OF THE PERPLEXED *(see ch. 4). Guttmann is excellent on Maimonides, as is David Hartman's* MAIMONIDES: TORAH AND PHILOSOPHIC QUEST *(Jewish Publication Society, 1976).*

Maimonides' Thirteen Principles appear at the conclusion of his "Introduction to Helek*" (ch. 10 of tractate* Sanhedrin*), part of his* COMMENTARY TO THE MISHNAH. *An excellent English translation— indeed, an excellent anthology of all of Maimonides' writings—is* A MAIMONIDES READER, *edited by Isadore Twersky (pb Behrman, 1972).*

Twersky's introduction to the volume illuminates Maimonides the man, his times, and his thought as a whole. Maimonides' description of the eternal bliss, reserved for the righteous in the world to come, is also in his "Introduction to Helek,*" p. 412 in the Twersky anthology.*

Maimonides' MISHNEH TORAH *is available in a 14-volume annotated translation published by Yale University Press in the Yale Judaica Series (Yale University Press, 1956).*

A more contemporary reworking of this approach is in ch. 6 of Robert Gordis' A FAITH FOR MODERNS *(Bloch, 1960).*

VII

Encountering God:
Existentialism

The Existentialist Temper

A FRIEND COMES TO YOU FOR ADVICE. SHE IS PREGNANT. THE pregnancy was unanticipated and it couldn't have come at a worse time. The family will be relocating in a few months and money is tight. Her youngest child is just into nursery school and she had been looking forward to a few years of freedom to finish her own professional training. Now this. An abortion would solve this problem—but create others. She has heard a good deal about the emotional trauma that accompanies an abortion, and she does have some feelings about the ethics of abortion on demand. She wants your advice.

Depending on who you are, you might refer her to a clergy-person or psychotherapist, help her sort out the issues yourself, tell her straight out what you think she should do, simply hold her hand and comfort her—or any combination of these.

Or, you may say something like the following: "Nancy, it's a rough problem, but it's the kind of problem that nobody can resolve for you. There are no rules here, at least no rules that apply to everyone across the board. You're going to have to make your own decision and whatever you decide will be right, right for you. That's as much "right" as you can hope to have because ultimately, nobody else *is* you, nobody else shares your situation, nobody else can put themselves in your place. Whatever you decide is risky and you, above all, will have to live with that risk and with the anxiety that accompanies it. Your family and friends can stand by you, hold your hand, comfort and console you, but it's your fetus, your body, your pregnancy, and your abortion. You alone will deliver the baby or undergo the abortion. You will have to live with the consequences, whatever they may be."

A more concise version of that elaborate response would be: "Nancy, you're confronting an existential decision." When we apply an approach of this kind, systematically, not only to significant moral decisions but also to the choice between value systems, to the search for the ultimate meaning of human life, to questions of personal identity, and to the range of issues raised by religion—the existence of God and the nature of religious faith—we are adopting a philosophical approach that has come to be called existentialism.

Existentialist philosophers are a highly individualistic group of thinkers, many of whom either refuse to allow themselves to be called existentialists or are not philosophers in any technical sense of the term. It is a comparatively youthful movement, originating in nineteenth-century Europe with the work of the Danish Christian theologian Sören Kierkegaard (1813–1855), the German philosopher Friedrich Nietzsche (1844–1900), and the Russian novelist Fyodor Dostoyevsky (1812–1881). However, existentialists also like to trace their lineage back to thinkers such as the seventeenth-century Frenchman Blaise Pascal, the fourth-to-fifth-century Church Father Augustine, to Socrates, and even, as we shall see, to the Bible.

In our own century, existentialism has attracted thinkers as diverse as Jean-Paul Sartre and Albert Camus in France, Martin Heidegger in Germany, and Miguel de Unamuno in Spain. Kierkegaard's work, in particular, has stimulated a radical rethinking of the nature of religious faith in the writings of Gabriel Marcel among the Roman Catholics; Karl Barth, Karl Jaspers, Reinhold Niebuhr, and Paul Tillich among the Protestants; and Martin Buber and Franz Rosenzweig together with their younger disciples Emil Fackenheim, Eugene Borowitz, and the late Will Herberg among the Jews.

What unites this variegated group of thinkers is first and foremost the distinctive mood or temper that pervades their writings. Terms such as "anxiety," "risk," "loneliness," "despair," and "absurdity" are omnipresent in their writings. Illness, death, and suicide are recurrent themes. They are not, by and large, an optimistic or cheerful lot. Intellectual historians have noted that existentialism, as a philosophical movement, flowered in Europe, roughly from 1850 to 1950—when the continent was ravaged by war and revolution—whereas it had minimal impact on American thinking until the 1940s and on American Jewish thinking until after the Holocaust. The more positive, progressive, optimistic American temper of the first half of our century did not identify with existentialism's pervasive seriousness.

But existentialism is much more than emotion or mood. It is based on a number of serious philosophical assumptions, preeminently the conviction that to speak in a general, universal, or abstract way about "the human situation," "human life," "human beings," or "people" is precisely to miss what is most important about me and my life. There is no generalized "human situation," "human life," or "human being"; there is only *my* situation, *my* life, *my* being—or, more precisely, *my* existence in all its concrete particularity. What is most important about me is not what I have in common with every other person, but, rather, what makes me a singular, distinct individual.

The corollary to this sharp individualism is the affirmation that nothing significant can be applied or addressed to all human beings as a class. There are no value systems, meaning structures, or philosophical or religious truths that can claim objective, universal validity. The kind of truth that mathematics or science strives to attain may be valuable for certain purposes, but it becomes progressively less relevant the closer the issue impinges on my own, personal life experience. In these personal issues, what is true is whatever I decide is true. In fact, I make it true by clinging to that decision and by acting on it in my life experience.

On a broader scale, the same can be said for the range of answers that philosophies and religions have proposed to the human search for the meaning of life. None of them has intrinsic value, significance, or truth; any one of them can become true when I appropriate it as mine. The very act of appropriation makes it true—true for me—and that is the only kind of truth I can hope to have.

Thus the existentialist temper. Life is serious and perilous. Death is the ultimate absurdity. I am largely alone. How to live, what to make of my life, what ultimate structure of meaning to adopt, is my decision to make. Only *I* can make that decision, and in making it, I am utterly alone. I have nothing on which to base myself, apart from my own, totally personal sense of who I am, what I hold dear, and how I want to conduct my life. The decision is risk-filled for what is at stake is my one-and-only life. No wonder I am anxious—not the kind of anxiety that I face before an exam, but a root or "existential" anxiety which stems simply from my being alive, and from which I will be freed only when I die.

Essence and Existence

The term *existentialism* stems from a philosophical distinction that, like so much else in philosophy, has its roots in Plato. Plato distinguishes between an entity's "essence" and "existence." A thing's essence is that quality which makes it a member of a class of entities that share that same quality. Thus, with apologies to English usage, we can speak of "watch-ness," the quality that makes a watch a watch, or of "brown-ness," or of beauty itself, the quality that makes an individual flower or painting beautiful. Another way of referring to essences is to call them "ideas" or "universals" or, more technically, "forms."

But apart from the essence or form of watch, brown, and beauty, there are also particular, individual, concrete "existents": this watch on my wrist, my brown chair, the beautiful, red anemone on the table. An essence is actualized, or embodied, in a concrete existent. The particular watch "participates" in its idealized form. Essences, ideas, or forms are abstract and general; existents are concrete, particular, and individualized. Ideas are eternal; existents live and die.

While philosophers may disagree on the precise interpretation of Plato's theory of forms, it is clear that Plato himself believed that they were much more than linguistic conventions designed to facilitate communication, or even concepts "located" in the human mind. Plato wove an elaborate myth whereby these forms inhabit a timeless, changeless, disembodied world of their own. Our everyday world contains individual, time-bound watches, chairs, and flowers. In Plato's transcendent and superior world, these forms are arranged in a hierarchy according to their degree of abstractness.

This myth, like all others, enabled Plato to answer a number of basic philosophical questions about the world, our experience, and the goal of human life. What is the nature of ultimate reality? What is the world made up of? How did it come to be? What is authentic knowledge? What is of ultimate value? Wherein lies human fulfillment?

Plato deals with all of these issues by positing a series of dualisms; there are two dimensions to the human being, two methods of knowing, two worlds, two ways to live. But the dualism is not simply structural; it is also very much valuative. One of the two poles is always and inherently superior to the other: the soul over the body, reason over sensation, the timeless world of forms over the concrete world of particulars, detachment from the world over engagement.

Plato's assumption that the ultimate guide to truth and value was through "essentialist" thinking became the guiding principle of much medieval and modern thought. It is the underlying assumption of all forms of rationalism. Essentialism reached its acme in eighteenth- and nineteenth-century German Idealism, particularly in the work of Georg Wilhelm Friedrich Hegel (1770–1831) and his immediate successors, who taught that Mind or Spirit is the whole of reality and that the process of universal history is but the outward face of an evolutionary and progressive development within Spirit itself. The emergence of existentialism in Europe, toward the end of the nineteenth century, can then be viewed as a reaction against the excesses of essentialism in German Idealism.

Most existentialists are not opposed, in principle, to an essence-oriented approach to the world. Most of them are not overly concerned with metaphysical questions such as the ultimate nature of reality. What does trouble existentialists—what they believe to be the only truly significant philosophical question—is the nature of the human being. Or, to formulate that same question in existentialist terms: "Who am I?" They are all fundamentally philosophical anthropologists. Their root assumption is that to the extent that we try to understand the human being by focusing on the *idea* of the person, on abstractions such as "the human condition," "humanity," or "man," we have overlooked the single, most significant dimension of any human being: the individual's sense of his own "existence" in all its concrete, ineluctable particularity.

As far as the human being is concerned, then, Plato must be stood on his head. What is most real, most true, and most valuable is not a timeless, disembodied, eternal "essence" or "idea" of the human being but, rather, *this* very time-bound, changing, concrete individual: *me* and my own life experience as it is lived in all its idiosyncratic detail. If the core philosophical question is "Who am I?", then I am the only one who can answer that question, and I must answer it from within my individual situation. Third-person thinking is replaced by first-person thinking, a philosophy of the "grandstand" by one of the "playing field," the spectator by the participant. Abstractions are mistrusted, for the further we remove ourselves from concrete life as it is lived, the more irrelevant we become. Conversely, passion, so mistrusted by the Greeks, is prized by the existentialist; for nothing is more personal to me than my emotional life.

The full weight of the move from essentialist to existentialist thinking can be captured in this brief illustration. The essentialist will claim, "All men are mortal." The existentialist will say, "I must die." The first is a detached intellectualization; the second, my personal coming to terms with my fate. The first is objectively true but irrelevant; the second is a personal cry of pain, and of infinite significance.

Existentialism as Critique

Because existentialism prizes individualism and subjectivity, its representatives are free to disagree on many of the positive implications of their basic approach. But what they all share is a strong critical stance toward any system of values that comes from outside the individual and claims to have universal, objective validity. Much of existentialist literature is devoted to this systematic ground-clearing operation, to exposing the irrelevance of all abstract systems, to opening our eyes to the intrinsic meaninglessness of all philosophical and religious structures of belief and practice.

Existentialists evoke this gaping absence of *intrinsic* meaning or value in human life—what they refer to as the "absurdity" that characterizes our life experience—through a variety of striking metaphors. Two of these metaphors are central to the existential portrait of the human condition in the work of the French Nobel Prize-winning author, Albert Camus (1913–1960). They appear in his philosophical tract, *The Myth of Sisyphus,* and in his novel, *The Plague.*

Sisyphus was a figure in Greek mythology who was condemned to roll a boulder to the top of a mountain, watch it fall, and roll it back up again, to eternity. His fate is a metaphor for the absurdity of every human life. The first sentences in the book pose the challenge: "There is only one serious philosophical problem: suicide. To judge whether life is worth living is to respond to the fundamental philosophical question." If life is absurd, if death is the ultimate absurdity, then why not take my death into my own hands and exercise at least that degree of control over my life? Camus eventually rejects the option of suicide because it is incompatible with human pride and dignity. But he insists that we must also remain free of any illusion that there is any meaning or purpose to what we do beyond the very fact of our living. What makes Sisyphus the authentic existentialist hero is that his eyes are open. He accepts and understands his fate.

The Myth of Sisyphus was written in 1942; *The Plague,* in 1947. In the intervening years, Camus lived through the Nazi occupation of France and fought with the French resistance. The later work reflects Camus' struggle to find other possible responses to Sisyphus' stance. The novel is set in a North African city that becomes infested with the plague and is quarantined from the rest of the world. The plague is another metaphor for the absurdity of human life. In effect, we all live all of the time in the face of death; the plague merely heightens our awareness of our fate. Camus then studies the reactions of his main characters as they live and work with the knowledge that any day may be their last. Here, the existentialist hero is Dr. Rieux, a modest, saintly man, who goes from bed to bed, treating and comforting the sick and dying. He has no answer to the questions that everyone is asking; he can't explain why the plague occurred. He simply accepts it as there, to be lived with and struggled against. But his response goes beyond Sisyphus'. Awareness is not enough. We must fight the absurdity, not in the hope of conquering it, but simply to make it more bearable.

Camus' denial of any intrinsic meaning to human life must never be understood, then, as a denial of the very possibility of meaning. Instead, meaning and value emerge in the very act of choice or appropriation of a value system. A value becomes a value *because* I appropriate it as mine, *if* and *when* I choose it and live it. I remain the supreme authority for myself because, after all, who is better qualified to legislate value and meaning for my own life than I! Rieux's response to the absurdity of the plague is his personal way of infusing his life with meaning. It is "true" because he espouses it. Similarly, my decision determines what is true—not objectively or universally true, but "existentially" true—true for me. This truth is verified not by appeal to any outside standard or authority but by my living it out in my concrete life situation.

The common task of all existentialists is to open our eyes and to bring us face to face with the ultimate absurdity that confronts us—to expose our cop-outs, our attempts to escape our situation. It also impresses us with the fact of our radical freedom to decide for ourselves—and with the loneliness, risk, and anxiety that accompany that decision. What it can never do is dictate the substance of our choice. That is our task, alone.

Camus' metaphors, Sisyphus and the plague, lend a sharp, realistic edge to his existentialist critique. But they also open the way for the next question: Given that critique, where do I go from here? How then do I deal with my life? How should I live?

The Existentialist Leap of Faith

Existentialism is in constant danger of allowing its denial of *intrinsic* meaning or value to shade into the denial of *all* meaning or value. It then becomes nihilistic and self-defeating. Camus' humanism is a valuable corrective to that threat. What makes Dr. Rieux an existentialist hero is not where he ends up but how he gets there. He too has no illusions. His struggle against the plague is simply his personal attempt to extract a measure of meaning out of his life and work.

We can understand then why existentialism has served as the seedbed for both radical atheism and passionate religious faith. The atheist existentialist accepts the realization that there is nothing in the world outside my individual self that can answer my search for meaning. The believing existentialist will concede that there is no such ground of meaning in the world, but that meaning can be discovered through a "leap of faith" in the transcendent God beyond the world. But in fact, the tension between belief and nonbelief pervades the life experience of all existentialists, especially those we formally dub "believers," but even, for example with Camus, the so-called "atheists." They are all constantly on the move between these two poles. Rarely do they achieve any sense of stability.

The founding document of modern religious existentialism is Sören Kierkegaard's *Fear and Trembling*, an extended *midrash* on the story of the binding of Isaac in Genesis 22. In Kierkegaard's retelling of the story, Abraham is the paradigmatic existentialist hero. God's command is the epitome of absurdity. Everything in Abraham's experience suggests that he should ignore it. Yet he obeys, out of his passionate, personal, and lonely conviction that it is the transcendent God who has spoken to him and that he must obey. Abraham is the "knight of faith," the embodiment of authentic belief.

On Kierkegaard's path to God, there is certainly no rational demonstration of God's existence, no proof or argument from anything in the external world. If anything, the evidence is totally ambiguous. Nor is there a distinctive "religious" experience as the experientialists claim to have, neither of God Himself, His presence in the world, nor of patterns in nature and history that reveal His concern or His majesty. Nothing in the world testifies to God. There is no evidence. Thus the metaphor of the "leap." We leap because we have nothing to stand on, no basis, no ground for our affirmation.

Existentialist faith is the epitome of "belief in . . . ," not at all "belief that . . . ." It is trust, commitment, loyalty, a turning of the entire self toward God, a living, vital relationship. It is an act of the whole person, not of the mind, the will, or the emotions alone. It is a risk because it has no basis in reason or experience. It can neither be proven nor disproven. It is the ultimate risk because I stake my only life on its outcome. It is never secure, never permanent, nothing I "have" as an acquisition. It must be renewed moment by moment because every moment brings renewed temptation to capitulate to the illusionary faiths of reason or experience or to abandon the search. Finally, it is the result of a decision. And in making that decision, I am ultimately alone. Existentialism flaunts the individualism and subjectivity of religious faith.

Subjectivity is the cornerstone of all existentialist thought, but this has not diminished the ferocity of the dispute between atheistic and believing existentialists. The atheist accuses the believer of copping out, of succumbing to an age-old delusion; the believer accuses the atheist of trying to dictate the outcome (as opposed to the process) of the search for meaning, and hence of betraying the very premises of existentialism.

But Jewish existentialists have faced an even more powerful critique from the more traditional wings of the believing community. Their espousal of radical individualism has been viewed as an affront to Judaism's strong communal orientation and to its insistence on providing a universally binding and all-encompassing structure for the life experience of the Jew. That's why Kierkegaard's reading of the binding of Isaac has been vigorously attacked by Jewish thinkers who counter what they view as his "Christian" understanding of the story with the "Jewish" rabbinic reading that downplays the absurdity of God's command. The rabbinic *midrash* on the story highlights the legitimacy of God's command to Abraham to sacrifice his son. It claims that God, Abraham, and Isaac all understood that the command was completely justified. Beyond this, Kierkegaard's Abraham confronts God in his ultimate loneliness; the rabbinic Abraham, at the moment of his testing, pleads for all of Israel—which is why this story is read on Rosh Hashanah, when Jews come before God for forgiveness as a community, not as a set of individuals. This rabbinic reading of the biblical story—which is, of course, also a *midrash*—portends the difficulties that modern Jewish existentialists faced in their attempts to approach Judaism as existentialist religion.

A Believing Existentialist: Martin Buber

The earliest such comprehensive reading was provided by the German and later Israeli thinker, Martin Buber (1878–1965). Not at all paradoxically, from what was said above, Buber has had a far greater influence in Christian and humanist circles than in the Jewish world. His use of traditional Jewish sources is highly selective. He draws heavily from certain portions of the Bible and from mystical and Hasidic literature, but very little from the rationalist tradition. And he views much of the rabbinic tradition—particularly the traditional *halakhah*—as the prototype of what, in an early paper, he calls "religion" as opposed to "religiosity." "Religion" is characterized by structure, discipline, traditionalism, dogmatism, and legalism; "religiosity," by creativity, spontaneity, emotion, decision making, and living communion with God. In short, religion is faith in an essentialist mold; religiosity, in an existentialist mold.

Buber's *I and Thou* is one of the few generally recognized

masterpieces of twentieth-century philosophy. Buber teaches that we relate to the world in two possible ways, as expressed by the two "primary words," "I-Thou" and "I-It." The I-Thou relation is a meeting of two persons, two subjects who recognize, acknowledge, and address each other as persons. Their meeting is reciprocal and each becomes fully a person in and through their relation. The I-It relation, in contrast, is one of subject to object, of person to thing or to another person who becomes a thing by being addressed as an It. Here, the I uses, controls, manipulates, or dominates the It—which remains passive or allows itself to be used by the I. Finally, in the I-Thou relation, the I is totally individualized; in the I-It, the I is an "anyone," a "no one in particular." Thus the mutuality of the I-Thou relation and the impersonal nature of the I-It. The difference between the two ways of relating can be captured in this way: I-Thou is the relation between two lovers; I-It, between a prostitute and a customer. The first is personal. The second is impersonal; each party is infinitely replaceable.

Much of our interaction with the world is justifiably of the I-It variety, reflecting our need to control the world in order to function. For example, I-It is the foundation for science, which is properly impersonal. But the I-It approach tends to become imperialistic, to claim that it is our exclusive way of relating to the world. The danger here is that the human being also becomes an It, an object to be controlled and manipulated by other people. Ultimately, the I-It world dehumanizes both the It and the I.

We can have I-Thou relations with nature (such as the painter with his landscape), with other persons, with a work of art, and, ultimately, with the transcendent God. God is the supremely personal Thou Who goes out of Himself to enter into relationship with the believer; the believer, in turn, goes out to meet God by opening himself to God's presence. This is religious faith at its most authentic. Buber's characterization of faith draws heavily on the model of an intense interpersonal relationship, even though God is never physically present to the believer. Similarly, when two human beings are intimate with each other, what is loved is not the beloved's physical presence but rather the "person" that lies within the body. Love does not end with the physical absence or death of the beloved.

This I-Thou relation with God is the core of what Buber earlier called "religiosity." It is the opposite of I-It "religion," which is preoccupied with evolving complex theological systems that reduce God to a concept, aim at demonstrating His existence and comprehending Him in intellectual terms. To Buber, "thinking about" God in this way is antithetical to "living with" God. When the believer's relation to God becomes embodied in a theology, when it is reduced to concepts and words, it is inevitably betrayed.

But that betrayal is inescapable, for no one can live on the sharp edge of the I-Thou relation for very long. Our very humanness impels us to think and talk about our experience. To Buber, this is part of a dialectical process that is omnipresent in the history of religions. Religion begins with religiosity, with the spontaneous, living encounter with a Thou-God. Inevitably the Thou-God becomes an It-God, *about* whom people think and speak, and around whom they construct institutionalized religions with rules and regulations, dogmas, and rituals, and with clergy to propagate and oversee them. Eventually this idolatrous It-God is exposed as no-God, as unworthy of ultimate allegiance, as incapable of meeting the need for a living faith, and is dismissed. This critical atheism is an entirely legitimate stage on the path to a renewed encounter with a living Thou—and the process begins again. This cycle repeats itself, over and over, in the life experience of the individual, and, on a broader scale, in the history of all the great religions.

Of course the believer alone in the throes of I-Thou knows that the Thou is truly present. The very notion of having to prove this is ludicrous. Proof implies a social context; we prove something *to* someone else. But here there is no someone else. What happens, then, when the Buberian believer encounters the skeptical atheist who insists that there is no "real" Thou out there, that the believer's experience is an illusion or wish fulfillment? The clash is unavoidable and unresolvable, for each position is legitimate on its own terms. The Buberian believer insists that in the moment of openness what he encounters is a very real Thou-God. The skeptic argues that he encounters nothing. Neither can demonstrate anything to the other. We are left with two conflicting faiths, two conflicting decisions—and no possible dialogue between them. The skeptic and the believer are like ships passing in the night. The distance between them is unbridgeable.

This confrontation with the skeptic exposes the full weight of the believer's risk. The believer knows full well that along with moments of genuine encounter come those terrifying moments of total eclipse, moments when the I and the Thou are unavailable to each other. The Bible is replete with testimonies to God's "hiding His face," sometimes in anger (Deuteronomy 31:18, Isaiah 54:8), sometimes for no apparent reason (Psalm 13:2, 102:3, 143:7), and to the sense of abandonment and vulnerability that such moments inspire. Again, just as the believer alone experiences the encounter, so he alone experiences the eclipse. But who is to say that this experience is not simply a momentary eclipse but the exposure of what, all along, has been an illusion? Perhaps the hidden God is a nonexistent God after all. The believer can only live, work, and wait for a renewal of the relationship.

The radical nature of that choice is illuminated in a striking way by one of Buber's disciples, Emil Fackenheim, in his discussion of the theological implications of the story of Elijah on the Carmel as related in 1 Kings 18. On the face of it, this is a story of how Elijah put to a decisive test the "hypothesis" that the God of Israel is indeed the living and only God, and proved beyond doubt that the hypothesis is indeed true. But Fackenheim poses a startling question: What would Elijah have done if God had not manifested His presence—if Elijah's sacrifices were not consumed, or worse, if the sacrifices of the priests of Baal alone were consumed? Fackenheim's answer is indisputable: Elijah would not have abandoned God and worshiped Baal. Instead, "He would have lamented that, already forsaken by men, he was now forsaken by *Adonai* as well—and continued to do His work, alone." If Elijah seems a remote figure, and his story primitive in its simplicity, consider the contemporary Holocaust survivor who emerged from the Nazi death camps—surely as graphic an experience of divine hiddenness as human beings have ever endured—with faith intact. This kind of religious faith has nothing to do with hypotheses and the weighing of evidence; it is, rather, a turning of the whole person to God.

What is existentialist about *I and Thou?* Clearly, its avoidance of abstractions, proofs, and systems; its appeal to living experience, its sharp individualism, its emotional coloration, its refusal to provide demonstrations of objective truths, its insistence on simply opening windows and pointing the way. *I and Thou* is the most personal of philosophical documents. It traces one man's journey. It testifies to his personal experience and invites us to set out on our own equally personal quest. Buber, like Camus, teaches that we conquer absurdity through relationship. But he goes beyond Camus' humanism in insisting that the ultimate relationship, the one that colors all the others and makes them possible in the first place, is the relationship we have with an Ultimate and Eternal Thou. And we emerge from this I-Thou experience with an overwhelming sense of completion, of resolution and meaning.

What is Jewish about *I and Thou?* Buber would say, "Everything." By definition, an existentialist thinker cannot be disembodied, can never live in a social and historical vacuum. He is shaped by the memories, values, and sensibilities of his cultural roots, and Buber's roots are in Judaism and the Jewish people. Beyond this, Buber sees the I-Thou relationship everywhere in the Jewish experience, in the biblical account of Israel's encounter with God, in the experience of prophecy, in the homiletical portions of rabbinic literature, in the testimonies of Jewish mystics, and in Hasidic literature. He sees it verified again and again in Judaism's religious vitality, in its innate capacity for self-renewal over the centuries. He counters the charge that existentialism leads to an isolationist and privatistic view of religious faith by invoking Israel's powerful sense of community. Israel becomes a collective "I" in and through its relation to the "Thou-God."

Yet by and large, the Jewish community has remained skeptical about the legitimacy of Buber's thought as an authentic expression of Judaism. Unquestionably, this skepticism stems from Buber's stubborn refusal to attribute any religious significance to the established structures and institutions of the Jewish religion. Most offensive of all was his pointed rejection of the binding quality of *halakhah*. The very notion that a behavioral discipline is to apply across the board to all members of a community, and that this universally binding behavioral system provides an access to God, violated every one of his religious instincts. The I-Thou relation is nothing if not spontaneous, an expression of our radical freedom and individuality. Law can only get in the way.

A Jewish Existentialist: Franz Rosenzweig

The impact of Buber's friend and colleague, Franz Rosenzweig (1886–1929), was very different. Although these two monumental thinkers share a wide range of philosophical and theological assumptions, they nevertheless end up in very different places on one of the most central issues in Jewish theology: the authority of the *mitzvot* as the authentic form of Jewish religious expression. Rosenzweig's position on this issue, while far from popular traditionalism, has had a decisive impact on post-1950 Jewish thinking.

Rosenzweig's biography is as important as his thought. He was born into a highly assimilated, German Jewish family and imbibed the best of German intellectual life. Early on, he decided to follow the path of most of his friends and convert to Christianity, which they regarded as the consummation of Judaism. But Rosenzweig felt that the only respectable way to become a Christian would be through an understanding of authentic Judaism, which he had really never known. So he turned to the study of Judaism, only to discover that there was no need to go beyond it. In October 1913, after spending Yom Kippur in a synagogue in Berlin, he writes: "After prolonged, and I believe thorough, self-examination, I have reversed my decision. It no longer seems necessary to me, and therefore, being what I am, no longer possible. I will remain a Jew."

Rosenzweig devoted the rest of his tragically short life—he died at age 43 from amyotrophic lateral sclerosis—to living and teaching his new understanding of Judaism. In his last years he became a mentor to some of the brightest and soon-to-be most influential of young German Jews. These disciples later translated his writings and transmitted his thought to the Jewish world outside of Germany.

Rosenzweig's turn to existentialism did not come easily or quickly. His early years were devoted to a study of Hegel and philosophical Idealism, and much of the abstruse quality of his major work, *The Star of Redemption,* reflects his struggle to rid himself of Idealist ways of thinking. But a later essay, "The New Thinking," could well serve as a manifesto for Jewish religious existentialism. In contrast to the old essentialism, the new, existentialist way of thinking is inextricably time bound; it reflects the concrete, particular, personal situation of the thinker instead of aiming for timeless and universal abstractions. It is "dialogical," revealing a "speaking thinker" rather than a "thinking thinker," because it is speech that brings two concrete individuals into relation at a specific moment. The "new thinking" yields subjective truth and is hence inherently pluralistic. Truth *becomes* true when it is appropriated by the individual, when it is verified in the individual's life experience. It is then a truth that one must live for, and, if called upon, die for as well.

This was not a purely academic issue for Rosenzweig. In 1920 he declined an invitation to teach at the University of Berlin, opting instead to open the Lehrhaus, an institute for adult Jewish education in Frankfurt. His letter of refusal traces his personal struggle with Idealism and his decision to return to Judaism via the new thinking of existentialism. That very impulse, he writes, makes it impossible for him, now, to work in a purely academic setting. He is no longer interested in dealing with ideas for their own sake. He is unmoved by the issues that are raised by scholars. Instead, he wants to struggle with those issues that are raised by human beings—the human beings that are within the scholars—in the course of their struggle with their concrete life situations.

Rosenzweig translated this concern into a philosophy of

Jewish education that he embodied in his Lehrhaus. His opening address in August 1920 spoke of the need for a new kind of Jewish learning, a learning "that no longer starts from the Torah and leads into life, but the other way round: from life, from a world that knows nothing of the Law, or pretends to know nothing, back to the Torah." This new style of Jewish learning acknowledges the fact that every modern Jew is, to a significant degree, alienated from his Jewish roots. The direction, then, is "from the periphery back to the center; from the outside in." But because we are all different one from the other, because we begin with different experiences and different degrees of alienation, our paths back to the center will be different as well. In fact, to go beyond Rosenzweig, the very notion of *a* center or *the* center may no longer apply. This is the inevitable mark of our age. Rosenzweig then is the paradigmatic, modern Jew who, in his maturity, rediscovers and reaffirms his Jewish roots. In true existentialist fashion, his thought mirrors his personal life experience.

We can now take a second look at Rosenzweig's celebrated exchange with Martin Buber on the issue of the authority of *halakhah*. Both thinkers understand revelation as God's entering into relationship with Israel. Both understand revelation in I-Thou terms as God and Israel's mutual self-revelation. What was revealed, then, was not a text, not a body of doctrine, and certainly not a set of laws. The only content of revelation is God's self-disclosure, the fact of His presence, and thereby, His concern for Israel.

But at this point Buber and Rosenzweig part company. Buber insists that revelation can never be legislation, that the laws of the Torah reflect the deterioration of the intimate God-Israel relationship, its dilution from the realm of I-Thou to that of I-It. Although Rosenzweig agrees that revelation itself is never legislation, he goes on to claim that revelation can still have a *commanding* quality. In fact, every relationship implies an expectation. The relationship itself commands. And command, in contrast to law, is very much an I-Thou phenomenon, for it is a totally personal and spontaneous expression of the sense of obligation that I feel toward the Thou that reveals Himself to me.

To Rosenzweig, then, revelation leads not to legislation but to a sense of being commanded. True, the deterioration that Buber describes inevitably sets in, and Rosenzweig condemns this development as harshly as Buber does. The personal sense of being commanded can never be transformed into a universally binding code of law. Rosenzweig agrees with Buber that such a body of law has no authority. However, while Buber insists that the dialectic ends at this point, Rosenzweig claims that law *can* be transformed back into command and then obeyed, precisely as command. That transformation can only be done by the individual Jew, and only at the moment of his renewed encounter with the commanding Thou-God.

Note the thoroughgoing existentialist impulse that pervades Rosenzweig's position. In fact, paradoxically, Buber's blanket rejection of the very possibility that an individual Jew might choose, freely, to accept a *mitzvah* as God's personal command, seems to be a violation of the very assumptions of existentialism. It is Rosenzweig who gives full weight to the individual's right to shape his own religious response to God's presence in whatever way he wishes.

Rosenzweig's position on the authority of *halakhah* seems to straddle the gap that separates Buber and Abraham Joshua Heschel, whose experiential approach to God frequently shades into existentialism. But Heschel disagrees even more sharply than does Rosenzweig with Buber's rejection of the disciplines and institutions of Jewish religion. Here Heschel's experientialist intuitions come to the forefront: the *halakhah,* the synagogue, the established liturgy, the cycles of Sabbaths and Festivals, and the rituals of daily living—all these provide the indispensable context for the experience of God. God can never be experienced spontaneously; our entire environment militates against that experience. The patterns of Jewish religious living serve to draw us out of the everyday and enable us to look at the world afresh. They also make the religious experience truly communal. In fact, they create community in a way that an I-Thou encounter can not possibly do. On the issue of *halakhah,* then, Heschel may not be a thoroughgoing traditionalist but he is also very far from an existentialist. The Bible may be *midrash,* but the body of Jewish observances is the community's classical way of experiencing God and is hence authoritative as a body, however much we may reject some of its individual provisions.

Small wonder, however, that modern Jews have turned more to Rosenzweig and Heschel than to Buber for a contemporary reading of Jewish theology. Buber's influence has indeed been monumental; the I-Thou/I-It distinction has become part of our native vocabulary. But he is read more avidly in Christian, particularly Protestant, theological circles because his characterization of the religious experience coincides neatly with the Protestant view of religion as centered on a highly personal, spontaneous turning of the individual to God. He has had a strong influence on humanist philosophies of education and on contemporary social and political philosophy. Yet to Judaism, his thought remains an ongoing challenge.

The Impact of Existentialism

Although *I and Thou* was published (in German) in 1923 and Franz Rosenzweig died in 1929, existentialism had little influence on American Jewish theology until the late 1940s and early 1950s. But when it came, its impact was powerful and widespread. It quickly established itself as the dominant theological temper among thinking Jews. Selections from Rosenzweig's writings were not translated into English until 1953, but when *Commentary* published its symposium, "The Condition of Jewish Belief" in 1966, the editor summarized the conclusions of the symposium by noting that "the single greatest influence on the religious thought of North American Jewry" was Franz Rosenzweig.

Christian thinkers had embraced existentialism for decades. But for Jewish thinkers, World War II and the Holocaust were turning points. The war was, as Camus noted, the ultimate absurdity. The Holocaust cast into question all of the familiar assumptions that had governed Jewish thinking and living for centuries. It demolished the comfortable reliance on human reason, science, and technology as the most effective ways of dealing with the human situation. And to the experientialists who claimed to see God's presence in nature and history, it posed the terrifying question: Where was God in the era of Auschwitz? Never before did we feel so radically alone, abandoned, insecure, and afraid.

This pervasive mood was tailor made for the existentialist critique of the illusory substitute faiths that people had used in their quest for ultimate meaning. Nothing in the world can satisfy our search for completion. The world itself is devoid of intrinsic meaning. There is no alternative but to "leap" beyond the world of familiar experience to the God who transcends that world— beyond history and its ambiguities, beyond reason and experience. Therein lies a resolution to the dilemma of being a human being in the post-Auschwitz era.

Existentialism also spoke to the individualism that was always part of the American temper. Here, Franz Rosenzweig's insistence that the decision as to what *mitzvah* is to be observed and when lies in the hands of each individual Jew, has been widely embraced, especially by the less traditionalist segments of the community. The position itself is anarchic at the root and easily abused. For Rosenzweig himself, the process of transforming law back into command was undertaken in "fear and trembling," hardly with the casual attitude of many of our contemporaries.

When a Jew says that he observes the Sabbath in a way that is "meaningful" to him, or that he does not pray regularly because he finds no meaning in the discipline of prayer, he is echoing, however unconsciously, existentialist individualism. The very fact that a Jew feels he has the right to make that decision for himself, that he *alone* has the right to make that decision, is a strikingly new and modern departure from the more authoritative and communal style of traditional Jewish thinking.

Of our three approaches to religious faith—rationalism, experientialism, and existentialism—existentialism is the most elusive. Its methodological rejection of abstract thinking and its emphasis on faith as a living relationship with God lends it a certain a-theological or a-philosophical thrust. One senses that the very attempt to write on existentialist faith is a betrayal. The questions we raised under the umbrella issue of subjectivity, and which for centuries have been central to the agenda of the philosophy of religion, are dismissed as irrelevant because they stem from essentialist assumptions. But then how can we believe in a God who is totally beyond experience? How do we know that God is really there? What about wish-projection, illusion, and hallucination? All irrelevant, says the existentialist. I know He's there. I know it's not a wish-projection. And if you wanted to, you too could know. The skeptic can only react in bewilderment and dismay.

To one who shares the existentialist temper, who is uncomfortable with theological abstractions, who turns to religion not for intellectual reasons but as an anchor in the face of the absurdities and stresses of living, the appeal of existentialism is indisputable. Indeed, it is difficult to conceive of a human being who has not been an existentialist at some point or other of his or her life. When we confront major surgery, for example, or struggle in the throes of some other life-threatening situation, or when we face some deeply personal and apparently insoluble dilemma, many of us will begin to think or feel as existentialists do all the time—even without recognizing it.

And if our ultimate criteria for evaluating the authenticity of a reading of Jewish religion is its effectiveness in making it possible for Jews to identify, with emotional and intellectual integrity, with Judaism and the Jewish people, we can easily dismiss the accusation that existentialism is un-Jewish. Countless of our contemporaries owe their own return to Judaism to the work of Buber, Rosenzweig, and their disciples. Finally, if there is any possible way for post-Holocaust generations of Jews to make sense of their experience, it will have to incorporate a dimension of existentialism.

FOR FURTHER STUDY
The material on existentialism is more than abundant. A good place to begin is with the appropriate entries in the ENCYCLOPEDIA OF PHILOSOPHY *(see ch. 3). See also any number of general surveys of*

existentialist thought, such as James D. Collins' THE EXISTENTIAL-
ISTS: A CRITICAL STUDY *(pb Greenwood, 1977). The original, classic
statement of religious existentialism remains Sören Kierkegaard's* FEAR
AND TREMBLING *(pb Princeton University Press, 1954).*

On Martin Buber, the authoritative version of I AND THOU *is the
translation (with prologue and notes) by Walter Kaufmann (pb
Scribner's, 1970). The anthology,* ON JUDAISM, *edited by Nahum N.
Glatzer (pb Schocken, 1972), is a compilation of some of Buber's classic,
shorter pieces from 1909 through 1951, including his paper, "On Jewish
Religiosity." Will Herberg's introduction to* THE WRITINGS OF MAR-
TIN BUBER *(pb Meridian, New American Library, 1956 and 1974), an
excellent anthology of selections from all of Buber's writings, is a clear
exposition of the central thrusts in Buber's thought. For a book-length
study, see Maurice S. Friedman,* MARTIN BUBER: THE LIFE OF
DIALOGUE *(pb Harper Torchbooks, 1960).*

*On Franz Rosenzweig, the indispensable starting point is Nahum
N. Glatzer's anthology,* FRANZ ROSENZWEIG: HIS LIFE AND
THOUGHT *(see ch. 1). Glatzer's extended biography, which takes up
the first half of this volume, is required reading for anyone who wants
to understand Rosenzweig's thought. "The New Thinking" appears
on pp. 190–208 of that anthology, and Rosenzweig's discussion of
existentialist truth is on p. 206. His return to Judaism is traced on pp.
23–31 and his decision that it was no longer necessary for him to become
a Christian is reported on p. 28. His letter justifying his decision to
reject the invitation to teach at the University of Berlin is reproduced
on pp. 94–98, and his address on the opening of the Lehrhaus appears
on pp. 228–234.*

Glatzer's second anthology of Rosenzweig's writings, ON JEWISH
LEARNING *(see ch. 1) includes Rosenzweig's existentialist approach to
Jewish law. The first book-length study on Rosenzweig is a compila-
tion of scholarly articles,* THE PHILOSOPHY OF FRANZ ROSENZWEIG
*(University Press of New England, 1988), edited by Paul Mendes-
Flohr. Rosenzweig's impact on post-Holocaust, American Jewish
thought is addressed in Milton Himmelfarb's Introduction to* THE
CONDITION OF JEWISH BELIEF, *p. 2 (see ch. 1).*

*Among the second generation of Jewish existentialists, see in
particular Will Herberg's* JUDAISM AND MODERN MAN *(see ch. 1).*

THE JEWISH THOUGHT OF EMIL FACKENHEIM: A READER, *edited and introduced by Michael L. Morgan (pb Wayne State University Press, 1987) is a useful compendium of Fackenheim's work, and his* GOD'S PRESENCE IN HISTORY *(New York University Press, 1970; pb Harper Torchbooks 1972) is a classic statement of the religious existentialist approach in Jewish terms. Fackenheim's "On The Eclipse of God," included in his* QUEST FOR PAST AND FUTURE *(Indiana University Press, 1968; pb Greenwood, 1983) is a serious attempt to respond to current trends in the modern philosophy of religion—specifically the issues of verification and falsification as discussed in the Hick anthology,* THE EXISTENCE OF GOD *(see ch. 3)—from a Buberian, existentialist position. The encounter between the existentialist believer and the contemporary skeptic is discussed on pp. 235–243 of this volume. Fackenheim's discussion of Elijah on the Carmel is in ch. 1 of his* ENCOUNTERS BETWEEN JUDAISM AND MODERN PHILOSOPHY *(Basic Books, 1973; pb Schocken, 1980). His conclusion that on no account would Elijah have abandoned his own faith is on p. 22.*

The most lucid expositor of religious existentialism from the perspective of Judaism remains Eugene Borowitz. His A LAYMAN'S INTRODUCTION TO RELIGIOUS EXISTENTIALISM *(pb Delta, 1965) is out of print but remains a classic. His more recent* CHOICES IN MODERN JEWISH THOUGHT: A PARTISAN GUIDE *(pb Behrman, 1983) is a masterful survey of the issues and the personalities.*

Finally, for a critique of Jewish versions of existentialism, see Marvin Fox, "Kierkegaard and Rabbinic Judaism," anthologized in FAITH AND REASON: ESSAYS IN JUDAISM, *edited by Robert Gordis and Ruth B. Waxman (Ktav, 1973); and Milton Steinberg's "Kierkegaard and Judaism," in* ANATOMY OF A FAITH *edited by Arthur A. Cohen (Harcourt, Brace and Co., 1960).*

VIII

Suffering:
Why Does God Allow It?

The Many Faces of Evil

THE MOST PERSISTENT CHALLENGE TO FAITH IN GOD COMES FROM the cluster of issues that we call "the problem of evil." In its starkest form, the challenge is this: If God exists, if His will is sovereign, and if He is just and compassionate, why are pain, suffering, and evil so intractable a dimension of human living?

But we have to go beyond this formulation. First, we have to distinguish between the suffering caused by one human being to another (homicide, slander, theft), and suffering that has a natural cause, such as disease or an earthquake. The first type directs our attention to human nature. We want to know why people are capable of inflicting pain on other human beings, sometimes inadvertently, but often deliberately and consciously. We usually account for this by positing human freedom and making the case that, on the whole, the benefits of freedom outweigh its negatives. But when we confront as massive a trauma as the Holocaust, we are struck by the inadequacy of that explanation. It doesn't begin to explain the suffering.

The second kind of suffering directs our attention to the nature of things in the world at large. We want to know, for example, why nature itself is so constructed that it can produce the AIDS virus—not how, but why? Why does a seven-year-old child suddenly develop cancer of the brain? Why are some babies born with congenital heart defects? Why are people killed in hurricanes, tidal waves, and tornadoes?

Both kinds of suffering raise the existential question: "Why me?" Sometimes the answer is clear: I neglect my health so I get sick. My life situation is so stressful that I will abuse my children. But then a psychotic goes berserk and empties his rifle randomly into a crowd of people. Or a beam detaches itself from a building under construction, falls to the street, and kills a passerby. Or an airplane crash kills a group of people who happen to have chosen this particular flight. The sheer randomness of the event poses the existential question in its sharpest form.

Overarching all of these formulations is the frequent gap between the virtue of the sufferer and his pain. The traditional Jewish formulation of the problem is: "Why do the righteous suffer? Why do the evil prosper?" For the believer, the issue is God's alleged justice. Thus the name "theodicy" (Greek: *theos*, God; *dike*, order, right, just) for that area of theology that attempts to "justify" or vindicate God, to maintain His justice in the face of random, apparently unjustified suffering. No other theological problem has proven to be so intractable. There simply are no totally adequate explanations for the death of an innocent child from leukemia, or the lightning bolt that kills an innocent young man.

But the word "adequacy" here is ambiguous; it can be measured objectively or subjectively. I can give a five-year-old an objectively, or scientifically, fuzzy explanation of why his father died of cancer, but he will leave with a five-year-old's subjective sense of having been satisfied. On the other hand, a neurologist can give me an accurate scientific account of how a child suddenly became brain dead, though she was apparently quite well just hours before, but I leave the conversation with a vague, subjective sense that my questions have not been stilled. I now know how the brain works and how it can suddenly die, but I still want to know why.

When we explain the death of six million Jews in the Holocaust by positing human freedom and God's reluctance to blunt the freedom even of the Nazi murderers, we have offered an explanation that is, in a limited sense of the term, "true." The classic Jewish claim is that God did create human beings with freedom and in the exercise of that freedom, human beings may well behave with unfathomable cruelty toward others. Yet subjectively, psychologically, many of us are left with a tortured sense of dissatisfaction. This happens all the time in the course of our theodicies, and then we have to ask: How do we handle that dissatisfaction? Where do we go from here?

Paradoxically, however difficult the issues, the impulse to pursue theodicy is very powerful because we are driven to make sense of our world, to order our experience into some meaningful whole. Suffering constitutes the greatest challenge to that sense of order. It is absurdity in its most threatening form. We strive with all our might to banish it and to plug the gap in our structures of meaning. The problem of apparently unjust suffering, then, is not simply one more issue that has to be dealt with in the context of a comprehensive theology. It is, rather, the supreme theological—or religious—issue, the issue *par excellence,* the issue that threatens to undermine one's entire theological and religious structure.

The challenge is two-dimensional. On one level, the problem is an intellectual one; we want to understand how God's justice can be reconciled with suffering. Here, we seek answers to questions posed by the mind. On a second level, the challenge is more existential: how to cope with suffering, how to go on living in the face of the pain. By and large, no religious tradition has been able to deal with the intellectual issue in a totally adequate way, but every tradition has evolved many experiential ways of helping the sufferer handle pain. In general, the less adequate our explanations, the more valuable our existential responses. This chapter will study characteristic Jewish responses to both dimensions of the challenge.

Suffering as Retribution

The classic explanation for suffering throughout the Bible—with the notable exception of the Book of Job and some of the Psalms—is that it is God's punishment for the sins of the community. The Bible assumes God's power and justice. God rules nature and history as a single, unified panorama. And He is not malicious. How else, then, can we account for both humanly caused suffering—such as military defeat—and naturally caused suffering—such as disease, famine, drought—than by seeing it as divine retribution for the community's rebellion against Him? Deuteronomy 11:13–21, the second paragraph of the *Shema*, and Deuteronomy 28:1–68 set forth the equation: If we obey God, we will be blessed; if we rebel, we will be punished by all kinds of suffering—military defeat or exile, plague or famine.

In the later rabbinic literature, the doctrine of divine retribution is captured in the liturgical passage that opens the *Musaf* (or "additional") service on the Festivals: "Because of our sins were we banished from our land. . . ." Exile was, of course, the paradigmatic, specifically Jewish, form of suffering.

Sometimes God's punishment takes the form of the withdrawal of His protective concern over Israel, leaving the community vulnerable to afflictions of all kinds. This seems to be the meaning of the oft-repeated reference to God's "hiding His face" (in Deuteronomy 32:20 and frequently in prophetic literature such as Isaiah 54:8), which is the obverse of God's "lifting up His face" in favor and affection (Numbers 6:26). In most cases, God's hiding of His face is understood as punishment. Psalm 13:2 is one notable exception to this rule. It reflects a different, Jobian tradition in dealing with the fate of an individual, and in claiming that sometimes the sense of abandonment by God is simply inexplicable.

By and large, the doctrine of retribution works because the Bible applies it to the fate of the community as a whole, rather than to individuals. In much of the Bible, at least, the destiny of the individual is submerged in the fate of the community. From time to time, the narrative does single out an individual for punishment: Moses' sister Miriam (Numbers 12:1–15) for having slandered Moses, and Moses himself (Numbers 20:7–13) for having hit the rock instead of speaking to it. By contrast, Abraham is singled out for reward because of his loyalty to God (Genesis 15:6). But these individual instances are rare. The result of this communal emphasis is that the doctrine of suffering as retribution becomes unchallengeable. The individual Israelite who may have been totally virtuous still suffers from the famine that God imposes on the community as a whole. Famines don't discriminate between individual members of one community.

The suffering that one individual can inflict on another is viewed as the inevitable concomitant of human freedom. This is spelled out unambiguously in the paradigmatic tale of Cain and Abel. Abel is the first innocent victim of human cruelty, and God explicitly warns Cain, the paradigmatic murderer (Genesis 4:6–7), that though sin may exercise a powerful attraction, he may yet rule over it and over himself, if he wills it. Nowhere in the Bible is the fact of human freedom questioned, apart from the episode where God hardens Pharaoh's heart (Exodus 7:3 and elsewhere in the Exodus narrative), before the Exodus from Egypt. But the Pharaoh episode is precisely the exception that proves the rule, for the biblical account assumes that under all normal conditions Pharaoh too would be free to release the Israelites. This is not a normal situation because God has a broader purpose to accomplish. That's why God has to intervene directly to limit Pharaoh's freedom. It takes a specific divine intervention to rob Pharaoh of his freedom—so much is freedom a natural part of the order of creation.

The Bible is clear that however God may grieve over the effects of human freedom, he does not restrain Cain's hand. The startling conclusion is that God is also ultimately responsible for humanly caused evil. Later, in prophetic literature, God's complicity becomes the impulse behind the development of the doctrine of repentance as preempting divine punishment. Psalm 103:10–14, for example, tells us that God is eager to accept our repentance because "He knows how we are formed; He is mindful that we are dust"—a clear reference to the Genesis 2:7 account that "the Lord God formed man from the dust of the earth." Indeed He knows how we are formed; He was the one who formed us that way!

Throughout this material, it is absolutely clear that suffering can be accounted for. Moses was denied entry to the Holy

Land because he sinned. The community suffered military defeat, plague, famine, and exile because it rebelled against God. God's complex relationship with His world is fully explicable. His justice is intact. But this tidy package is shattered by the Book of Job.

Job

The Book of Job introduces two new elements into the picture. First, it highlights the fate of an individual human being; second, it breaks completely with the doctrine of suffering as divine retribution. These two departures from the earlier tradition combine to make this complex book a theological landmark. In fact one might ask what this book is doing in the Bible in the first place—so much is it in conflict with the dominant biblical tradition.

Identify with Job. *We* the readers know, from the outset, why you suffer, but *you* don't, and you never find out. You were taught to believe in a just and caring God who is not malicious, who does not toy with His creatures, and who inflicts suffering only as retribution for sin. His behavior is always predictable, and you have conducted your life on this basis. Suddenly, chaos breaks loose; your children are killed, your possessions are destroyed, and you are afflicted, head to toe, with a severe skin ailment. You sit in mourning on an ash heap, scratching your skin with a potsherd. Your wife protests: "Blaspheme God and die!" (2:9). But you can not.

The traditional doctrine of retribution is then propounded by three friends who come to comfort you, but in the throes of your pain, you find the doctrine simply unacceptable. *Your personal experience testifies against it.* You may have sinned, little sins here and there, but nothing to justify this fate. Your punishment is totally out of proportion to your sin. This is a decisive moment in Jewish—and in fact, in world intellectual history. One person's experience clashes with a community's *revealed* tradition, and to our amazement, the tradition yields! First, God Himself dismisses the traditional doctrine as untrue (42:7), and He tells Job's friends that only if Job himself intercedes on their behalf will they be spared punishment; and, second, the book becomes canonical.

What replaces the traditional doctrine? It emerges in God's speeches to Job out of the tempest, in chapters 38 to 41. The speeches are a paean to God's power and majesty, and to the sheer grandeur and complexity of His creation. God tells Job: "Who are you to try to package Me, to try to fit Me into your human, moral, or epistemological categories? What kind of a God would I be if you could understand Me! I am God and you are a simple human being. What seems to you to be good or evil, just or unjust, purposive or nonpurposive, rational or irrational are simply your own, puny, human conceptualizations. My reality totally transcends them all. Don't try to account for my behavior." The ultimate, natural, and by implication moral order of reality is beyond human perception. But both are there.

Job emerges from his experience with a new perspective on God and on human life. "I had heard You with my ears, but now I see You with my eyes" (42:5). His previous perspective was "hearing"; his new one is "seeing." It is clear that Job considers this newly acquired understanding to be more adequate, more comprehensive than his previous one. There is also a clear sense of closure in this last response, a feeling of resolution. Job has acquired the kind of wisdom that emerges out of a profound personal experience, possibly the wisdom that pain alone can teach. Job has learned to accept life with all of its apparent complexities, and with this new understanding comes a sense of serenity.

But note the nontheological character of God's response. It is, in fact, an explicit denial of the very possibility of theodicy. Suffering is simply part of God's complex plan; it has no further explanation. Job emerges with no new knowledge, no new facts about God and His relation with the world. His new "seeing" is, paradoxically, an acknowledgment that he can not see the ultimate make-up of creation. Only God has that kind of vision. What reassures Job is that the order—both the natural and the moral order—is there. And that reassurance brings him peace.

That paradoxical resolution is the clue to Martin Buber's understanding of God's final speeches. What is important to Job at the end, Buber suggests, is not *what* God says but rather *that* he speaks to Job again and anew. The once-hidden God is now revealed again, and in that renewed self-revelation, Job is reassured. God is there for Job—and with God's presence comes a sense of His order and sovereignty over the world. Job may not be able to understand that order, but this is less important than the fact that it is there.

The book leaves us, however, with a frightening dilemma. We are commanded to trust an all-powerful God who deals with us in ways that we can not understand and are seemingly unrelated to how we conduct our lives. With all of the problems of the doctrine of retribution, at least it gave us security and predictability. We knew that if we lived virtuously, we would be well; if we rebelled, we would be punished. Job destroys that neat equation. Of course human beings, long before the author of Job, must have been aware of the discrepancy between virtue and its reward. But our human impulse to deny is very powerful. After Job, that denial becomes more problematic.

It is not surprising, then, that the later tradition distanced itself from the message of Job. One quick test of the impact of a biblical book on the later tradition is the extent to which it is quoted in the traditional liturgy. Jeremiah, for example, is omnipresent, especially in the High Holiday liturgy; Job is represented by only a few brief phrases, the most important being a portion of one verse, the familiar "The Lord has given, and the Lord has taken away; blessed be the name of the Lord" (1:21), which appears in the burial service. The problem is not that God is directly responsible for suffering; if His sovereignty is indeed absolute, how can He avoid that responsibility? The problem is that we have to live with the apparently capricious exercise of that sovereignty. Job accentuates that dilemma.

The Eschatological Resolution

The key to how the later tradition escaped this dilemma lies in the emergence, early in the rabbinic era, of a radically new doctrine of the afterlife of the individual. The ensemble of teachings that deal with what is commonly called "the end of days" or "the Messianic Age" is called "eschatology" (Greek: *eschatos*, last; *logos*, discourse), or "discourse about the last things," or about the "final events."

Though the Bible is positively voluble about the national and universal dimensions of its eschatology, with the exception of one verse in Daniel (12:2), it is totally silent about the fate of the individual human being after death. In the Bible itself, death is final. "Put not your trust in the great, in mortal man who can not save," the Psalmist advises. "His breath departs; he returns to the dust; on that day his plans come to naught" (Psalm 146:3–4). And again: "The dead can not praise the Lord, nor any who go down into silence. But we [i.e., the living] will bless the Lord now and forever" (Psalm 115:17–18). Death marks the end of everything, including our relationship with God.

But as the rabbinic era dawns, this picture changes radically. Two doctrines enter into Judaism and rapidly acquire almost dogmatic standing—the resurrection of the human body at the end of days and the immortality of the soul. We can speculate on the different impulses that led to the absorption of these doctrines; one of them was almost certainly the need to deal with Job's dilemma. If our relationship to God is not exhausted by our life experience on earth, if our experiential span is extended to include an eternity after death, then the framework is broadened and God has further opportunity to bring virtue and reward into line. Thus the belief in His justice can be maintained intact.

The new eschatology then becomes a new theodicy. Whatever suffering the righteous may have endured on earth will be more than compensated for by the reward they will enjoy in an eternal Paradise hereafter. Note that throughout Job there is not a single hint that Job's problems will be resolved after his death. On the contrary, Job's fortunes are restored during his lifetime; when this book was written, there was nothing after death. With the new eschatology in place, the pre-Jobian sense of harmony is restored. God's behavior can be accounted for once again.

In this eschatological context, we can understand why rabbinic law commands us to "praise God over evil as we praise Him over good" (*Mishnah Berakhot* 9:5), by reciting the benediction, "Blessed be the righteous judge" (9:2). To this day, the Jew recites this benediction upon hearing news of a death. But note the formulation of the benediction. We praise God as a "righteous judge." The judgments of God are still righteous—if not now, then in the long run. The technical name for the liturgy recited at a burial is *Tzidduk ha-Din,* literally "Justification (or Vindication) of (God's) Judgment." Both the benediction and the liturgy assume that God is just, and also that His justice can be trusted to become manifest.

The richest expression of rabbinic eschatological affirmation in the face of tragedy is the *Kaddish* that is recited at the graveside. There are many different versions of the *Kaddish* in our liturgy, the most familiar being the mourner's *Kaddish* that we recite during the period of mourning and on the anniversary of a death. The graveside *Kaddish,* which is less familiar, begins with a paragraph that affirms the entire package of eschatological doctrines that had become normative in rabbinic Judaism. The text reads: "May His great name be magnified and sanctified in the world that is to be created anew, where He will revive the dead, and raise them to eternal life; and will rebuild the city of Jerusalem, and establish His Temple in its midst; and will uproot all alien worship from the earth, and restore the worship of Heaven to its place."

Beyond this, every form of the *Kaddish* prayer ends with the same affirmation: "May He who creates *shalom* in His celestial realms, create *shalom* for us and for all Israel." *Shalom* is usually translated "peace" but a more accurate translation is "harmony," "order," or "cosmos," the original Greek opposite to "chaos." If death represents the eruption of chaos, then we respond by reaffirming the fact of cosmos, or harmony and order—if not now, then in the eschatological future. There is nothing intellectual about this affirmation. It is neither theology nor theodicy for it explains nothing. It simply *affirms* the conviction that ultimately cosmos will vanquish chaos.

Note that we have invoked a distinction that has appeared elsewhere in this volume between theology—here specifically in the form of theodicy—and religion. Theology speaks to the mind. Theodicy is an attempt to deal intellectually with the problem of suffering by explaining why a just God allows people to suffer. Religion has a much broader scope. It is more concerned with the texture of life as a whole, including its emotional, behavioral, and experiential dimensions. The *Kaddish* is more a religious affirmation than a theological one. We respond to suffering not by explaining it but by affirming our conviction that there *is* an ultimate order of things—if not now, then soon, literally "in your lifetime and during your days and in the life of the entire house of Israel."

When we distinguish between theological and religious responses to suffering, we in no way imply a difference in value or significance. Both are important. We have to understand suffering *and* we have to respond to it. The genius of the rabbinic response to Job's dilemma is that it includes both theology and affirmation. Both stem from one single impulse: the inveterate human need to banish chaos and restore cosmos to our world.

Evil and the Power of God

The focus of all theological speculation about the place of evil in the world is its relationship to God. The dilemma is clear: If God is omnipotent, then He is in some way responsible for evil. If He is not responsible, then He is not omnipotent; then evil exists independently of God's will and God's sovereignty is severely impaired. The choice lies between an omnipotent God who is responsible for evil and a limited God who is not.

If these are the two options, then normative Jewish theology really had no choice. Monotheism was so deeply ingrained in Judaism and dualism so deeply abhored that there was no way evil could be allowed an independent reality of its own. Isaiah 45:6–7 puts it unambiguously: "I am the Lord and there is none else, I form light and create darkness, I make weal (Hebrew: *shalom*) and create woe (Hebrew: *ra*)—I the Lord do all these things." But there is no discounting the palpable discomfort that accompanies this unambiguous attribution of evil to God. In fact, note that when this verse was inserted into the daily morning liturgy, the last phrase was softened to read "I make weal and create all things," instead of "and create woe." Of course, "all things" includes "woe," but who thinks of that meaning when we recite the daily liturgy?

Once we establish God's ultimate responsibility for evil, the problem then becomes reconciling evil with His justice and His benevolence, in short, with the personal character of the monotheistic God. That is the substance of all theodicies. The biblical doctrine of retribution is one way of accomplishing this reconciliation. The rabbinic doctrine of individual eschatology is another. Still a third is a view of human freedom as evidence of God's self-willed limitation of His power. This last doctrine sees human beings as the proximate cause of much of the evil in the world but God as the ultimate cause, for it is He who created us free. That's why the efficacy of repentance as preempting punishment becomes so fundamental to Judaism. Because God created the possibility for humanly caused evil, He had to provide us with the means to escape its consequences.

Finally, God's responsibility for evil is explicit in Job, though what distinguishes this book is its stark rejection of any attempt to reconcile God's sovereignty with His benevolence. God Himself is above such a reconciliation. We must simply accept Him and His creation as they are—from our human perspective, infinitely ambiguous.

If the options are an omnipotent God who is responsible for evil or a limited God who is not, it wasn't until our own century that a Jewish thinker opted for the second of these choices. To be precise, the notion that God may, in His own freedom, *choose* to limit Himself and His power, is as old as the Bible; it is at the heart of Moses' claim that God must not destroy the Israelites after the golden calf episode (Exodus 32:11–14). He clearly has the power to do so and He may even be justified in doing so, but first, what will the Egyptians say? And second, what about His promise to the community's forebears that their progeny would be "as numerous as the stars of the sky"? Moses argues, here, that God should not exercise His power in this instance because of a commitment that He Himself freely entered into.

That God may *will* to limit His power, then, is familiar. But that He may be *intrinsically* limited is a startling contribution of a modern Jewish theologian. Not surprisingly, that thinker was Mordecai Kaplan. Recall Kaplan's definition of God as the power (within nature) that makes for salvation, where salvation means the actualization of all values. The actualization of all values means the elimination of all evil. The Kaplanian God, then, is the very drive, inherent throughout the natural order, to rid the world of evil. But that drive has not as yet won out; evil is still very much part of the natural fabric. Hence Kaplan's God as innately limited—not a self-willed limitation but an inherent one. Evil has not as yet been eliminated simply because God is incapable of eliminating it.

The purely theological dimension of Kaplan's work lies in his radical redefinition of how we conceive of God. The traditional approach begins with the fact of a personal God and then considers what kind of a Being He is and how He functions in nature and history. Kaplan proposes that we stand this approach on its head. Instead of beginning with a personal Being, we should begin with those of our experiences that reveal our set of values, then use these experiences to define God.

The tradition begins by postulating a being—God—who is good, compassionate, just, and the rest. Kaplan begins by seeing goodness, compassion, and justice in the world and then identifying these as "godly," in fact, as God Himself. We define God by His activity. God is what He does. To the extent that our experience of the world reveals goodness, compassion, justice, morality, creativity, and the rest, the world reveals God—not a personal Being but a quality or dimension of the natural order.

A particularly poignant elaboration of Kaplan's position—and the problems it raises—lies in his response to a reader's question: "How would you answer the question of a child who asked: 'Why did God make polio?' " Kaplan answers: "God did *not* make polio. God is always helping us humans to make this a better world, but the world can not at once become the kind of world He would like it to be." He continues by enumerating what God is doing: He gives us the intelligence to understand, prevent, and cure disease; He enables us to develop the technology to make polio more bearable; He gives us friends and families who care for us when we are ill. All of these are manifestations of God at work in the world. He is the sum total of all the good things we discover in our lives.

But the stubborn reality is that however much all of these manifestations of goodness are true and real, so is the child's polio. Both the good and the disease are part of the natural order. We wonder why Kaplan focuses on and unifies the ensemble of goodness in nature and calls them God, but refuses to unify the ensemble of evil qualities in nature and call these Evil. The dualistic implications of Kaplan's position are clear: If God is one of many processes in nature, there can be others, and these others can also be unified. Potentially, then, we can have two Gods—a good God and an evil one—or even more.

Kaplan himself stubbornly refuses to go that route. But once we begin by defining God through our human experience of goodness, and once we admit that this human experience is ambiguous—that we experience evil as much as goodness—the dualistic conclusion seems entirely legitimate. That's why traditional Jewish thinking preferred to postulate God's omnipotence and deal with the problems that position raises, rather than accept a Kaplanian, inherently limited God and its implications.

A more recent formulation of Kaplan's position is spelled out in Harold Kushner's *When Bad Things Happen to Good People*. Kushner's book, written out of the deeply felt personal trauma of the death of his son at age 14 of progeria, is not primarily a theological treatise, even though he addresses the theological problems raised by his experience. Kushner writes to counter our intuitive—and the traditional—inclination to see God as responsible for human suffering. He sees the random instances that we encounter daily as manifestations of a leftover chaos that God's creative impulse is not able to control, what Milton Steinberg called "the still unremoved scaffolding of the edifice of God's creativity." Again, a limited God. God does much for us; He has created a world where the good outweighs the evil. But He does not, He can not, eliminate evil from the world.

If there is a difference between Kaplan and Kushner, it reflects the fact that Kaplan wrote in the first part of our century and Kushner, some decades later. There is a pervasive optimism in Kaplan that is absent in Kushner. Kaplan seems to believe that evil is progressively being eliminated, that the drive for salvation is gaining ground. Kushner seems resigned to the inevitability of evil and suffering as an inherent part of nature.

But if Kushner's theology recalls Kaplan, the impulse behind his book brings to mind Job. Here again, a personal experience is pitted against a long-standing theological tradition, and here again, the tradition is asked to yield. It is simply inconceivable to Kushner that God could in any way be responsible for his son's illness. The more traditionalist of Jewish theologians may be offended by Kushner's radical redefinition of the Jewish God, but the immense popularity of the book testifies to the readiness of many believing Jews to accept his redefinition.

God and Auschwitz

With the Holocaust, the problem of evil acquires a new and terrifying urgency. Jewish theological responses to the Holocaust can be grouped into two broad classes.

The first sees the Holocaust as one more instance of human cruelty, perhaps more massive than ever but not intrinsically different and hence not posing significantly new theological or religious challenges. The death of six million Jews and countless other human beings is not necessarily more problematic than the death of one innocent child. The Jewish theological tradition, in this view, has developed resources to deal with the problem and these resources are applied to the Holocaust.

The other view sees the Holocaust as totally unprecedented. The sheer scope of the massacre, the malevolence with which it was perpetrated, the machinelike efficiency of the Nazi death camps, the active involvement and passive acquiescence of countless, ordinary human beings, the fact that the world of Auschwitz was conceived and carried out by the most cultured of European nations—any or all of these factors make the Holocaust totally unique. In this view, the resources that the tradition has evolved for dealing with suffering are simply inadequate. We can not write this trauma off as one more instance of human cruelty. The vexing theological question "Where was God?" will not go away by simply postulating human freedom. In fact, it is made all the more poignant by Judaism's cardinal claim that God and Israel share a unique intimacy. Indeed, then, where was He? Why did He let it happen?

One response that is almost universally rejected by all thinking segments of the community is that the Holocaust is God's punishment for Israel's sin. If the Holocaust accomplished anything, it effectively killed the doctrine of retribution as the key to Jewish theodicies. It may have worked for centuries, but today it is viewed as an obscenity. It has not been invoked by any but the most traditionalist wings of the Jewish community, by those who maintain the sanctity of the past, come what may. To everyone else, the sheer disparity between the "explanation" and the event is so wide that it just does not merit serious consideration. This is our paradigmatic instance of the death of a portion of the Jewish myth. It must be replaced—but by what?

Rubenstein's "Death of God" Theology

The most radical answer to that question is Richard Rubenstein's striking claim that after the Holocaust "we live in the time of the death of God." Rubenstein's assumption is that the Holocaust represents a radically new phenomenon that demands an equally radical response. His use of the "death of God" imagery is but one of many radical positions that this imaginative theologian has proposed. It is typical of his readiness to stretch or even ignore the commonly accepted parameters of Jewish theological inquiry, even to the point of offending most of his contemporaries. But his thinking can not be ignored.

The "death of God" movement developed in the 1960s as a Christian theological response to that era's sense of social and religious alienation. It drew heavily on the thought of Friedrich Nietzsche and Jean-Paul Sartre and the theological idiom of Paul Tillich, in claiming that the traditional God of the Judaeo-Christian tradition had become irrelevant to the culture and social issues of the day. More specifically, it emerged as a response to the stubborn and persistent presence of evil in society and to God's seeming indifference to that evil.

The very phrase "the death of God" carries a powerful

Christian resonance. The Christian God had to die in order to accomplish His preordained mission. His death symbolizes God's paradoxical identification with humanity and becomes the instrument for the vicarious remission of human sins. It is also but an interim step toward His ultimate resurrection. Rubenstein adopts this image, minus its specifically Christian connotations, because of his conviction that it is the only way Jews can deal with the issue of God in the era of the death camps.

Rubenstein is forthright in admitting that no human being can say that God "really" died. What *has* died is our conception of God, our theological and religious symbols and myths. The statement "God has died" is a statement about human beings; it is a cultural fact. It says that the way we have conceived of God and His relation to humanity and particularly to Israel no longer works. It has been decisively killed by our historical experience. "[T]he thread uniting God and man, heaven and earth, has been broken. We stand in a cold, silent, unfeeling cosmos, unaided by any purposeful power beyond our own resources. After Auschwitz, what else can a Jew say about God?"

Note the distinction between claiming that God has died and claiming that our myth has died. The first is considerably starker than the second. But, ultimately, if all we have is our myths about God—if no human being has access to what God is in Himself— then the two claims are functionally equivalent and equally final. After Auschwitz, we can no longer speak of a caring, compassionate, personal God. Radical events require a radical *midrash,* a radically new myth.

Paradoxically, Rubenstein proceeds to argue that in an age of the death of God, we need religion—its communities, traditions, rituals, norms, and institutional structures—more than ever. They provide us with the shared context that enables us to deal with the crises that are inherent in human existence.

As for God, the death of the traditional God of Judaism does not mean the death of all of our concepts of God. In its place, Rubenstein suggests we return to the God of the mystics, God as Holy Nothingness, the totally indeterminate and indeterminable God who is the source of all creation and to which all of creation returns. Rubenstein is aware of the heretical implications of this new image. Since the all-powerful, free, and personal God of traditional monotheism has failed us, we fall back on the God who is the embodiment of the implacable rhythms of nature. Rubenstein finds there the renewed sense of security and serenity that comes from knowing our place in the cosmic order of things—and that the traditional image of God is no longer able to provide. In fact, Rubenstein reverts to an image of God that is very close to that of the pagan religions in which everything in the world is ultimately subject to blind, implacable natural forces. Our salvation lies in resigning ourselves to their sway over our destiny as well.

Paradoxically, Rubenstein's source of comfort is close to that of the author of Job, though with one significant difference. Both appeal to an ultimate cosmic order that may not be immediately apparent, but that underlies the anarchic and discordant dimension of overt human experience. The difference is that in Job, that cosmic order is the work of the omnipotent God who Himself transcends the natural order; in Rubenstein, the cosmic order is inherent in nature. There is simply no power or Being that can transcend nature.

Rubenstein's God, like Kaplan's, is then very much within nature. Yet the two thinkers are far apart. Kaplan's God is the embodiment of a system of values that is closely tied to the liberal-progressive context of early-twentieth-century America. Rubenstein's God is much more the embodiment of the cycles of nature and hence totally neutral in regard to value. From Rubenstein's perspective, Kaplan's theology can't even begin to deal with the Holocaust. If nature does indeed manifest a quasi-biological drive toward salvation, how can we account for the kind of stubborn, radical impulse to evil that emerged during that period? It is simply not adequate to posit the fact of human freedom and our innate human reluctance to ally ourselves with the salvational impulse. But what else can Kaplan say, given his theological assumptions! Kaplan never wrote a systematic response to the Holocaust, we may surmise, not only because his creative period was well behind him by the time Jews became aware of the issues.

What do we do with a theological proposal, such as Rubenstein's, that breaks so sharply with all of the accepted parameters of Jewish theological inquiry? More than any other thinker, Rubenstein forces us to consider the broad methodological issues of authority and authenticity in Jewish theology. If we view past formulations of theological positions as grounded in an explicit revelation and hence as strongly authoritative, we have no choice but to reject Rubenstein. If, on the other hand, we view these positions as evolving in the context of the community's ever-changing historical experience, we are saying that the received tradition is no longer *ipso facto* authoritative. The locus of authority then passes into the hands of the community and the community decides which theological path, or paths, it is prepared to follow.

It is significant, then, that Rubenstein's proposals have failed to strike deep roots even among the less traditional of contemporary Jewish thinkers. The issue is less the fact of his break with tradition—we have seen equally radical departures in the writings of many of his predecessors—than the point on which he breaks and the problematic nature of his alternative. To do away with the notion of a God who cares deeply for the fate of Israel is to reject the cornerstone of the Jewish myth; without this, the entire myth collapses. Further, however much Rubenstein stresses the need for religion in an age of the death of God, one can only wonder how that religious tradition can have any authority whatsoever. Finally, did Judaism successfully resist the inroads of paganism for four millennia only to return, at this stage, to a prebiblical, pagan way of viewing our place in nature?

The issue, then, is less one of authority and more one of authenticity. Authenticity is not a new issue for us; we have encountered it in dealing with Job, and earlier, with the thought of Martin Buber, Mordecai Kaplan, and Harold Kushner. There are no clear-cut ways to predict which stretchings of the parameters of authenticity will be accepted and which not. Rubenstein is prepared to sacrifice authenticity in order to capture the monumental quality of the trauma. In his case, his contemporaries have, by and large, disagreed with that choice.

Buber's "Eclipse of God"

The alternative path is to return to the tradition and rework its own internal resources for dealing with human suffering on the assumption that, however massive this particular trauma, the tradition has had a long history in dealing with this type of experience.

Paradoxically, the most influential representative of this approach is Martin Buber—hardly the most traditionalist of contemporary Jewish thinkers. Buber's answer to the question "Where was God?" is to speak of an "eclipse of God," an image that evokes the familiar biblical "hiding of His face."

In the Bible itself, God's hiding of His face is most frequently a form of retribution—but not always. Sometimes—Psalm 13 is an excellent example—it represents a mysterious ebb in the divine-human relationship that the human being simply can not fathom but experiences as palpably real and terrifying. For Buber, the "eclipse" represents an inherent stage in the dynamic of the I-Thou/I-It relationships. All relationships know both their moments of intimacy as well as their moments of withdrawal. I-Thou becomes I-It, which eventually can become I-Thou again. Only the partners in the relationship can testify to the presence or the absence of their partner, and only in the moment of each experience.

The term "eclipse," when applied to God, is as much a symbol as the term "death." The difference is that an eclipse is temporary but death is final. Rubenstein explicitly rejects Buber's image because it is too soft; for him, it does not capture the impact of the Holocaust. But for Buber, it does.

To use another idiom, if a *midrash* exists in a state of tension between past and present, between the claims of authenticity and of contemporaneity, Rubenstein is prepared to strain the pole of authenticity to capture what he feels is a radically unprecedented event. Buber takes the opposite path and works to integrate the event into the categories of classical Jewish theology. The decision between these two *midrashim* can not depend on any external criterion; each of us has to decide which of the two images speaks to us, moves us, captures our own sense of the meaning of the experience, and provides us with a renewed sense of purpose.

But we should not underestimate the terror that is inherent in the sense of God's eclipse. In Buber's existential framework, the leap of faith is filled with risk for it has no basis in reason or experience. Buber's disciple, Emil Fackenheim, poses the particularly devastating nature of our contemporary awareness of God's absence: Is it indeed temporary, or is it "the final exposure of an age-old delusion?" The believer can never know for sure, but in the meantime, must continue to trust. This is the subjective quality of existentialist faith.

Buber understands Job's experience as the paradigmatic eclipse of God and Job himself as the paradigmatic existentialist believer who trusts, despite all. We saw that Buber understands God's speeches out of the tempest as the renewal of His relationship with Job. What is significant is not *what* God says but *that* He speaks to Job again, and in that speaking, He turns His face to him again. Job is reassured not by the substance of the speech but simply by his renewed sense of God's presence.

The Buberian response is also reflected in the thinking of a contemporary theologian, Irving Greenberg. Greenberg seizes on the dialectical tension between the Buberian I-Thou and I-It, on the alternating moments of presence and absence, affirmation and denial, faith and nonfaith. Both moments are an inherent part of the process; the error is to fix on either one of the polarities as exclusive and final. Neither classical theism nor atheism can do justice to the complex nature of our relationship with God. The tension itself, the very tenuous and indeterminate nature of religious faith, its fragmented quality is simply inevitable. God is a "moment God"; faith is a "moment faith."

The full implication of this position is that atheism is an integral part of the experience of faith. There is no faith without moments of despair, just as there is no despair without moments of affirmation. It is not at all clear who is the believer and who the atheist. They differ only in the frequency of their moments of despair or affirmation, not at all in the certainty or demonstrability of their positions. Applying this perspective to the Holocaust, Greenberg suggests that it reveals, with particular urgency, the full weight of the tension inherent in the life of religious faith.

Still a third discussion of these issues from a Buberian perspective is in Eliezer Berkovits' *Faith After the Holocaust.* To Berkovits too, Auschwitz does not stand alone. Jewish history is littered with Holocausts just as it is studded with expressions of God's love for Israel. Both are true, both part of the complex pattern of Jewish history. Berkovits takes the daring step of balancing Auschwitz with the reestablishment of the State of Israel. Both have to be integrated simultaneously into the larger pattern of Jewish history. To isolate either one is to misread that pattern.

In fact, Berkovits sees God's presence even in the throes of the Holocaust. He refers to the countless instances of courage, determination, and humanity that occurred even in the death camps. He reminds us that in fact, the Jewish people did survive the Holocaust, despite its powerlessness. The Holocaust, then, reveals both aspects of God's relationship to Israel—His presence as well as His absence.

On the issue of theodicy, Berkovits reaffirms the biblical notion of a God who withdraws from history so that human beings may exercise their freedom. God's tolerance of human cruelty becomes, paradoxically, an affirmation of His respect for humanity. This may lead to human suffering, but there is no escaping that outcome. If God exalts human freedom, He must tolerate evil, and if He tolerates evil, people will suffer. Yet God waits, even for the sinner and even despite the suffering of the victims. That's what makes Him God.

Heschel's Suffering God

The Holocaust then represents a human, not a divine failure. It is surprising that Abraham Joshua Heschel who, more than any other contemporary Jewish thinker, addressed an entire range of social evils, wrote very little on the Holocaust itself. From another perspective however, all of his thought is implicitly pervaded by an awareness of his generation's historical experience.

His reclaiming of the supernatural, pathos-infused, biblical God, his reaffirmation of the fact of human freedom and the responsibility that comes with it, his insistence that what God demands, above all, is that we recognize His presence and respond by creating a certain kind of social order, his sense that God is in search of and waiting for us—all of these Heschelian motifs can be understood as responses to our post-Holocaust situation.

Heschel did publish one brief statement that speaks openly about the Holocaust. It was originally delivered in March 1938 at a conference of Quaker leaders in Germany, and then was revised and published as "The Meaning of This Hour" in 1943, after Heschel had settled in America. It is a searing indictment of the human responsibility for Auschwitz. Indeed, Auschwitz is but one example of the pervasive human tendency to ignore God's voice, for He is "everywhere or nowhere, the Father of all men or no man, concerned about everything or nothing." Where is God? "[He] will return to us when we shall be willing to let Him in. . . ." In the meantime, He waits for us to redeem the world.

As He waits, He joins in the suffering of his people. This sharing of human suffering is the ultimate expression of His pathos. Throughout prophetic literature, Heschel sees God's anger as suffused with pain. "And do you speak to them thus: Let my eyes run with tears, day and night let them not cease, for my hapless people has suffered a grievous injury, a very powerful wound" (Jeremiah 14:17). God cries over the suffering of His people for despite everything, they are still His "hapless people." The intimacy remains throughout. God may not be able to prevent suffering but He can share in it, and in this sharing provide a measure of consolation and strength to a suffering humanity.

Cosmos and Chaos

This survey of positions has shown that the enterprise that has come to be called Holocaust theology, though but a few decades old, has already produced a rich and diversified literature. But the second dimension of the challenge, the attempt to develop a more generalized religious response to the event through liturgy and ritual, has not proven nearly as fruitful. A glance at the various ways in which we celebrate *Yom Ha-Shoah* will confirm that our community has not as yet reached a consensus on a memorial that is Holocaust specific. Thus far, we have been drawing on other familiar patterns: We light candles, some of us fast, we recite Psalms and the memorial prayer from the burial service, and of course, we say the *Kaddish*.

This should not be surprising. Liturgy and ritual are infinitely more complex to work out, particularly on a communal basis, and particularly when we haven't as yet reached a consensus on the theological issues. What should the liturgy say? What should be the implicit message of the ritual? Until those questions are answered, we are all groping in the dark. But we are also desperately in need of a set of religious responses, so we draw from the familiar patterns of our past.

The Holocaust is simply too close to us. But it is not too much to expect that the same vitality that enabled our ancestors to develop elaborate ceremonial pageants for Passover, Hanukkah, Purim, and Tishah b'Av will, in time, enable us to develop equally gripping memorials for this event as well.

If the ultimate impulse behind a religious perspective on the world is to introduce a sense of cosmos, order, or harmony into our experience of the world, then suffering and evil are properly perceived as profoundly threatening. In fact, the problem of evil is the greatest theological problem because it threatens the central function of any religious system as a whole. It represents the eruption of the chaos that destroys our cosmos.

When that happens, we can respond in two ways. Intellectually, we try to account for the evil, explain why it had to be so, and thereby integrate it into our cosmic pattern. In effect, we reknit the pattern with the evil included. This is properly the task of theodicy. The evil becomes God's punishment, or the result of God's self-limitation to make room for human freedom, or it will be rectified in some eschatological future. These are all intellectual accountings, designed to maintain the integrity of our fabric of understanding.

But sometimes these explanations just don't work. To return to one of our initial distinctions, they may provide objective explanations and yet leave us with a sense of emotional irresolution. Heschel, for example, can insist that the Holocaust is our failure, not God's, and objectively that may be perfectly true. But on some other level, it explains nothing at all. We are still haunted by questions: Why did this have to happen? Why does this have to be the price we pay for our freedom? Why is the world this way?

At this point, our response to chaos has to move in a different, less intellectual, and more affective direction—or, to use our earlier distinction, a "religious" direction. At that point, we stop trying to explain, and instead, somehow existentially affirm our conviction that our cosmos will be restored intact. Jews say the *Kaddish,* which in its last line becomes a prayer for an eschatological *shalom,* for harmony, for cosmos in human affairs.

Of course, we don't always consciously think of this affirmation when we say the *Kaddish,* or for that matter, any liturgy that we recite over and over again. But this gives us a clue to the role and function of ritual in religious life. In a sense, the medium becomes the message. It's not so much what we say, but rather that we say it, again and again, predictably, as a structured portion of our daily life. We counter chaos by infusing our life with structure. In fact, the main reason why in all cultures death, burial, and mourning are so highly ritualized is precisely this intuitive human impulse to restore structure at the very moment when it is most threatened.

In the final analysis, most theodicies are inadequate. That's probably why the Book of Job is in the Bible. It's almost as if our ancestors said, "We really don't have any conclusive answer for why human beings are doomed to suffer. So here's another approach." The genius of most ancient and rich religious traditions is that they give us multiple ways of accomplishing the same purpose.

FOR FURTHER STUDY
Begin with Clifford Geertz' "Religion as a Cultural System" in his THE INTERPRETATION OF CULTURES *(pb Basic Books, 1973). This seminal article in the anthropology of religion provides an indispensable*

background to understanding the impact of the problem of evil on religion.

On Job, Moshe Greenberg's "Reflections on Job's Theology" (see ch. 5) remains the most succinct and suggestive statement of the theological "message" of the book. For a more comprehensive translation and study of the book as a whole, see Robert Gordis' THE BOOK OF GOD AND MAN: A STUDY OF JOB (pb University of Chicago Press, 1965). Nahum N. Glatzer's THE DIMENSIONS OF JOB (pb Schocken, 1969) includes an anthology of interpretations of the book, including Martin Buber's, that reveal both its endless fascination and intrinsic mystery.

On the eschatological resolution of the problem of evil, see the material listed at the end of ch. 10. Mordecai Kaplan's approach to the problem is captured in pp. 115–120 of his QUESTIONS JEWS ASK: RECONSTRUCTIONIST ANSWERS (see ch. 4). Kaplan's response to the child who is suffering from polio is on pp. 117–120 of this volume. Harold Kushner's WHEN BAD THINGS HAPPEN TO GOOD PEOPLE (Schocken, 1981; pb Avon, 1983) is a restatement of an essentially Kaplanian position with emphasis on its pastoral implications. Harold M. Schulweis' EVIL AND THE MORALITY OF GOD (Hebrew Union College Press, 1984) deals with the more technical, theological assumptions of that approach.

On Holocaust theology, Richard Rubenstein's "death of God" theology is expressed concisely in his contribution to THE CONDITION OF JEWISH BELIEF (see ch. 7), and more extensively in a number of papers collected in AFTER AUSCHWITZ: RADICAL THEOLOGY AND CONTEMPORARY JUDAISM (pb Bobbs-Merrill, 1966). On the metaphor of God's "eclipse," see Emil Fackenheim's "On the Eclipse of God" in his QUEST FOR PAST AND FUTURE and the material on the Holocaust collected in THE JEWISH THOUGHT OF EMIL FACKENHEIM (see ch. 7). Eliezer Berkovits' FAITH AFTER THE HOLOCAUST (pb Ktav, 1973) has been widely read, and Irving Greenberg's "Cloud of Smoke, Pillar of Fire: Judaism, Christianity, and Modernity after the Holocaust" in AUSCHWITZ: BEGINNING OF A NEW ERA?, edited by Eva Fleischner (pb Ktav, 1977) is a significant restatement of the Buberian position. Elie Wiesel, of course, has struggled with the implications of this event for Judaism. To this reader, his novel NIGHT (pb Bantam, 1983) remains his starkest and most powerful statement. Relatively unknown and now out of print but incredibly suggestive is another novel, The Third Pillar, *by Soma Morgenstern (Farrar, Straus and Cudahy, 1955), which uses themes from Jewish mysticism to deal with the impact of the Holocaust. Heschel's "The Meaning of This Hour" is included in his* Man's Quest for God *(Scribner's, 1954; pb title,* Quest for God, *Crossroad, 1982).*

Finally, Steven T. Katz' Post-Holocaust Dialogues *(New York University Press, 1983; pb 1985) is a critical study of all of these responses.*

IX

Ritual:
Why Do We Need It?

THERE IS NO PRECISE HEBREW EQUIVALENT FOR THE WORD "RITual." Traditional Jewish texts refer to observances such as the dietary laws; Sabbath and Festival practices such as lighting candles, eating *matzah,* and fasting; rites of passage such as circumcision and marriage; or daily prayer with *tallit* and *tefillin* as *mitzvot shebein adam lamakom,* that is, commands that deal with the relationship between a human being and God. These ritual commands are distinguished from *mitzvot shebein adam lehavero,* those that deal with the relationship between one human being and another. In the Bible, the distinction is apparently between God's *hukkim* and His *mishpatim.* The former, according to the rabbinic interpretation of passages such as Leviticus 18:4, are arbitrary divine decrees; the latter, had God not revealed them, would have been decreed by humanity itself, for they are the totally reasonable axioms of our social order. In medieval philosophical texts, the distinction is between *mitzvot shimiyot,* or heavenly (i.e., revealed) decrees, and *mitzvot sikhliyot,* or rational, reasonable decrees.

Rituals, then, are practices that have no obvious interpersonal or ethical impact and no rational basis; they are binding simply because they are said to represent God's explicit will for us. Is it any wonder, then, that many of us have trouble making sense of these practices? In an age that places a premium on individualism and autonomy, obedience to arbitrary divine decrees does not come easily. For those of us who were not raised in observant homes, ritual observances demand a choreography that is unfamiliar and threatening. It is not easy for adults to begin observing the dietary laws, turn their kitchens inside out, and accept the social limitations that this discipline demands. It is not easy to begin putting on *tefillin* in a public forum such as the synagogue chapel, or to adopt the practice of ritual immersion after menstruation—just to cite a few more examples. How can we justify these dramatic changes in lifestyle, first to ourselves and then to our families and friends?

Is it any wonder that many of us prefer to view religion as a matter of faith and belief alone, as inwardness or emotion ("I'm a Jew at heart!"), or as affecting primarily our interpersonal, ethical behavior? We may accept the fact that religion can dictate giving charity, dealing honestly with our fellows, remaining faithful to our spouses, and avoiding gossip or slander. What more can it legitimately require of us? Isn't it enough to be a good person?

Yet we are also aware of the genuine power of certain ritual practices in our lives. Some of us, for example, will remember days of total immersion in the television coverage of John F. Kennedy's assassination and funeral, because the ceremonies and the pageantry surrounding the burial of a president helped us cope with the grief and the sense of absurdity that enveloped us. Many of us feel an inner thrill when we sing "The Star Spangled Banner" (or *Hatikvah*) on state occasions or at convocations (though perhaps less so before a ball game). We feel there is a certain appropriateness about the rituals that govern an appearance of, or before, the President of the United States or the Queen of England. The family gathering around the dining room table on Thanksgiving Day, with its ritual carving of the turkey and the rest of the traditional menu, are recalled with warmth and anticipation. We are grateful that at certain peak moments in our lives—when we get married, for example, or when a dear one has died—there are specific, familiar, and predictable behavior patterns that are available to help mark the transition. Ritual behavior patterns, then, are not limited to formal religious situations alone.

The scholarly study of the place and function of ritual in human situations is a new and rapidly growing discipline, to date conducted largely by social scientists and scholars in the study of primitive religions and of Christianity. The results of this inquiry are only beginning to be incorporated into the scholarly study of Jewish religion. But the material is extremely important if we are to make sense of Judaism in our modern context.

The Varying Functions of Ritual

Religious rituals play many different roles in people's lives. The list that follows focuses on these functional distinctions, that is, on the varying ways that people use ritual behavior. Some of these uses can be more easily identified with one specific branch (e.g., Orthodox, Conservative, or Reform) of the Jewish religious community, but there is no intrinsic correlation between any one of these functions and membership in a particular religious community or movement within that community. In fact, any one of us, at any moment of our lives, may use a specific ritual in any of the following ways. To complicate the problem even further, frequently only the individual knows just how he or she is using a particular ritual. More frequently, we are barely aware of just how we are using the ritual, so much is ritual behavior a part of our natural life experience.

RITUAL AS MAGIC: According to this view, the ritual, if performed correctly, has the power to coerce the force, or forces, that govern nature and history and so produce a desired result. The distinguishing features of this position are, first, the believer's conviction that the ritual can change the course of events; and second, that this change takes place by cause-and-effect and as a clear and direct result of performing the ritual in the proper way. It is the ritual itself, pure and simple, that produces the effect, and it does so automatically and consistently. Failure to perform the ritual, or to perform it in the proper manner, can lead to disaster.

It is the mind set of the believer, then, that will reveal if a ritual is being performed magically. This mind set is molded by an implicit theology, or world view, which assumes that the world is governed by a body of blind and implacable laws. The magical ritual works because it taps into these laws and draws on their power for the benefit of the ritual community. Certain words, substances, and gestures are themselves charged with this magical power, and whoever knows how to use these powers is able to produce the desired effect. The ritual rain dance, for example, will always produce rain because the dance itself has the power to affect the laws of nature in a totally predictable way; if it doesn't produce rain, there was something wrong with the way it was performed.

This magicalist view of ritual is most frequently associated with pagan religion. All forms of paganism view the world as governed by a set of transcendent laws to which even the gods are subject. Both the human community and the pagan gods have to resort to ritual in order to activate the powers that ultimately rule the world so that they may survive in the face of nature.

But however pagan its origins, this magicalist approach to ritual appears everywhere, even in the most sophisticated of religions. There, however, it will frequently be dubbed a "superstition" by other members of the community. In Judaism, for example, the conviction that kissing the *mezuzah* before leaving the house will protect the believer from any harm during the course of the day can reveal a magicalist position, depending again on the individual's mind set; or, it can simply be understood as one of a series of customs through which an individual identifies with a certain community.

In other words, we can't always tell how the ritual functions simply by looking at the act itself. Even the believer may not always be consciously aware of its function. One of the clues could be the amount of anxiety generated by not performing the ritual. For example, a Jew who forgot to kiss the *mezuzzah* before leaving home on an extended journey, might actually return home to perform the ritual—so great is the anxiety engendered by the failure to do it the right way at the outset. The greater the anxiety, the more magical the ritual; for if the world is governed by implacable laws, failure to act in the appropriate way can be terrifying.

Most of us, at critical moments in our lives, become implicit magicalists. Whenever we are overwhelmed by natural events and feel powerless to control our destinies, we intuitively seek some device that we believe will enable us to regain control and bend nature to our will. On another level, we resort to religious ritual as a way of getting rid of our guilt for some misdeed which, we assume, has resulted in the "punishment" to which we have been subjected. In extreme situations (for example, before going in for major surgery), even those of us who are confirmed monotheists may find ourselves resorting to such devices. We may even, for example, use perfectly acceptable Jewish ritual forms, such as reciting chapters from the Book of Psalms or asking our rabbi to recite the prayer for the sick. The magical quality of these rituals, in such instances, lies in the expectation that they will coerce God's will, which, in other situations, we would acknowledge as uncoercible by human beings.

As a conscious theory of Jewish ritual, the magicalist position is unacceptable, then, for the simple reason that it denies the notion of the monotheistic God who is supremely free. No true monotheist can believe that the world is governed by transcendent laws that operate independently of God; without this assumption, the magicalist approach is undermined. We can not shape a formal Jewish approach to ritual on these grounds.

RITUAL AS SACRAMENT: Here, too, ritual is motivated by the belief that it has the power to effect a substantive change in the nature of things out there, beyond the believer. In contrast to the magicalist, the sacramentalist insists that it is not simply the ritual itself that produces the desired effect; rather, the ritual must be accompanied by a whole set of appropriate inward states and explicit belief structures. Without this set of conditions, the ritual itself is either ineffective or it even becomes an act of desecration. Although the magicalist also has an implicit theology and mind set, they play no role in determining the efficacy of the ritual. For the sacramentalist, they are indispensable.

The classic expression of religious sacramentalism is in the Roman Catholic understanding of the Eucharist. The wafer and the wine actually become the flesh and blood of Jesus (the technical term is "transubstantiation") when the proper words are recited by the proper person (an ordained priest) at the proper point in the Mass. The Christian who then consumes the wafer has become "one with Christ" and thereby saved.

The sacramentalist position differs from the magicalist in two ways. First, the ritual works not because it taps into the blind forces that govern nature but because, according to Christian belief, Jesus himself, prior to his death, commanded his disciples to perform this ritual and promised that when they do so, they will earn salvation or eternal blessedness. This promise, in the context of his subsequent crucifixion, opened what Catholics call "a source of grace," which gives the ritual its salvational power. Second, the ritual is efficacious only if both the priest and the communicant explicitly accept its theological basis and are free from sin.

The full weight of these conditions emerges strikingly in one of the most moving of contemporary "religious" novels, Graham Greene's *The Heart of the Matter*. The novel revolves around the experience of an obscure British civil servant trapped in an out-of-the-way African outpost during World War II. While his wife is temporarily out of the country, Scobie drifts into an affair with another woman. When his wife returns, her suspicions are aroused but instead of confronting her husband, she pleads with him to go to Mass and take the Eucharist. He knows that he must not take the Eucharist without first confessing his sin to the priest; otherwise, the ritual not only loses its saving power but becomes an obscenity. But he also knows that in that tightly knit community, confessing his sin will destroy his marriage.

Scobie's tragic resolution of his dilemma is less important than the dilemma itself. It would simply never assume that kind of weight outside of a sacramentalist framework. Nowhere else would Scobie's inward state or the taking (or not taking) of the Eucharist make such a difference. Note that the more liberal wings of Protestant Christianity transformed the Eucharist into a symbolic act (see below), or a historical reenactment of Jesus' self-sacrifice. Either way, the Eucharist loses its sacramental character. A liberal Protestant version of Scobie would never have his dilemma.

The only formally articulated Jewish version of ritual sacramentalism in post-Temple Judaism is in the mystical theology of Isaac Luria. Lurianic mysticism views each *mitzvah* performed with the specific intent of "repairing" the world and bringing redemption to Israel, to the world, and even to God Himself, as a cosmic and efficacious instrument for redemption. Kabbalistic prayer books, for example, frequently insert brief introductory prayers, prior to the performance of a ritual act (such as donning the *tallit*). These brief prayers, called *kavannot,* are literally "declarations of intent" (Hebrew: *kavannah,* intention), and are designed to help the worshiper focus on the esoteric, cosmic purpose of the prayer, which is nothing less than restoring the unity of creation and of God Himself. With this mind set in place, the kabbalist believes, the subsequent performance of the ritual will have the desired effect.

Jewish sacramentalism, then, requires a set of theological assumptions that are highly esoteric and hardly within the popular grasp. We may be fascinated by the poetic nature of these doctrines, but they are simply not representative of normative Jewish thinking. There is no Jewish ritual that carries the weight of the Roman Catholic Eucharist, no ritual that has the power to convey authenticity within Jewish religious life or to guarantee salvation. No Jew, for example, would ever find himself in Scobie's position. A Jewish Scobie would know that genuine repentance can erase most sins, certainly the sin that he committed, and that he has the ability to reconstitute his own life and his marriage as well. In the meantime, there is simply no area of Jewish ritual life that is closed off to him.

There are multiple rabbinic passages that explicitly deny that Jewish ritual has substantive power. Note, for example, the claim of Rabban Yohanan ben Zakkai in the first century C.E. that "neither does the corpse itself convey substantive ritual impurity nor do the waters [with the ashes of the red heifer] convey substantive purification, but rather I [God] have issued a set of arbitrary decrees that you are simply not permitted to flout" (*Numbers Rabbah* 19:8). This rabbinic teaching assumes that Jewish rituals are simply exercises in obeying God's will.

Moreover, there is not one single Jewish ritual that may not, on occasion, be suspended. Even circumcision, which must be performed on the eighth day after birth, including the Sabbath and Yom Kippur, may be postponed indefinitely if the infant is ill. The *onen* (the mourner between the moment of death and burial) must not perform ritual acts such as putting on *tefillin* (because the overriding *mitzvah* is to arrange for the burial). The laws of the Sabbath, the Yom Kippur fast, and the dietary laws may all be waived in order to save a human life. By contrast, neither the magicalist nor the sacramentalist can tolerate the suspension of such central ritual practices.

Because the sacramentalist position inherits the assumption of magicalism that ritual can have a coercive power over nature, it compromises the monotheistic God. Further, because the inward conditions that are so crucial to sacramentalism are relatively intangible, this position can easily shade into magicalism, where the proper performance of the ritual itself is viewed as automatically efficacious, irrespective of the mind set of the believer. This, some contend, is precisely what has happened in some debased forms of contemporary Hasidism.

RITUAL AS OBEDIENCE TO GOD: Here we enter more familiar, classically Jewish territory in which ritual is no longer viewed as automatically or coercively affecting the world. Judaism views the world as governed by a God who is supreme, omnipotent, and completely free. God has revealed the rituals to the community and has commanded us to perform them. These rituals may have many desirable effects, but the only genuinely religious reason for performing them is to obey, and hence please, God. God may, or may not choose to reward us for obedience. The reward (or, conversely, the punishment for not performing the ritual) is never automatic or inevitable because, above all, God is supremely free.

Note that performance of the ritual as obedience to God's

will can have a substantive effect on nature and history. For example, according to Deuteronomy 11:13–17, which is the middle of the three biblical passages included in the twice-daily recital of the *Shema*, observance of God's commands can bring rainfall and bountiful crops. But that effect is never an automatic result of ritual performance itself. Rather, it is a totally free God who may *choose* to act in the world in response to the believer's act of obedience—or He may choose not to. In this latter case, what we have called "the problem of evil" (i.e., how can a just, omnipotent God allow the righteous to suffer) raises its head.

An almost inevitable corollary of the obedience position is to elevate ritual commands over the interpersonal in the hierarchy of spirituality. The ethical commands were also revealed and commanded by God, but they can all too easily be performed for humanistic or rational reasons. Since the rituals are totally arbitrary, to fulfill them is to perform the purest act of obedience, and hence to acknowledge God as supreme and His will as binding.

Therein lies one of the problems of the obedience position. Prophetic religion, for example, assigns a clear priority to the ethical command over the ritual. Justice, compassion, righteousness—these are absolutely divine, for they define God's relationship to us. But God does not participate in the ritual, nor is He affected by the Temple cult. If God were to choose, Hosea 6:6 tells us, He prefers *hesed* (acts of lovingkindness) over Temple sacrifices. Isaiah 1, which we read liturgically on the Sabbath prior to the Tishah b'Av fast, has God denouncing Israel's sacrifices and festivals as meaningless unless we cease to do evil, devote ourselves to justice, aid the wronged, uphold the orphan, and defend the widow.

In fact, what more dramatic repudiation of the priority of ritual can there be than God's decision, twice, to destroy His Temple, as punishment for Israel's moral shortcomings, thereby depriving Israel of the opportunity to perform the central rituals of biblical religion. To the obedience position, the destruction of the Temple poses most sharply of all the question of religious priorities.

Beyond this, the obedience position assumes a literalist understanding of revelation. The believing community views its sacred texts as the literal word of God. Thus God's explicit will underlies the ritual system. Abandon that theology of revelation and the position becomes increasingly tenuous. In contemporary Jewish religious life, if there is a theological basis for the distinction between Orthodoxy on one hand, and Reform, Reconstructionist, and most readings of Conservative Judaism on the other, it lies in how each of the movements understands revelation and hence the authority of the system of *mitzvot,* primarily the ritual *mitzvot.* Contemporary Orthodoxy fits squarely into the obedience camp; Conservative and Reform Judaism will adopt one of the positions described below.

RITUAL AS SYMBOLIC BEHAVIOR: Once we reject a literalist understanding of revelation, we can no longer view God as the active, initiating source of ritual practice. The alternative is to view ritual as emerging, in some way, out of the religious life of the community—a position that the three remaining approaches all share.

The first of these perspectives views ritual as a symbolic expression, in behavioral language, of the community's religious myth. Ritual is "symbolic" behavior in the sense, first, that it has no substantive effect on the world out there, except on the feelings of the one who performs the ritual; and second, because it shares the characteristic of all symbols, namely, that of standing for, pointing to, or participating in a reality that lies beyond itself. It is thus an expression, in behavioral language, of the community's religious myth. This myth, in the sense of the term discussed in chapter 4, renders this ultimate reality in more discursive or narrative terms; the ritual, in behavioral terms. Together, they form one complex whole, duplicating and reinforcing each other. The Bible, for example, refers to two powerful Jewish rituals, circumcision and the observance of the Sabbath, in each case, as an *"ot,"* or symbol; the first, for the covenant between God and Israel, and the other, for God's original ordering of the world at creation. This understanding of ritual reflects the theological perspective of this volume as a whole and we will return to it in greater detail below.

RITUAL AS RELIGIOUS FOLKWAY: The view that the Jewish religion emerged out of the life experience of the Jewish people was first propounded by Mordecai Kaplan, who was a thoroughgoing religious and theological naturalist. In Kaplanian theology, God is a process or power within nature; revelation is a form of human discovery or creativity; and religion itself is a totally natural expression of the group experience of the community, not at all (as the traditionalist would have it) imposed on the community by a supernatural, personal God. It is no longer possible, then, to view ritual as *mitzvah,* as commanded, for the Kaplanian God is not a commanding God. Kaplan does away with the entire notion of religious law and with the correlative notion that failure to fulfill a ritual is a "sin." He proposes instead that we view the rituals of Judaism as "religious folkways." As the term implies, these practices are expressions of the distinctive lifestyle of the community. They serve, in a tangible way, to distinguish this community from others, to promote group identity, to give the individual a sense of unity with the larger group. They can also be viewed as "poetry in action," as adding a dimension of sensory richness to Jewish life experience.

The net result of Kaplan's naturalist perspective is to locate the authority for ritual in the community itself. What the community created, the community can decide to preserve, ignore, or change in line with its ever-changing needs and sensitivities. Specifically, the folkways position will be alert to the fact that a ritual practice, such as the exclusion of women from the performance of synagogue rituals, can sometimes become morally offensive. When this happens, the community is thoroughly justified in substituting alternative ritual forms. This process is never painless or easy and should never be undertaken casually or precipitously, but there is no question that, in this view, the authority behind the ritual system is significantly diminished.

Finally, the folkways position differs from the symbolist position to be described below in viewing ritual as an expression of the cultural or civilizational life of the community, whereas the symbolist position views it as linked to a community's religious myth. Although the two positions may shade into one another, they can be distinguished in two ways: First, the folkways option will have more difficulty specifying the distinctive quality of *religious* as opposed to *cultural* folkways; and second, the symbolist will tend to view the ritual system as more authoritative (though clearly not as authoritative as in the obedience position), more tightly tied to the religious vision of the community, and hence less easily modified than the folkways position would have it. We will return to these issues below.

RITUAL AS ANACHRONISM: This position equates ritual with "ritualism," purely outward forms of behavior that have lost any of the religious, spiritual, or emotional content they may have had centuries ago. As such, they should be abandoned. They may have had meaning in earlier, more primitive times, but today our preferred forms of religious expression are more "spiritual" (i.e., inward, emotional) or interpersonal (i.e., ethical).

The classic Jewish formulation of this position is in American Reform Judaism's Pittsburgh Platform of 1885 and its European and American antecedents. The Pittsburgh Platform views the traditional laws that regulate diet, for example, as having originated in ages and under the influence of ideas that are totally foreign to modernity, and if anything, obstruct rather than further spiritual elevation. Hence their abandonment is thoroughly justified.

In more recent years, however, Reform Judaism has decisively rejected many of the planks in this early document, including its view of ritual as anachronism. American Reform's 1976 Centenary Perspective affirms the legitimacy of traditional Jewish observances in the home and synagogue and urges the Reform community to confront the claims of this tradition—all within the classical Reform framework of individual autonomy. Although the Perspective itself, understandably, offers no conceptual understanding of the place of ritual in religion, in practice ritually observant Reform Jews will usually fit into either the symbolic or folkways position. The view that Jewish ritual is a total anachronism would today be espoused only by Jewish secularists.

These final three positions—symbolist, folkways, and anachronist—are all prepared to take the decisive step away from a literalist understanding of revelation and to locate the authority for determining the content of revelation in the community. It is the community that becomes the conduit for God's will and shapes the ritual system. The result is that religious authority becomes much more open and flexible, some rituals can fade away while new ones are created, and pluralistic ritual practices within the community become viable. Those who prefer a more absolutist or authoritarian religious structure will shun any of these options, probably in favor of the obedience position.

With these six views on the function of ritual in Jewish religion in place, note again how difficult it is for an outsider to know how any particular ritual is being used at any one time. A critically ill person, for example, will want someone to recite a prayer for healing. In a magicalist framework, the very recital of the prayer will be viewed as automatically and coercively effective. The sacramentalist will view the prayer, recited with the proper mystical *kavannah,* as helping to repair the fault in creation, thereby eliminating the illness. In an obedience framework, the prayer will be viewed as a plea that God freely choose to heal this person. In a symbolist or folkways position, it will be viewed as a device to help the patient express his feelings of helplessness, resignation, and/or hope—but never (unless the illness is psychosomatic) as an effective way of healing. The anachronist will dismiss the notion that prayer can have any effect at all as a primitive superstition. The differences between the positions are subtle and frequently hidden from view—but still quite genuine.

Our task now is first to address the anachronistic position and then to weigh the strengths and weaknesses of the symbolist and folkways options. These two remaining options are particularly vulnerable to the charge of anachronism, because once we have rejected the possibility of literal revelation, it is tempting to conclude that the entire fabric of religion is a human fiction—a useful fiction perhaps, but a fiction nonetheless, and thus to be rejected by sophisticated, modern Jews.

The answer to the challenge of anachronism is clear and

direct: The issue is never ritual or no ritual, but rather which ritual, for significant portions of our life experience are inevitably ritualized. Contemporary Jewish secularists may well believe that they have relegated all of ritual to the backwater of civilization. But even a cursory glance at their lifestyles will disclose the multiple ritual systems—of country club, suburban community, socioeconomic class, corporation, law firm, or profession—in which they quite comfortably participate.

Rituals and Communities

There is no escaping ritual. Rituals are intrinsic to communities, be they as small as a family, a corporation, or a baseball team, or as large as the United States Army or the Jewish people. The nexus between ritual and community rests on our viewing ritual as a language; just as a community creates its language, the language itself creates the community. People who speak a common language share a sense of belonging. But in the company of people who speak a foreign language, we feel excluded. In fact, *every* community includes and excludes—and one of the ways it does so is through its distinctive language.

We are familiar with verbal languages that are unsurpassed for specificity and accuracy of content. They communicate the most complicated pieces of information clearly and distinctly. Ritual languages replace (or frequently supplement) words with specific gestures, ways of dressing and eating, or of shaping the most ordinary tasks of everyday life, such as preparing for sleep at night or getting up in the morning, of courtship patterns, life transitions, and the like. We call these behavioral patterns "rituals" because they carry absolutely predictable meanings—that's what makes them a language. These highly specific meanings enable them to be understood, or "read," by other people who "speak" the same ritual language, and thus to do the work of creating a community.

Take the community of contemporary adolescents, a striking example of how a community is held together by a set of highly coercive ritual patterns. In order to belong to this community, adolescents pay impeccable attention to how they dress, how they wear their hair, how they hold their bodies, what they eat, what songs they sing, how they court each other, how they deal with parents and teachers. To flout any of these rituals is to invite ostracism. It may have been fine a generation ago for an adolescent girl to go to school wearing penny loafers, a plaid skirt with a large safety pin on the side, a white blouse, and a cashmere sweater, but in the America of the late 1980s, this outfit would invite exclusion from the group. Such is the coercive power of these rituals—none of which, it need be added, were revealed at Sinai.

Rituals, like verbal languages, confer identity. That's how they create communities, for who we are depends in large measure on where we belong. They garb the social experiences of everyday life in the distinctive values of a particular group. In the process, a group acquires a distinctive identity, separate from others.

This "separated" quality is probably the basic meaning of the Hebrew word *"kadosh."* Much like the English word "distinguished," which can mean both "separate" and "special," *kadosh* begins by meaning "separate" and ends by meaning "special" or "sacred," "holy," "elevated." So the Sabbath day, according to Genesis 2:3, begins by being separated out from the other days of the week and then becomes a special day. The people Israel (according to Leviticus 19:2) are commanded to be *"kedoshim"* or distinct/special from other peoples, and the rest of that chapter describes the specific lifestyle that will accomplish this goal. Leviticus 11:44 also exhorts the people to become *kedoshim* as the climax of an extended list of forbidden foods. In both of these passages, the community is to be *kadosh* because God Himself is *kadosh*—the absolute paradigm of "separate"/"special"—in relation to the world and to other gods.

As much as these rituals serve to distinguish a community, they also transmit its identity from generation to generation. They are powerful pedagogic devices, largely because of their inherent theatricality. This theatrical quality is less evident in the rituals of daily life, but is very much evident in the grand set pieces of communal ritual such as the rites of passage—circumcision, marriage, and the rites surrounding death, burial, and mourning—or, in the celebration of the Festivals of the year, such as the Passover *seder*. The Passover Haggadah is both script and textbook; the *seder* table is both theater set and classroom; the rituals of drinking the wine, dipping the herbs, and eating, lifting, and lowering the *matzah* are both stage directions and experiential learning devices. The whole forms an elaborate pageant designed to teach the founding, or "master," story of this community to a new generation.

This metaphor of ritual as theater illuminates both its community-building role and its pedagogic function. Theater, too, creates community; in a play's most powerful moments, the proscenium collapses and the players and audience are drawn together in a shared experience. Again like great theater, ritual carries a powerful emotional charge. Verbal language may be highly specific, but body language is much more effective in expressing emotion. We hug our children, for example, but it would take pages of prose to convey the affection that emerges in the hug. Great educational moments always have an affective or experiential dimension; they speak to the heart and the senses as much as to the mind. Eating the bitter herbs and dipping our fingers into the wine at the Passover *seder* leaves an infinitely longer imprint on the child than the recitation of the Haggadah.

Rituals and Myths

Even the most convinced of secularists will find it difficult to deny the power of ritual to confer identity on a community and lend a sensory or poetic quality to its communal life. This, in effect, is the response of the folkways position to the challenge of anachronism. The question is: Can we go beyond this?

The symbolist position says that we can—by viewing ritual as an experiential expression of the community's myth. We have seen, in Chapter 4, that the signal function of a religious myth is to structure reality, to create a sense of cosmos or order in our lives. In the process, we acquire a place in the cosmic order and an accompanying sense of identity, security, and meaning.

The heart of the myth is its structuring role. Some structures are inherent in reality: day and night, for example, or animal and vegetable, male and female, heaven and earth, and life and death. These are part of the very nature of things. But other structures are cultural artifacts. Space and time, for example, in themselves are undifferentiated or homogenous; the division of space into inches, feet, yards, and miles; or the more complex differentiation of space through architectural design, the creation of special spaces such as temples and monuments, and the establishment of national boundaries and city limits is the work of human beings. So is the division of time into seconds, minutes, hours, days, weeks, months, and years; and certainly the determination of special times such as weekends, birthdays, anniversaries, or Sabbaths and Festivals.

The structuring work of the myth is reflected in both the intrinsic and the cultural distinctions. In the latter, it literally creates the structure: It determines, for example, when a day or a year begins and ends, when a week begins and why it has seven days; it establishes Festival days and special spaces, such as monuments and museums; and it creates sacred spaces, such as cathedrals and synagogues. Even where certain structures are inherently real, the myth determines which of these inherent structures it wants to highlight, which it chooses to ignore, and how it chooses to do the highlighting. Meat and milk, for example, may be inherently distinct but there is no intrinsic reason why they can not be consumed together, whereas meat and vegetables, also inherently distinct, can. Or why males and females should be prohibited from sitting together in the synagogue but not around the dining room table.

Above all, a myth abhors undifferentiation or homogeneity, which it understands as incipient chaos, for human beings can not tolerate chaos. Cartons, for example, can be stored in a large, undifferentiated warehouse space; human beings demand rooms. If the space is to be lived in, it has to be divided into a kitchen, living room, bedroom, dining room, and the rest. The alternative engenders feelings of insecurity, rootlessness, and anxiety. The same applies to time. Try to imagine the sense of rootlessness that would result from going through life without the notion of a "day" or a "week," without a sense of when either begins and ends, without hours to mark off the working day or to tell us when the opera begins, or without special days devoted to leisure or celebration.

Myths function unconsciously. They are so ancient and authoritative that they become quasi-invisible. But those myths that shape human experience in a rich and distinctive way, that provide a living community with its *raison d'etre* and shape its sense of destiny can not afford to remain invisible. They must be brought alive, into experience. To accomplish this, the community generates rituals. Rituals are public dramatizations that bring the myth into experience. They enable a community to bond together, live its myth in an overt way, and transmit it from generation to generation.

Rituals reflect the myth by almost invariably focusing on the interface between two structures, either two inherent structures or two structures that the myth wants to highlight. Wherever we find a ritual, we almost always find a structural distinction. The operative metaphor seems to be that of a "threshold," that is, the point where two structures meet. The ritual illuminates the threshold between these two structures, guides us from one structure into the other, and in so doing, brings the structural distinction into our awareness.

A number of examples. First, on the most literal level, the threshold of a Jewish home is marked by a *mezuzzah,* literally a "doorpost," but by extension, a tiny case containing the parchment with passages from the Torah that (according to Deuteronomy 6:9 and 11:20) we are commanded to place on the doorposts of our homes. The *mezuzzah* separates my home—with its associations of privacy, possession, security—from the outside world which is public, open, and hence potentially perilous (recall the blood on the doorposts of the Israelite homes in Egypt which protected our ancestors on the night of the Exodus, in Exodus 12:7). The *mezuzzah* effectively creates my private space which, by law, is inviolable.

On a much broader canvas, the Bible is replete with instances of the attempt to structure space. God commands Abraham (Genesis 13:17) to "walk about the land [of Canaan], through its length and breadth," as if to establish the coordinates of the space that he has been promised. Later, in the course of their trek through the wilderness—precisely!—the Israelites march in a highly structured order with the sanctuary at the center of the camp and the tribes arranged in precise order around the periphery (Numbers 2). This anticipates the later hierarchy of sacred spaces in biblical religion—the world as a whole, the land of Israel, Jerusalem, the Temple, the Holy of Holies, the Ark, and ultimately, the point between the two cherubim that were placed on the cover of the Ark, from where, according to Exodus 25:22 and Numbers 7:89, God will speak to the community.

Note, however, that in the desert experience, there is no inherently sacred space, no one spot that is fixed as a point of orientation for the spatial hierarchy. That point is wherever the Israelites set up their camp and locate the Sanctuary. Here, the community determines the spatial hierarchy. In the later tradition, the central point of orientation in the Jerusalem Temple is fixed by identifying it (according to 2 Chronicles 3:1) as Moriah, the place where God revealed Himself to Abraham as he was preparing to sacrifice his son (Genesis 22:14). This ambivalence prefigures the ambiguity with which later formulations of Jewish religion viewed the entire notion of sacred space for, in time, Jews were exiled from their land, the Temple was destroyed, and, in the course of an extended experience of exile (or displacement), Jewish religion reverted to the earlier notion that any spot on earth can become sacred simply by the decision to establish a synagogue for prayer.

But there is no ambiguity about Judaism's interest in structuring time. An elaborate set of rituals are designed to distinguish thresholds in time. We have liturgies to recite immediately upon waking up and immediately before going to sleep. We pray at sunrise and at sunset, and in each case, the liturgy notes the transition from light to darkness or from darkness to light, from day to night and from night to day. We mark the end and the beginning of a week with a Sabbath day and we separate the Sabbath from the rest of the week by rituals of transition at its beginning and at its end. The rituals are called, respectively, *kiddush* and *havdalah,* which are synonyms and which literally mean "separating out." We have a ritual that marks the beginning of each month and a festival that marks the beginning of a new year. Two of our major festivals, Sukkoth and Passover, occur exactly six months apart and mark the natural transitions from summer to winter and again from winter to summer. Finally, we use rituals to mark the stages of human life: birth, puberty, marriage, and death.

Like space and time, social structures are also designated. Judaism has a ritual for creating a family (marriage), for dissolving a family (divorce), and for entering into a community (conversion). A Jewish male infant is brought into the covenanted community through the ritual of circumcision. The community as a whole celebrates its founding through a complex Passover festival during which it reenacts the events that brought it into being as a distinctive people. An elaborate set of rituals distinguishes the status of the male members of the community from the female, the adult members from the children, and in biblical times, the priests and Levites from the rest of the community.

Finally, a complex series of ritually determined distinctions shape the everyday life of a member of this community. They affect eating, dressing, sexual relations, interpersonal relations, and the rest. On the microcosmic level, the dietary laws, for example, force us to make explicit distinctions between meat products and milk products. Within the groupings of animals, fish, and birds, we distinguish between those members of each class that we may eat and those that we may not. On the macrocosmic level, the ensemble works to perpetuate a daylong and even lifelong sense of distinction between the life experience of this community and that of other communities, making this community *kadosh*—that is, "separate" and, eventually, special or "holy."

There is a clear overlap between the folkways position on ritual and the symbolist position; both see ritual as a way of conferring and transmitting identity within a communal structure. But the symbolist position goes beyond the folkways by locating the authority for the ritual pattern not solely in the community but, more significantly, in the community's sense of a cosmic order. Ritual draws its power from our intuitive human need for structure, which is the obverse side of our equally intuitive fear of chaos. That deeply human need is what makes ritual compelling. Jewish religion captures this compelling quality by viewing the Jewish ritual pattern as a system of law that it ascribes to a revealing God. But from this anthropological perspective, the reason this legal system is taken as binding in the first place rests in its responsiveness to the human need for order.

Finally, we call this position "symbolic" because it views these ritual patterns as having no substantive effect on the world. They don't change anything out there; they don't bring rainfall, assure safety and security, or cure illness. These ritual behavior patterns are themselves symbols in the sense described in chapter 4. They are not "signs"—mere human conventions that can be changed at whim like traffic lights. Rather, like a national flag, they point to, stand for, participate in, or draw their power from some dimension of reality that lies beyond them, precisely that dimension of reality that the community's myth tries to capture.

The Bible itself captures the symbolic quality of ritual by using the Hebrew term *"ot"* in reference to two major Jewish rituals, the Sabbath (Exodus 31:17) and circumcision (Genesis 17:11). The word itself is usually translated as "sign," but it is clear that in our technical, contemporary usage, "symbol" would be more accurate. Neither is a mere convention. Both have enormous affective power. Both draw their power from a central, founding event captured by this community's myth: in one case, God's original ordering of the universe in creation; in the other, the primitive binding together of God and Abraham, now Israel, in an eternal, covenantal relationship. In each case, the performance of the ritual is a reenactment—not merely a recalling—of that primal event. We recreate that original cosmic order by distinguishing the day on which God completed the work of creation and by stepping back from our own creative work, as He stepped back on the seventh day. In effect, every Sabbath is a temporary restoration of that primal sense of cosmos—which is why the talmudic tradition also understands the Sabbath as a foretaste of the age to come, when that original cosmos will be restored for eternity. We also reenact the primitive covenant with Abraham by introducing each newborn Jewish male into that same covenantal relationship.

On a broader scale, we as a community are commanded to be *kedoshim* (holy, separated out, distinguished) as God is *kadosh* (Leviticus 19:2). Our separateness points to God's. As we are distinct from other nations, so is He distinct from other gods. Each time we perform our rituals, we affirm His distinctiveness, for Israel is that community on earth that stands for, represents, or, in our terminology, "symbolizes" God's distinctive presence in the world.

The ultimate goal of the entire Jewish ritual system, then, is not simply to enable us to identify with this particular community, as the folkways position would have it but, rather, to capture in our personal lives an elaborate cosmic order which extends to God Himself as the ultimate cause and embodiment of that order. That's why our communal life is replete with divisions between the permitted and the forbidden—in what we eat, how we dress, how we conduct our sexual activities. The ritual system, then, points to, or brings into awareness the cosmic structures through which our community has organized its picture of the world.

Prayer as Ritual

No other form of religious expression is as challenging as prayer. Part of the problem is that the word "prayer" is an all-purpose term that covers many forms of activity. But Judaism fine-tunes the act of prayer. It can be an act of praise (as in the Psalms that we recite throughout the service), or of petition (for healing, for forgiveness, for food), or of articulating theological beliefs (as in the passages immediately prior to the *Shema* in the daily morning liturgy), or of gratitude (as in the Grace after Meals). In one form or another, all of these are instances of what we may call "expressive" prayer. Here, we use the act of prayer to express something—sometimes a set of theological claims, but more often a powerful emotion. In its ideal form, expressive prayer begins with the words of the prayer but then takes us well beyond them to the point where we are totally one with the feeling, so involved or caught up in the experience that the words of the prayer seem to fall behind.

The problem with this model is that in Judaism, at least, prayer is subjected to a rigorous discipline. Jewish law tells us when, where, and in what company we must pray, even what words we must use on each occasion. This discipline of prayer casts into question the very possibility of that more spontaneous or emotional model of expressive prayer. Most of us can not be commanded to be spontaneous or to feel intensely. We all experience moments—for example, when we are seriously ill—when we do spontaneously *need* to and *want* to pray, and in those moments our prayer is genuinely expressive. But we resist the notion that we should be *commanded* to pray when we don't feel the need to do so.

It is this structured, disciplinary dimension of prayer in Judaism that makes it a form of ritual expression. In reality, for most of us, expressive prayer is a relatively rare experience. Most of the time we pray because that is what is expected of us as Jews. Sometimes ritual prayer can lead into expressive prayer, but many times it doesn't—and we are left sitting in the synagogue, perhaps enjoying the experience of community, but often wondering why we are there. Our thoughts and our hearts drift away; eventually we just stop praying or even coming.

A common response to this problem is to tinker with the prayer book or with the service by adding English translations or readings from other sources, or by involving the congregation through unison or responsive readings in translation—in the hope of generating some feeling. When the theological content of the liturgy seems to be out of sync with our own, we either shade the translation or even change the Hebrew liturgy to bring it into line with our own beliefs. Thus, when Mordecai Kaplan concluded that contemporary Jews could no longer believe that Jews were the chosen people, he simply eliminated all references to this claim from the liturgy.

There is no question that expressive prayer is an ideal, and that we should be concerned with the theological content of the liturgy. But there may still be wisdom in the traditional demand that we should pray even when we don't feel intensely and don't pay particular attention to our theology. Sometimes the act of prayer is simply a ritual act, and it confers the same benefits that all our ritual behavior patterns confer.

Mourners who recite the *Kaddish* following the death of a parent are rarely conscious of the theological content of the prayer and after a while, no longer feel intense grief. Yet many of us continue to say the *Kaddish* on a regular basis, three times daily, for eleven months, and the very act of reciting this sacred text in this absolutely predictable way can carry religious significance. Here is one of those instances where the medium is very much the message. Most people who have followed this practice in a serious way testify to the power of this ritual in structuring the day-to-day flow of living. Twice a day, morning and evening, we know that we have to enter the synagogue with a community of fellow Jews and read prescribed liturgical texts, and these two moments become fixed points of orientation around which our entire day revolves. Precisely at a time of our lives when we are most easily vulnerable to the threat of meaninglessness and chaos, our religious tradition gives us a ritual that puts order back into our lives in a very concrete way.

The *Kaddish* experience is probably the most striking example of how prayer functions as ritual. But by extension, the larger discipline of daily prayer can work the same way, as long as we are not intimidated by our almost intuitive expectation that genuine prayer must always be an intense, spiritual experience. Those moments are precious but rare, and when they do occur, it is frequently because of, not in spite of, the more structured experience of ritual prayer.

Three further issues bear upon the role of prayer in Jewish religion. First, Judaism recommends that prayer take place among a *minyan* (or quorum) of ten Jews. The *minyan* symbolizes the Jewish people as a whole. We are permitted to pray alone and many of us do that rather frequently. But many prayers—the

Kaddish is an excellent example—require a *minyan* before they can be recited. Beyond this, almost all of the liturgy is couched in the plural form (*"our* Father, *our* King," not *"my* Father, *my* King") and our classical texts are replete with homiletical urgings that we pray only in a synagogue and with a *minyan*.

This expectation is much more than a pious platitude. It reflects both the powerful communal dimension that was part of Jewish religion from the very outset, as well as the conviction that ritual behavior demands a public setting to be effective. If ritual is a form of language, there has to be a community to whom we "speak." Beyond this, the broadest structure that Jewish religion imposes on our lives is the distinction between this people and other peoples. At the very least, then, particularly in our pluralistic society, the place where we encounter other Jews is in the synagogue and in prayer. Whatever else transpires or fails to transpire in the synagogue, it serves as the setting for our sense of community.

Second, the challenge raised by the conflicts between the theological content of the liturgy and our own theologies merits more serious consideration. The liturgy expresses the classic Jewish myth. More than any other text—with the exception of the Bible—here is where we encounter normative Jewish teaching. In reality, the liturgy is a Jewish form of the Catholic Credo—that portion of the Mass where the Catholic articulates the belief content of Christianity. And because Jewish law requires us to recite specific prayers on specific occasions, our religious tradition hands us a built-in opportunity to articulate what we stand for theologically as Jews.

But what happens when we no longer believe what the liturgy says, for example, that we are the chosen people, that God will resurrect the dead at the end of days, that abundant rainfall or drought are God's reward or punishment for our behavior, or that we hope for a restoration of the Temple cult with its sacrificial rites?

The two most familiar strategies for dealing with this problem are either to poeticize the translation so as to soften the impact of the traditional text, or to change the Hebrew text itself in line with our own beliefs. Thus, to illustrate the first approach, some of our prayer books preserve the traditional Hebrew text of the benediction in the *Amidah,* which praises God as One who is *mehayei hametim* (literally: "revives the dead"), but we translate the phrase as "Master of life and death" (as in *Siddur Sim Shalom,* published in 1985 by Conservative Judaism's Rabbinical Assembly and United Synagogue of America). This alternative translation stretches the meaning of the original to make it more palatable to modern ears. The question is how much can the meaning of the text be stretched? At what point does it become a dishonest translation that plays on the fact that most of our congregants do not understand Hebrew?

Proponents of this strategy do not want to provide an accurate, literal translation of the Hebrew text. Their goal is, rather, to render the Hebrew in devotional or poetic English that enables those who can not read Hebrew to use the traditional liturgy in prayer. But even devotional English can have theological content, which may be more or less in line with that of the original Hebrew.

The second strategy is more radical. It confronts the fact that the original Hebrew text of the liturgy has a precise meaning, that this meaning has become unacceptable to the editor and his community, and hence that it must be changed. To continue the example from above, Mordecai Kaplan changes the Hebrew text of the *mehayei hametim* benediction to read "who in love rememberest Thy creatures unto life." This strategy is not vulnerable to the charge of dishonesty. But its inevitable trade-offs are, first, that the prayer book loses its role as one of the classic, unifying texts of our religious community. Second, the liturgy is in a state of constant flux, as passages are added, dropped, or added again in line with changing theological fashion. Finally, the liturgy can no longer be studied as the authentic formulation of the classic Jewish belief structure. In fact, it can be claimed that Kaplan misunderstood the central purpose of liturgy which is, precisely, to create a religious community in the first place by propounding a classic formulation of its belief structure.

A third possible strategy would be to preserve the Hebrew

text *and* to translate it accurately and literally. The contemporary Jew, then, is asked to confront that text in its original meaning with full awareness of the discrepancy between what the text says and what some contemporary Jews in fact believe. This option acknowledges that the liturgy embodies classic Jewish teaching and therefore should not serve as the setting for the ongoing task of theological reformulation. That task has to be done, but elsewhere. In fact, it can not be done without an awareness of what the normative tradition has to say on any issue, and where else can we discover that but precisely in the liturgy.

Our task, then, in this view, is to confront the liturgy as formulated by preceding generations simply because that is what our community teaches, and then to struggle with the tension. In the synagogue, we say the words that our community has said for generations. At home and in class, we struggle with them and work on what we can appropriate as our own and what we can not. But we always return to the synagogue and to the prayer book to recite the traditional texts—as we always return to the original Bible, even though its contents sometimes disturb us.

This last strategy is also not universally effective. The reality is that our Hebrew liturgy is by no means totally inviolate. It has changed over the centuries in response to changing historical conditions. We too will want to make certain liturgical changes, most notably when a liturgical text has become offensive to members of our congregation today. For example, many Jewish men now find it difficult to praise God (in the early morning benedictions) "for not having made me a woman." Here, a poetic translation will not help. There is no alternative but to change the Hebrew text so that we now praise God for having "made me in His image." None of these three strategies excludes the others, then, and in reality, we use all three at different times. But some of us feel that we should be notably conservative about changing the Hebrew liturgy itself.

Finally, the great moments in the Jewish year and in a Jewish life are sanctified by elaborate pageants where liturgy and ritual—the language of words and the language of the body—come together, each doing what it does best. The ritual provides the drama and the affect. It is the visible, public expression that knits the participants into a community. The words provide the specificity. They tell us, clearly and distinctly, just what is happening and how the community understands this moment.

Thus as the foreskin is cut at a circumcision, the words tell us that what we are doing goes back to Abraham and binds still one more Jew to Israel's covenant. At the Passover *seder* we eat the bitter herbs, and the words tell us that we are tasting the bitterness of our ancestor's slavery. After a death we rend our garments, and the words tell us that though our lives have been torn by the death of a loved one, God's judgment is true and just. At a wedding, the bride and groom stand together under the *huppah,* and the words tell us that they are recreating the coming together of the first man and woman in Eden.

The greatest testimony to the power of these pageants is the sense of emptiness that we feel when we have no way of marking some significant occasion. There is, as yet, no accepted memorial to the Holocaust on Yom Ha-Shoah, or fixed celebration of the establishment of the State of Israel on Yom Ha-Atzmaut, or an established ceremony to mark the birth of a female child. Some contemporary Jewish women have adopted the rituals of *kippah, tallit,* and *tefillin* in various permutations and have testified to the impact of these rituals on their lives as religious Jews. In all of these areas, we are in the midst of a process whereby new ritual forms are being created and tested. The experience is fascinating to watch, however anxiety provoking it may be. But it does give us some glimpse into the way in which ritual works in the living experience of a religious community.

"Isn't It Enough to Be a Good Person?"

There is no question that Judaism wants us to be "good people." In fact, according to Isaiah 1, Hosea 6:6, and most of prophetic literature, God wants us, *above all,* to be good people. He abhors the Sabbath and Festivals and Israel's sacrifices when they are accompanied by flagrant violations of His moral law. Above all, He wants us to be concerned with the oppressed and the disadvantaged, with justice and compassion. His destruction

of the Temple as punishment for the moral failings of the biblical community is powerful testimony to the hierarchy of values
in prophetic religion.

But it is also clear that Isaiah is not denouncing the Sabbath,
the Festivals, and the sacrificial cult themselves. After all, a later
prophet, Ezekiel, prophesied at length about the rebuilding of the
Temple, and the returning exiles did rebuild it with the explicit
approval of that generation's prophets (Haggai 1:2ff). What
Isaiah could not tolerate was the place that ritual had assumed in
the life of the community. Jeremiah 7:8–15 is even more precise.
The Temple had come to be viewed as a magical guarantor of
security. The Israelites seem to have assumed that as long as there
was a Temple, as long as the proper sacrifices were offered, they
could do anything else they wished and still be safe, for God
would never dare to destroy His Temple. But He did—and in
so doing, He said loudly and clearly that the Temple was created
not for His sake but, rather, for the sake of a community of
human beings. This seems to be the Bible's way of affirming what
modern scholars have recently rediscovered: that ritual serves a
powerful human—and not a divine—need.

The choice, then, is never between being a good person and
a ritually observant Jew, but rather between competing ritual
systems. Our problem is that we belong to multiple communities
with multiple ritual systems. Sometimes our different communities cohere; we can have a kosher wedding dinner at the Plaza
Hotel. But sometimes they don't; we can't serve shrimp cocktail
at a kosher wedding. And then we have to choose. Who are we?
Where do we belong? What is our identity? With that choice
comes the choice of a ritual system.

Of the six positions outlined above, most of us will under-
stand Jewish ritual as either obedience to God's will, as symbolic
behavior, or as a set of Jewish folkways. The issues involved in
making that choice are both theological and programmatic.
Theologically, obedience implies a literalist view of revelation.
Deny that and you are forced into one of the two alternatives.
Between these two, the folkways option—following Mordecai
Kaplan—usually assumes a more naturalist (as opposed to super-

naturalist) concept of God. The symbolist position will be able to accommodate a supernaturalist God, providing it is understood that all of our concepts of God are symbolic and mythical.

Programmatically, the latter two positions can accept the fact that rituals can "die" or lose their power to move us, and that new rituals can be generated by the community. The obedience position can not abide that possibility. Nor can it abide the possibility that a ritual can become morally offensive to segments of the community—as, for example, modern Jewish feminists claim some synagogue rituals have become.

But extreme caution should be exercised in doing away with rituals, however much they seem to have lost their power. We never know when they may be reinfused with meaning, and the process of creating new rituals from scratch is long and arduous. Both the symbolist and the folkways position will tend to be more tolerant of pluralistic ritual patterns and extended periods of indecision. They are more willing to let the process of eliminating, revising, retaining, or creating ritual anew work itself out within the life experience of a community.

Finally, it should be absolutely clear that neither of these latter positions advocates a contraction in ritual behavior. If we live in an age of communal fragmentation, anomie, and isolation, or rootlessness and emotional aridity, then more than ever we need ritual, even more theatrically performed than ever before— even if some of us no longer believe, as our ancestors did, that God explicitly commanded us to act in these seemingly arbitrary ways. If God did not command, then maybe we can discern a commanding voice in our very human nature and in our communal needs, and we may be prepared to hearken as obediently to this voice as our ancestors did to God's.

For Further Study
Much of the pioneering work on the role of ritual in religion has been done by social scientists. Emile Durkheim's The Elementary Forms of the Religious Life *(pb Free Press, 1965) is commonly acknowledged to be a classic statement. More recently, Victor Turner is consid-*

ered to have been a seminal thinker. See, in particular, his THE RITUAL PROCESS *(Aldine, 1969; pb Cornell University Press, 1977) and* THE FOREST OF SYMBOLS *(Cornell University Press, 1967; pb 1970). Mary Douglas'* NATURAL SYMBOLS *(Pantheon, 1970; pb 1973) and* PURITY AND DANGER *(pb Routledge and Kegan Paul, 1978) are extremely suggestive, particularly ch. 3 of the latter volume, which provides a conceptual scheme for dealing with ritual in biblical religion. The role of ritual in creating structures and distinctions in what we eat and how we dress is based on this chapter. Finally, Mircea Eliade's* THE SACRED AND THE PROFANE *(pb Harcourt Brace Jovanovich, 1959) discusses the way in which religious ritual structures space and time. Eviatar Zerubavel's* THE SEVEN DAY CIRCLE: THE HISTORY AND MEANING OF THE WEEK *(Collier Macmillan, 1985) is a fascinating study of the ways in which cultural factors influence our structuring of time. With the exception of the chapter from* PURITY AND DANGER, *little of this material focuses specifically on Jewish religion but all of it is extraordinarily helpful in dealing with our own problems with ritual today.*

Specifically on Jewish ritual, Abraham Joshua Heschel's THE SABBATH: ITS MEANING FOR MODERN MAN *(pb Farrar, Straus and Young, 1951) deals with much more than the Sabbath and is, in fact, a Jewish version, couched in Heschel's inimitable style, of the anthropological approach to religious ritual. A concise but suggestive discussion of the Sabbath ritual as a system of symbolic behavior is in ch. 7 of Erich Fromm's* THE FORGOTTEN LANGUAGE *(pb H. Holt & Co., 1951). Mordecai Kaplan's use of the term "Jewish folkways" is elaborated in ch. 29 of his* JUDAISM AS A CIVILIZATION *(enlarged edition, The Reconstructionist Press, 1957; pb Jewish Publication Society, 1981). Jacob Neusner has devoted a good deal of his scholarly writings to understanding ritual patterns in talmudic religion. His* THE ENCHANTMENTS OF JUDAISM *(Basic Books, 1987) is a remarkably accessible statement of many of his conclusions. Lawrence A. Hoffman's* BEYOND THE TEXT: A HOLISTIC APPROACH TO LITURGY *(Indiana University Press, 1987; pb 1989) is an extraordinarily rich exploration of worship in Jewish religion from an anthropological point of view. It extends our discussion of the symbolist approach in this chapter. See also my own "Rituals, Myths and Communities" in* THE SEMINARY

AT 100, *edited by Nina Beth Cardin and David Wolf Silverman (The Rabbinical Assembly and The Jewish Theological Seminary of America, 1987; pb 1987) and the further bibliographical references appended thereto.*

Graham Greene's THE HEART OF THE MATTER *(pb Penguin, 1978) is a stunning statement of the power of the Eucharist ritual in Roman Catholic Christianity.*

Nothing else in print even begins to approach the sensitivity of Abraham Joshua Heschel's discussion of prayer in Judaism in the first four chapters of MAN'S QUEST FOR GOD *(see ch. 8). This study is simply indispensable.*

X

The End of Days:
What Will Be?

ESCHATOLOGY IS THE BRANCH OF THEOLOGY THAT DEALS WITH the culmination of human history as we know it. The literal meaning of the word is "discourse about the final events" (Greek: *eschatos*, last, final; *logos*, discourse). In Judaism, these events include the coming of the Messiah; the universal recognition of the God of Israel as Lord of all creation; the end of warfare and the inauguration of an age of universal peace and justice; the end of the exile and the reestablishment of Jewish sovereignty in the Holy Land; the rebuilding of the Temple and the reestablishment of the sacrificial cult; the meting out of God's final judgment on all of humanity; the resurrection of the dead and the bestowal of ultimate immortality on the righteous.

In no other area of theology is dogmatism less justified since no human being can be certain as to how this scenario will evolve. Consequently, on this topic, the characteristic Jewish reluctance to speak systematically about its belief structure reaches its apogee. Since none of us knows what will happen at the end of days, Jewish thinkers have given their imagination free rein and espoused a wide spectrum of beliefs—including their opposites. Since Jewish theology has no formal or final authority structure for declaring one doctrine authentic and another heretical, the field is wide open. The only significant exception to this anti-dogmatic stance is the first paragraph in the tenth chapter of

Mishnah Sanhedrin. This tractate lists three types of people as having no "share in the world to come," including the one who denies the resurrection of the dead (or who denies that the resurrection of the dead is taught in the Torah—the text is in dispute). Apart from this significant instance, talmudic literature is replete with the most variegated descriptions of possible eschatological scenarios.

Judaism takes eschatology very seriously. Every liturgy, every rite of passage, every significant statement of Jewish belief, and every important movement in Jewish history in some way contains an explicit eschatological reference. Traditionally, every sermon delivered before a congregation of Jews concluded with the words: "He shall come as a redeemer to Zion . . ." (Isaiah 59:20) in conjunction with the fulfillment of the preacher's exhortations. Every Sabbath was experienced as a "foretaste" of the age to come. From early in the talmudic period to this very day, in every synagogue throughout the world, every service of worship concludes with the *Alenu* prayer, which reaches its climax with the words of Zechariah: "And the Lord shall be king over all the earth; in that day there shall be one Lord with one name" (14:9).

Even when Jews formally abandoned their religion in favor of a more national or cultural form of identification, they could not abandon Jewish eschatology. The most obvious example is political Zionism, which is simply Jewish eschatology in a modern, secular garb. Zionism's emphasis on the ingathering of exiles and the establishment of a Jewish state under Jewish sovereignty, the socialist ideology of the kibbutz movement, the vision that Jewish self-fulfillment would have redemptive value for the rest of humanity—all these echo Jewish eschatological teachings. Christianity, of course, presents itself as the fulfillment of the Jewish eschatological hope, by affirming that the birth of Jesus of Nazareth marked the onset of the end of days. The *eschaton* is here, at least in embryo.

We can not ignore the significance of this material, not only in Judaism but for the intellectual history of the West as well. Yet we have to proceed with caution. Here, especially, it is mandatory that we understand all of our claims as mythical. Since the events that we describe lie completely beyond our experience, our formulations have to be taken as poetic, dramatic, impressionistic visions—never objective, scientific forecasts. They are in no way provable or disprovable. They do what great myths have always done: infuse meaning into our lives, generate emotion, mobilize us to action, inspire loyalty, and reveal unsuspected dimensions in our experience.

The first of these functions—a response to our search for ultimate meaning—is indispensable. All of us live with the fear that in the cosmic order of things, our lives have little actual significance, that we really don't count, that what we do or don't do makes little difference beyond our immediate lives. An eschatological myth is the most effective weapon against this kind of nihilism and despair. It holds out the promise that however trivial or irrelevant our lives may appear, they still have transcendent import. History is not simply a random series of events; it had a beginning, and it moves toward an end that we can help shape. Our lives can make a difference. Whatever else religion can do for us, it must yield a sense of that ultimate significance. That's why every great religion has an eschatology.

The Three Dimensions of Jewish Eschatology
Jewish eschatology has a history of its own. In its maturity, from the dawn of the Talmudic era (first century C.E.) to our own day, it works on three interrelated levels: the individual human being, the people of Israel, and all of humankind. The first deals with the ultimate fate of the individual human being after death; the second, with the destiny of the Jewish people; the third, with a vision for society and the world as a whole.

Of these three, the latter two emerge almost fully formed in the Bible itself. The first is alluded to only in a late (second century B.C.E.) biblical text (Daniel 12:2). It appears, however, in a number of the apocryphal books (Greek: *apokruphos,* hidden, i.e., books that were "hidden away," or not accepted into the Hebrew Bible, but were included in its Greek and Latin translations) dating from roughly the same era, such as 2 Maccabees. It is not until the emergence of the Rabbinic era in the first century C.E. that Judaism has anything significant to say about the afterlife of the individual.

We can speculate about why this is so. First, the Bible is primarily concerned with the destiny of the community as a whole. Only rarely—Job and some of the Psalms are the most notable instances—does it express the concerns of an individual. Second, the Bible can not conceive that a human being would survive death. Only God does not die; if human beings survived death, they would become like God. To the extent that the Bible says anything about the ultimate destiny of the individual human being, then, that destiny is exhausted by what occurs during the individual's lifespan.

The Bible's resistance to offering the individual human being some form of an afterlife is expressed in the notion that contact with the dead causes ritual defilement *(tum'ah)*; anyone who touches a corpse, or even steps under the roof of a building containing a corpse, can not participate in the Temple cult or even enter the Sanctuary. These restrictions primarily affected the priests *(kohanim),* the biblical "clergy" who officiated at the cult. This body of law served as a barrier against any form of ancestor worship, a common practice in the ancient Near East that the Bible strenuously opposes. The Bible could not tolerate a cult of the dead.

None of the biblical personalities—not even Moses—survives death. The bereaved Jacob (Genesis 37:35 and 42:38) understands that if his children are dead, he is eternally cut off from them. Job never invokes an anticipated afterlife to ease his pain in this life; in fact, he knows that his death is the end (7:6–10). Psalm 115:16–17 insists that only the living can praise God, not the dead; and Psalm 146:3–4 teaches that we should trust only in God and not in mortals, for when man's "breath departs, he returns to the dust" and then "his plans come to nothing."

Numerous biblical passages do allude to a place called *She'ol,* some ill-defined netherworld where the dead go after death and where they lead some form of shadowy existence. But the Bible provides no systematic description of *She'ol,* and Psalm 6:6 insists that "there is no praise of You among the dead; in Sheol, who can acclaim You?"

Apart from this, two biblical personalities are described as never having died—Enoch who "walked with God; then he was no more, for God took him" (Genesis 5:24); and Elijah, who "went up to heaven in a whirlwind" (2 Kings 2:11)—but neither can be said to have survived death. The strange story (1 Samuel 28:7–24) of how "a woman who consults ghosts" raises Samuel from his grave on behalf of a despairing King Saul is totally idiosyncratic; it has neither parallels nor support in the rest of the Bible. Finally, Ezekiel's vision of the dry bones that are revived (Ezekiel 37:1–14) is clearly an allegory for God's national redemption of Israel (v. 11), and has nothing to do with a human being's bodily resurrection after death.

In the Bible itself, then, an individual's destiny is complete during his lifespan on earth. In contrast, the Bible is positively voluble about the national and universal dimensions of the eschatological scenario. Although the Pentateuch itself, which covers Israel's historical experience from the Exodus from Egypt to the eve of its entry into the promised land, knows of no future beyond that latter event, the scope of the vision expands dramatically during the age of classical prophecy (ca. 750–450 B.C.E.). Eschatological motifs emerge in the books of two of the earliest prophets, Amos and Hosea. Amos speaks of a "day of the Lord" (5:18–20, 8:8–10) on which God will wreak vengeance on those who defy Him, reversing even the order of nature as part of this cosmic upheaval. Out of this trauma will emerge "the remnant of Joseph" (5:15) who "seek to do good" or who "seek the Lord" (5:6) and who will become the foundation of the new order.

Hosea portrays this new order through the symbol of a new covenant that God will strike with a regenerated Israel, a covenant that Israel will be constitutionally incapable of flouting, so much will human nature itself be transformed (2:20–25; cf. Jeremiah 31:30–33). Indeed, the new covenant will have cosmic implications; it will affect even "the beasts of the field, the birds of the air, and the creeping things of the ground; I will banish bow, sword, and war from the land. Thus I will let them lie down in safety. . . . I will respond to the sky, and it shall respond to the earth; And the earth shall respond with new grain and wine and oil. . . ." All of these national and cosmic motifs remain at the heart of Jewish eschatology to this day.

The richest elaboration of this scenario is in the Book of Isaiah. Isaiah expands Amos' description of the "day of the Lord" (2:12–21) and the expectation that a remnant of the faithful who have returned to the Lord will be saved (10:20–22). But Isaiah goes well beyond Amos in prophesying the ultimate destruction of all idolatry (contra Deuteronomy 4:19, which accepts idolatry as the legitimate lot of the gentiles), leading to a universal age of peace and harmony (11:1–14). That vision of a renewed cosmic order remains one of the universally acknowledged masterpieces of world literature. Monotheism will become the faith of all people who will stream to learn Torah from Israel (2:2–4). The national and the universal motifs come together; Israel's redemption becomes the instrument for the redemption of the cosmos as a whole.

Note that all of these events will take place "in the days to come" (2:2), that is, at some specific date in historical time, not, as commonly translated, "at the end of days." By and large, Isaiah and his fellow prophets always address a concrete historical and social situation. When Isaiah prophesies the destruction of heathendom, he is referring to a specific empire, Assyria, originally the rod of God's anger (10:5), that is, designated by God to punish Israel for its rebellion, but now become haughty and self-righteous. Both the evils that Isaiah denounces and their obliteration are concrete and specific. God's judgment takes place within history. The emphasis is eminently "this worldly," not "other worldly."

Finally, it is Isaiah who teaches that this new age will be brought about by a charismatically endowed descendant of the Davidic line whose reign will be justice incarnate (9:5–6; 11:1–5). These passages were later to serve as proof texts for the post-biblical notion of *the* Messiah (literally, "the anointed one"), a uniquely designated being with extraordinary powers whom God will send to introduce the new order. But in the Bible itself, anointment with oil was simply the ritual whereby kings and high priests were set apart from the rest of humanity. Saul (1 Samuel 10:1), David (1 Samuel 16:13), and Solomon (1 Kings 1:39) were all anointed, as was the first of the High Priests, Aaron (Leviticus 8:30). In a derivative sense, the Persian emperor Cyrus, who had been chosen by God to restore Israel to its home after the exile, is referred to as God's "anointed one" (Isaiah 45:1). Throughout the Bible, then, the messianic king is a human being who is anointed as a ritual of appointment, not because he is a divine being. The change in the messianic image took place much later as Jewish eschatology evolved from the biblical "this-worldly" vision to a more apocalyptic, "other-worldly" one.

From This World to Another

The destruction of Jerusalem and the Temple in 586 B.C.E. and the experience of exile that followed was a watershed in Jewish history. From that time on, all eschatological scenarios envisioned the end of the exile, the restoration of Israel's sovereignty, and the rebuilding of the Temple as preconditions for the universal redemption to follow. Jeremiah teaches that the exile is the indispensable purgatory experience that must be undergone by all who sinned against the Lord (24:1–10). But it will end—Jeremiah assigns it a term of seventy years (29:10), a classical biblical round figure that signifies an eon—and it will be followed by the final destruction of heathendom and the return of the exiled community to its home, which Jeremiah portrays in rhapsodic terms (31:1–40). God's new covenant—following Hosea—will have a transformatory effect on human nature itself, making it impossible for anyone to rebel against God anymore (31:30–33). Once again, "I will be their God and they shall be My people." The old intimacy will be restored—this time, for eternity.

The exile did end, not in seventy years but in less than fifty (with the edict of Cyrus in 539 B.C.E.). But the new reality proved to be far from the dream. Only a portion of the people chose to return; the greater part remained in Persia. The land itself was impoverished, the neighboring peoples were a constant threat, and Judea remained under Persian, and later Hellenistic, rule for four centuries. But Israel was to undergo a far longer exile after the destruction of the second Temple (in 70 C.E.), and the prophetic visions of an ultimate redemption yet to come acquired a new urgency.

There was an undeniable gap, then, between the messianic vision of the prophets and the historical experience of the community in the six centuries that spanned the return from the first exile and the destruction of the second Temple. It was the awareness of this gap that led to a gradual extension of the eschatological scenario out of historical time and into some *olam habah* or "age (not world) to come," where the historical conditions of *olam hazeh,* "this age," would no longer be decisive.

If we can not find fulfillment in history, we will find it "beyond" history. Isaiah's "days to come" become "the end of days," an age that is liberated from the pain of this familiar one. The eschatological scenario takes on an increasingly fantastic coloration. The Messianic figure takes on increasingly superhuman powers; the "final judgment" becomes a cosmic event; the geographies of paradise and hell are elaborated in striking detail; God's war against the evil kingdom of Gog of the land of Magog, first described in Ezekiel 38–39, becomes a cosmic struggle against evil itself, leading to the establishment of a new social and natural order under the sovereign rule of God.

Once the eschatological scenario is liberated from historical time and from the conditions of this familiar world, it also becomes possible to free the destiny of the individual human being from the limitations of the grave. It is in this setting that the two doctrines of the resurrection of the body and the immortality of the individual human soul are absorbed into Jewish eschatological thinking.

The New Eschatological Individualism

The seedbed for this new vision had already been well prepared. First, prophecy had recognized that an individual's destiny should not be determined by that of the community or of anyone but the individual himself. Exodus 34:7 insists that the iniquity of the parents can be visited upon their children and children's children, but Jeremiah 31:30 and Ezekiel 18:4 (anticipated by Deuteronomy

24:16) countermand that decree: "The person who sins, only he shall die."

This new recognition that God cares as much for the individual as He does for the community adds a certain urgency to the problem of theodicy, of reconciling God's justice with the prevalence of human suffering. The earliest biblical resolution of that dilemma was to explain suffering as God's punishment for sin. That resolution worked as long as the focus was on the community as a whole. But it is difficult to explain the suffering of the virtuous individual by submerging his fate in the fate of the community as a whole. What, then, is to be done with the problem of an individual's apparently unjustified suffering?

The solution is to broaden the frame so that a human lifespan on earth is but a tiny portion of our engagement with God. The death of our physical bodies is no longer the end of our being or of God's ability to relate to us. God now has an eternity to establish His justice. Even more, the new eschatology of the individual becomes the last triumphant statement of God's sovereign power. If God is truly God, then why should my death stand in the way of His accomplishing His purposes for me? In one stroke, then, two of biblical monotheism's central doctrines, God's power and His justice, are reaffirmed, paradoxically, through two doctrines that have no explicit basis in the earlier tradition: the doctrines of the resurrection, in the Messianic era, of human bodies and of the immortality of the human soul.

In their purest form, the two doctrines are contradictory. The Greek doctrine that the soul is immortal assumes a dualistic view of the human being. We are composed of a material, hence perishable, body and a nonmaterial, hence immortal (for what is nonmaterial can never be destroyed) soul that preexists the body, enters into it at birth, and leaves it at death to continue its eternal existence. The soul is the real person. During life, it is imprisoned in the body. But since it governs the body, it is responsible for the quality of the individual life and will either enjoy eternal blessedness or suffer eternal misery in the hereafter. In Greek thought, none of this has anything to do with God; it is simply part of the natural order of things.

When this Greek doctrine enters Judaism, it becomes transformed. The notion of an eternal, preexisting soul, distinct from the body, has no basis in the Bible itself. There, the Hebrew terms *nefesh* or *neshamah,* which later came to designate the soul, simply means "person" (as in Exodus 1:5 and Psalm 150:6). The "breath of life" that God blows into the nostrils of the first man (Genesis 2:7) is clearly not an independently existing entity, but rather some vivifying power that animates the clod of dust.

Rabbinic literature, in contrast, does recognize the soul as a distinct entity that preexists the body and has a life of its own after the death of the body until, that is, the moment of resurrection and ultimate judgment. But perhaps because of its biblical precedents, even rabbinic Judaism could not tolerate the sharp dualism of the Greek doctrine. There is no trace of the deprecation of the body or of bodily pleasures that we find in Greek philosophical literature. Both the body and the soul are created by God, the two together define the individual, and both bear the responsibility for the quality of the individual life. In all cases, this is measured by obedience to God's Torah. Body and soul reunited will appear together before God for the final judgment and both will bear God's punishment or enjoy His reward.

Finally, the Jewish eschatological scenario centered on God's deliverance of Israel from exile and the regeneration of the community as a whole. There was no way that Jews who had died over the centuries and had endured the infamy and even the martyrdom that came with their Jewishness could be denied a share in this ultimate reward. They too, then, had to be restored to life as part of this final act in the drama of history.

The doctrine of bodily resurrection is the outcome of all of these impulses. It is of Persian origin and alluded to only once in the Bible, in a second-century B.C.E. passage in Daniel 12:2. But by the time of the Mishnah (ca. 200 C.E.), it is listed as one of three cardinal Jewish beliefs; one who denies it or its biblical roots is deprived of a "share in the age to come" (*Sanhedrin* 10:1). In the second of the three opening paragraphs of the *Amidah,* the central prayer in every service of worship, the notion that God resurrects the dead is invoked five separate times in the course of four sentences; apparently the doctrine was sufficiently under contention in this early rabbinic context to warrant its emphasis in the liturgy as a way of establishing its authoritative status. The details of this resurrection may be foggy but the thrust is clear: Whatever happens to the individual after death must include the body, for the body is indispensable to our sense of self.

These two doctrines, however contradictory they may have been in their original form, coalesce in rabbinic theology. At the final judgment, the immortal soul and the resurrected body will come together again, and judgment will be rendered on the individual person as a whole. The righteous and repentant will enjoy the blessedness of the age to come; the evil and unrepentant will suffer eternal condemnation.

In those Jewish circles that were more strongly affected by Greek thinking, this synthesis was awkward at best. Maimonides, for example, the most sharply dualistic of Jewish thinkers, was convinced that the state of ultimate blessedness could only be reserved for the soul alone. But as an authentic rabbinic Jew, he had to accept the resurrection of the body; it is one of his thirteen principles. He reconciles the two doctrines by arranging them sequentially. First, during the age of the Messiah, bodies will be resurrected and will reunite with their souls. But this Messianic age will also be temporary. Ultimately everyone will die again, inaugurating the "age to come," when only the souls of the righteous will gain their eternal reward.

By accommodating bodily resurrection but reserving the ultimate reward for the soul alone, Maimonides incurs the sharp criticism of his arch antagonist, Abraham ben David of Posquières (ca. 1120–1198), who comments flatly: "The views of this man are tantamount to denying bodily resurrection." He then proceeds to quote a number of talmudic homilies in support of his own view that bodily resurrection is the ultimate eschatological reward. Throughout his career, Maimonides was forced to defend himself against the charge that his position was inauthentic and even heretical. But in fact, the details provided in talmudic literature are so diverse and fanciful that almost any scenario could find some support.

From the age of the Talmud on, in one form or another and

despite their foreign origins, both of these doctrines—the resurrection of the body and the immortality of the soul—are accepted as authoritative Jewish teaching. In the process of their appropriation, these doctrines were thoroughly Judaized: The body/soul dualism was softened, the fate of the individual was integrated back into that of the community, reward and punishment were determined by obedience to Torah, and, finally, the entire scenario became a manifestation of God's power and justice. The result is that even though neither has an explicit basis in Scripture, in their Jewish form they emerge as a thoroughly natural extension of biblical monotheism.

This process of Judaizing two doctrines of foreign origin is a superb case study in the power of *midrash.* In their final form, they appear to be thoroughly natural extensions of biblical teachings. In fact, the new doctrines are then read back into the Bible and found to be supported by multiple proof texts that establish their authenticity. The biblical text itself remains closed, of course; it can not be altered. But it can be read and reread anew and in the process, infinite new layers of meaning can be uncovered. Thus an ancient tradition retains its vitality in multiple new cultural contexts.

Two Eschatological Voices

We are dealing, then, with a variegated and often contradictory ensemble of teachings, all of them projections into the indefinite future of whatever the believer imagined would embody the best possible conditions for the individual, the community, and the world as a whole. But how was it possible for any one thinker or movement to pull this material into a coherent and systematic whole, to give it shape and structure so that it could speak to the needs of the community?

In broad terms, over the centuries, Jews used two such integrating principles, that is, two dominant Jewish eschatological voices or tempers. One of the voices can be characterized as gradualist or evolutionary, the other, radical or revolutionary. These two voices differ on which of the various doctrines they choose to emphasize or ignore; how they knit these doctrines into coherent patterns; what roles they assign to God and to human beings in bringing about the eschatological scenario; how they understand the relationship between the current, familiar age and the Messianic age to come; and finally and most important, the emotional coloration that pervades the program as a whole.

Messianic gradualism sees the age to come *(olam habah)* as emerging slowly and imperceptibly out of the world as we know it *(olam hazeh),* as the natural culmination of a historical process. It rejects any sharp dichotomy or rupture between the two. This voice is patient and optimistic. It expresses a basic confidence that human beings can work on the details of their social and interpersonal lives and can achieve many small, partial redemptions as foretastes of the ultimate and complete redemption.

Evolutionary messianism sees the eschatological scenario not as an immediate demand but as a vision that yields hope for the future and infuses all human day-to-day activities with infinite meaning. It is more apt to portray the age to come in "this-worldly" terms, as taking place within the familiar world of space and time, within history. It sees the Messiah as a human being, extraordinarily endowed but human nevertheless, who will operate within familiar political structures to accomplish his goals.

In contrast, revolutionary messianism is pessimistic, despairing of humanity's ability to resolve its intrinsic problems in the normal course of affairs. It sees a radical discontinuity between the social order as we know it today and the age to come. This new age is viewed as post-historical rather than as the culmination of history, as "the end of days" rather than "the last days." At the core of this eschatological scenario is a cataclysmic event that will destroy the familiar order of nature and history and create a new one on its ruins. It describes this cataclysm in vividly "other-worldly" terms.

This voice demands a much more aggressive human role in bringing the new order about. It is less satisfied with partial redemptions. It views God as demanding that the community take its destiny into its own hands in a much more direct way, that it force His hand. This is the voice that leads human beings into radical political activity, or even into violent and militaristic behavior, in order to precipitate the end. In this view, the Messiah is more apt to be endowed with more-than-human qualities in order that he may initiate the final, cataclysmic act in the drama.

The gradualist voice is more sober, more low-keyed about its messianism, more quietistic, more apt to allow history to run its course. The revolutionary temper is more overtly messianic, more apt to put eschatology at the very top of its agenda, more aggressive about propounding and accelerating the scenario, more intensely involved in its outcome.

The core dispute between the two voices rests in the different ways they characterize the relationship between this familiar world and the Messianic age. The gradualist voice sees the two ages as essentially continuous; the first leads imperceptibly into the second. The revolutionary voice emphasizes the discontinuity between the two ages; it demands the collapse of the familiar world and, following a cataclysmic event that will overthrow the familiar patterns of nature and history, requires its replacement with a radically new era.

Finally, since theological speculation never takes place in a vacuum, specific historical contexts will encourage the emergence of one or the other of these two tempers. The revolutionary temper is more likely to emerge in periods of acute social conflict or oppression, as an expression of the community's despair about humanity, about the natural course of history or the fate of the Jewish people. However, in periods of relative calm, this radical temper tends to fade into the background and the more optimistic messianic temper becomes the governing voice. The interplay of these two traditions can be traced throughout the course of Jewish intellectual history to our own day.

Both of these voices have legitimate roots in the classical texts of Judaism. Amos's portrayal of a cataclysmic "day of the Lord" (5:18–20, 8:9–10) and Ezekiel's description of God's final defeat of the evil kingdoms of Gog and Magog (38–39) capture the urgency of the revolutionary temper. One of the distinctive themes of revolutionary messianism is the characterization of the events immediately preceding the appearance of the Messiah as "the footprints [or the "birthpangs"] of the Messiah," an age of unrelieved despair. Surprisingly, the classic portrayal of the bleakness of that pre-Messianic period is in the most sober of rabbinic texts, the Mishnah, in the main a code of law that occasionally strays into theological speculation: "With the footprints of the Messiah, presumption shall increase and dearth reach its height; the vine shall yield fruit but the wine shall be costly; the empire shall fall into heresy and there shall be none to utter reproof. . . . The wisdom of the Scribes shall become insipid, they that shun sin shall be deemed contemptible, and truth shall nowhere be found. Children shall shame the elders, and the elders shall rise up before the children. . . . On whom can we rely? On our Father in heaven (*Sotah* 9:15)." (It should also be noted, however, that scholars believe that this entire section is a later interpolation into the text of the Mishnah.)

That last poignant cry epitomizes the despair that underlies revolutionary messianism. Indeed, when the familiar structures of both nature and history have crumbled, whom else can we rely on if not our Father in Heaven? Since it is the community that designates a specific age as pre-Messianic, it is only natural for that same community to produce an explicitly messianic movement centered about a figure who claims to be the Messiah and who announces that the long-promised age to come has indeed arrived.

Jewish history is littered with messianic movements that at first fired the imagination of the Jewish community but later came to be viewed as deceptive and premature. The most noteworthy are the first-century C.E. movement that centered about Jesus of Nazareth and eventually produced Christianity, and the seventeenth-century movement that centered about Sabbatai Zevi. From the perspective of the Jewish community, both of these episodes—and indeed all similar episodes—proved to be traumatic. The messianic expectations never materialized, the movements themselves were deeply divisive, and the demoralization they left in their wake proved to be more paralyzing than the despair that impelled them in the first place.

But it was not only this bitter historical experience that engendered an intuitive mistrust of revolutionary messianism; the revolutionary temper is itself fundamentally incompatible with the basic structures of Jewish religion. In a word, this temper is at heart anarchic, while Jewish religion had produced a series of structures—social, communal, experiential, and behavioral—that lend a sense of order, integrity, and predictability to Jewish life. However fragile these structures may have appeared, they were at least familiar and they provided a certain security against the storms of history. It is only natural that religious authorities would seek to conserve these structures and be suspicious of any movement that threatened them.

Messianic quietism fed on biblical passages that portrayed the age to come in much more understated terms. The tone of Isaiah's eschatological "day of the Lord" (2:2–4, 11:1–10) is notably more subdued than in Amos, and the eschatological scenario seems to evolve naturally and progressively out of the current state of affairs, as part of the natural course of history. The verse in Song of Songs 2:7, "I adjure you, O maidens of Jerusalem, by gazelles and by hinds of the field, do not awaken or rouse love until it please," is quoted against those who would aggressively press for the coming of the Messiah. Rabbinic texts caution against the attempt to calculate the precise date of his coming, as epitomized in the homily attributed to the first-century C.E. talmudic master, Rabban Yohanan ben Zakkai: "If you have a sapling in your hand and they tell you that the Messiah has arrived, first plant the sapling and then go out to greet him" (*Avot de-Rabbi Natan* B 31); and in the third century C.E. Samuel's claim: "The only difference between this age and the age to come is Israel's subjugation to the nations" (*Berakhot* 34b). Apart from this, nothing else will be changed.

Indeed, much later in Jewish history, Maimonides quotes this last passage again and again in his attempts to disabuse the community of their more fanciful portrayals of the days of the Messiah. This most sober of rationalists, who tried to dictate the substance of authentic Jewish belief to his contemporaries, was also the leading rabbinic and political spokesman of his age. Above all, he was aware that revolutionary messianism threatened not only the established structures of the community, but also the authority of the rabbinic interpretation of the Torah and of its rabbinic interpreters as well. Hovering in the background was the lesson of Christianity—its antinomianism and its divisive impact on the Jewish community. It was a vivid example of what can happen when revolutionary messianism gets out of hand.

Thus a tragic dialectic was set into motion. Pray constantly for the Messiah, but don't do anything—apart from the normative demands of the Torah—to hasten his coming. Fashion elaborate images of the age to come, but don't try to calculate when it will arrive. Above all, suspect those who tell you it is at hand. Have faith that it will come, in God's good time, and in the natural course of events. Maimonides' twelfth principle (of the thirteen) says it all: "We are to believe as a fact that the Messiah will come and not consider him late. If he delays, wait for him [based on *Habakkuk* 2:3]; set no time limit for his coming."

In the meantime, the life experience of the Jew was sprinkled with tantalizing anticipations of messianism fulfilled. The rabbis romanticized the Sabbath as a "foretaste" of the age to come. Every High Holiday period provided a mini-experience of the final judgment. Every Grace after Meals prayed for the rebuilding of Jerusalem; every *Amidah,* for the restoration of the Temple. Every service of worship ended with the prophecy of Zechariah of a day when "the Lord shall be king over all the earth; in that day there shall be one Lord with one name" (14:9). These anticipatory experiences effectively served as an outlet for the messianic fervor that simmered beneath the surface of Jewish life throughout the long years of the dispersion. They remained anticipations, tokens, or substitutes for the real thing yet to come, but they succeeded in blunting the revolutionary impulse that seemed so threatening.

The tension persists to this day. After centuries of waiting, in our day Israel has regained its sovereignty. One of the classical dimensions of Jewish eschatology has been fulfilled—some would say in miraculous fashion. Yet the Jewish diaspora persists and remains vital and creative. And certainly, the broader, universalistic expectations of the prophets seem to be as far from fulfillment as ever. In this context, some Jews identify the establishment of the modern State of Israel (in the liturgy of the Grace after Meals and in the prayer for Israel composed by its Chief Rabbinate) as "the first flowering of our redemption." Others, reflecting on the very partial and incomplete nature of this modern development, seem to have inherited the age-old suspicion of too hasty messianic claims and prefer to continue to wait.

Modern Transformations

If any single event could possibly blunt the seductiveness of the revolutionary impulse in Jewish messianism, it would surely have been the collapse of the Sabbatian messianic movement in 1666, when Sabbatai Zevi converted to Islam, just one year after having proclaimed himself the Jewish Messiah.

Sabbatianism, the name given to the messianic movement that he inspired, is one of the most painful chapters in Jewish history. That this man proclaimed himself the Messiah is not by itself surprising—he was not the first Jew to do so. But that millions flocked to his banner, that the movement spread into eastern and western Europe, that its collapse traumatized the Jewish community for two centuries thereafter, and, most interesting of all, that in some circles his apostasy was justified as a legitimate phase in his messianic mission—all of this is testimony to the anarchic power of the revolutionary messianic impulse among the masses of Jews.

In the perspective of history, it is clear why some Jewish historians claim that the collapse of this dream also marked the collapse of a certain way of structuring Jewish religious life. It effectively marks the transition from the Jewish middle ages into modernity.

The inner, theological, and historical dynamics of Sabbatian messianism are not at all clear. The reigning interpretation, in place for the past half-century, was propounded in the writings of the late Gershom Scholem, the German-Israeli scholar who literally created the field of Jewish mysticism as a scholarly discipline and whose monumental biography of Sabbatai Zevi is commonly recognized as one of the masterpieces of contemporary Jewish scholarship. But more recently, Scholem's understanding of these events has been challenged in the work of a younger Israeli scholar, Moshe Idel, whose writings have forced us to take a new look at the entire episode.

Scholem insists that Sabbatai Zevi has to be understood as the almost predictable outcome of the mystical theology of Isaac Luria (1534–1572), developed in Safed in the Holy Land roughly a generation after the expulsion of Spanish Jewry. We have alluded to various aspects of Lurianic mysticism in other contexts. For our purposes here, the central theme of this elaborate system is the mystery of exile and redemption. Lurianic mysticism is in fact a complex myth that enabled Luria's generation to deal with its renewed sense of homelessness following the expulsion from Spain.

Luria transformed exile from a historical event into a metaphysical symbol for all that is wrong, out of joint, imperfect, or unredeemed in creation, for all historical and natural traumas. Exile is the symbol for the fault that cuts through all of God's creation. Not only Israel but all of creation and, shockingly, even God Himself is in exile. In Luria's mystical theology, God has two faces, two aspects: the *Ein-Sof,* or infinite, hidden face, God in Himself, in His essence; and the *Shekhinah,* or the revealed, accessible God, which, according to the Lurianic myth, is co-extensive with the created world. In our current unredeemed state, these two aspects of God are split apart; Luria refers to this condition as *Galut Shekhinah,* literally "the exile of the *Shekhinah,*" recalling a talmudic homily that God accompanied His people into exile, as an expression of His wish to cast His fate with Israel. Even God Himself, then, shares this state of disharmony.

Exile, then, is a metaphor for the state of the world in this period between the blissful harmony of paradise at the moment of creation, and the equally blissful messianic age to come when that original harmony will be restored. In the meantime, we live in the age of history, and to be in history means to be in exile—a fate that even God shares.

Luria's most startling claim, however, is that the responsibility for redeeming Israel, the world, and even God lies in the hands of Israel. If exile is a state of brokenness throughout, Luria's symbol for redemptive activity is *tikkun,* literally "repair." Israel's task is to "repair the world," and the redemptive tools are the *mitzvot.* Every single *mitzvah,* when performed with that specific intent, has immediate and cosmic redemptive power. When enough Jews perform enough *mitzvot,* all the exiles—not only Israel's national exile but the cosmic exile throughout creation and God's exile as well—will end. The coming of the Messiah will symbolize God's acknowledgment that the process of *tikkun* has been thoroughly accomplished.

There is no questioning the power and grandeur of this myth for the Jew who embraced it. However painful his or her own experience, it was but a microcosm of a far greater pain that transfigured the cosmos as a whole. But the myth did even more. It gave the Jew the power to bring this cosmic pain to an end. It infused every one of his or her everyday responsibilities with infinite significance. Is it any wonder, then, that the myth captured the imagination of the generation after the expulsion from Spain; or that, some decades later, when Sabbatai Zevi proclaimed that the process of *tikkun* had been accomplished, that the exile was at an end and that he was the Messiah, masses of Jews believed?

The Lurianic myth inherited not only the seductiveness of revolutionary messianism but its intrinsic problems as well: its tendency to see eschatology as the linchpin of the system as a whole; its aggressive, almost controlling temper; its vision that human beings can predetermine how and when God will work in history; and the fervor that animates the program as a whole. It was also excessively concrete, too narrowly tied to history. Great myths have to be concrete in order to have affective power, but their concreteness is always in tension with a certain elusiveness. Myths are sublime metaphors, poetic constructs that capture dimensions of reality beyond normal experience. Lurianic mysticism, precisely because it was designed to cope with a concrete historical situation, was prepared to sacrifice much of its elusiveness in favor of a highly concrete interpretation of history.

Sabbatianism as a heresy dates from the moment when the Lurianic myth came into conflict with historical events—in this case, Sabbatai Zevi's apostasy. When that happens, two choices are possible: either deny the myth or deny history. In an earlier age, the disciples of another messianic figure, Jesus of Nazareth, chose to deny history. Jesus may have died on the cross, but his disciples believed that he was resurrected, ascended to heaven, and would return to earth again. With this denial in place, the early Church proceeded to rationalize Jesus' death by remythologizing the events of his life. He was really a divine being all along, God incarnate, or the son of God, born miraculously of a virgin and hence spared of original sin. His death was preordained as his vicarious atonement for the sins of mankind. Paradoxically, Jesus' death then becomes his triumph. This denial of history made the birth of Christianity possible.

Some of Sabbatai Zevi's followers also chose to deny history: His apostasy was rationalized as a preordained, climactic act of *tikkun*. In order to vanquish evil, the Messiah had to embrace it in this direct and personal way. Only thus could he complete his mission. It was no accident, Scholem points out, that this ultimate defense was propounded among the Marranos—Spanish Jews who converted to Christianity under the threat of death but continued to affirm their Jewishness in secret. They, better than anyone else, understood the tragic paradox of Sabbatai Zevi's apostasy.

The opposite response, denial of the myth—or at least the overtly eschatological dimensions of the myth—led to the emergence of Hasidism. Scholem understands Hasidism as Lurianic mysticism minus its messianic core. In our terminology, Hasidism represents a return to the more gradualist messianism of the normative tradition. It provided a substitute eschatological experience through the Hasidic ideal of *devekut* (literally, "attachment") to God attainable through ecstatic prayer. Now the emphasis is on the individual, not the community, and on celebrating the normative institutions of the tradition as valid in and of themselves.

Of course, profound religious impulses such as revolutionary messianism never completely disappear. In this case, they simply went underground and emerged again, some generations later, in a secularized form, as political Zionism. The parallels between political Zionism and Lurianic eschatology are striking. Both assign the redemptive task to human beings and specify the concrete human actions that will bring about the desired redemption—the *mitzvot* in one, political activity in the other; both view the redemption of the community as the key to that of the individual; both place the eschatological goal at the center of the Jewish myth; and both have universal implications—an inherent part of the Zionist myth was the conviction that the redemption of the Jewish people would have an impact on society as a whole. Of course, Zionist messianism, at least in its early formulations, was strongly resisted by much of the religious community, not only for its secularism but also because of the painful memories of its previous incarnation several generations earlier.

Of the three original dimensions of Jewish eschatology—the universal, the national, and the individual—political Zionism focused on the national to the virtual exclusion of the other two. For its part, Reform Judaism, Zionism's competitor among nineteenth-century, western European Jewry, focused equally exclusively on the universal. Reform Judaism relegated the national life of the Jewish people to an early phase of its development. In the Modern age, Jewish national identity would be absorbed by the emerging European nation states and Judaism would become a religion alone. This led to the Reform movement's rejection of the hope for the return of the Jewish people to Zion and the reconstitution of Jewish national life on its own land. The national exile is no longer to be understood as a punishment. On the contrary, it is now part of a divine plan, the implementation of the Jewish mission to bring monotheism to the world. The Jewish messianic hope is now centered upon Isaiah's prophecy of an age of universal peace and justice when all peoples will recognize the God of Israel as Lord of creation.

This thesis—that the collapse of Sabbatian messianism led indirectly to the emergence of some decidedly nontraditional reformulations of Jewish religious teachings—is Scholem's most imaginative, far-reaching, and controversial contribution to modern Jewish intellectual history. Scholem sees Sabbatianism, for all its pernicious effects, as a liberating impulse that shattered the hold of rabbinic Judaism over Jewish religious life. Thus his claim that it marks the end of the Jewish middle ages and the transition into modernity.

Global scholarly claims of this kind are inherently controversial; they always seem overly simplistic when measured against the complexities they seek to understand. Indeed, the revisionist understanding of Sabbatianism, propounded by Moshe Idel, challenges Scholem's historical approach. Idel sees the roots of Sabbatian eschatology as deeply rooted in far earlier (i.e., Talmudic theurgic) traditions, not as a response to the expulsion from Spain at the end of the fifteenth century, and not as a simple extension of Lurianic mysticism. He views Scholem's attempt to trace a linear development from expulsion to Luria to Sabbatai Zevi to Hasidism and political Zionism as excessively simplistic. The ultimate resolution of this scholarly dispute, if indeed it can ever be resolved, lies in the hands of another generation of Jewish scholarship. But no one can question the impact of the Sabbatian episode on the narrower issue of Jewish eschatology itself.

Will Herberg on Jewish Eschatology

The most thoroughgoing contemporary reformulation of Jewish eschatology is attempted by Will Herberg, the late existentialist theologian, in his *Judaism and Modern Man.* Herberg discovered Judaism in his middle years via the writings of Martin Buber and Franz Rosenzweig. His earliest ideological commitment was to Marxism, which, from the perspective of his return to Judaism, he sees as a perfect secular parallel to revolutionary Jewish eschatology. Marxism imposes a three-phased scheme on history: first, an age of primal innocence (the Garden of Eden phase in Judaism), followed by a "fall" into the period of social evil and a class-oriented social structure (what we have called "history" or, in Lurianic mysticism, "exile"). This middle period culminates in social trauma (the "birthpangs of the Messiah"), which ushers in the final catastrophic upheaval, or the revolution (Amos' "day of the Lord"). Finally, on the ruins of this age will emerge a reconstituted, utopian, classless society (the new Eden)—the secular version of the Jewish "age to come."

The structural parallel, Herberg argues, is striking. But there is one major difference between the two systems. The Marxist believes that the entire process is impelled by dialectical forces that are inherent in history itself. Judaism, in contrast, maintains that history itself is fragmentary and ambiguous; only a transcendent God can redeem history and confer meaning on the historical process. Jewish eschatology has to be understood, then, as a complex myth that shapes the historical process by viewing God as the one who intervenes to clarify, complete, and redeem it.

With this broad picture in place, Herberg proceeds to extract the implicit meaning of each of the themes in Jewish eschatology. His most fascinating discussion is on the theme of bodily resurrection, which, he insists, is a much more Jewish idea than that of the immortality of the individual soul. The notion of bodily resurrection makes three important claims about the human being: first, that redemption of the individual person requires direct intervention by God; second, that what is redeemed is the entire person, the familiar, concrete person, for the doctrine affirms the inherent value of our bodily existence; finally, that by affirming the value of our bodily existence, history and society also acquire ultimate value, for it is in these contexts that we live our lives.

In effect, then, the doctrine of bodily resurrection is as much a statement about the here and now as it is a forecast of what will happen in the indefinite future. It teaches that my life and my world today are of infinite significance. Whatever will happen to me in the hereafter happens to *me,* the concrete me as I now know myself and am known to others. It also teaches that my ultimate fate will be determined by God, whose power to touch me can not be expunged by my death—as long as He is truly the monotheistic God.

Finally, Herberg claims that biblical eschatology alone permits us to avoid the two false eschatologies of our day, naturalism and idealism. Naturalism teaches that history, humanity, and the world can redeem themselves. The history of our century, Herberg insists, has exposed the absurdity of that claim. It has taught us that nature taken on its own terms is intractably ambiguous, that human nature can manifest both striking generosity and unbelievable cruelty, side by side. Nature and history alone can never redeem themselves.

Idealism, as exemplified in oriental religions, despairs of history and humanity and seeks redemption through an escape into an eternal, timeless realm. We must not despair of humanity and our world, but neither should we idolize them. The biblical alternative treds a narrow path between these two extremes: It affirms the significance of history and human striving while insisting that only a transcendent God can lend them ultimate meaning.

Of course, Herberg is a thoroughly modern thinker and so he understands Jewish eschatology as the myth that it is—as mythical as its Marxist and oriental alternatives. The choice, then, is between alternative myths.

Viewing these teachings as mythical makes it possible to respond to two constituencies that together make up the large majority of contemporary Jews. The first, Jewish secularists of all stripes, may espouse a secular version of Jewish eschatology in the form of Zionism, socialism, or both, but see its religious dimension as filled with fantasy and superstition. The other group is frankly bewildered by the entire topic of eschatology, can't accept its teachings about what happens after death or at the end of time as literally true, but doesn't have an alternative and hence avoids the issue entirely, or suspends belief.

The choice is not between secularism, literalism, or silence. The mythic approach sees these teachings as dramatic and poetic expressions of a reality that lies behind or beyond human experience. If they are "true," it is not because they are literal forecasts of what will be some time in the future; no human being can know that. Their truth lies in their ability to reveal unanticipated dimensions of meaning in our lives, to grip our emotions, to inspire us to act in certain ways and strive for certain goals, and most important, to lend infinite meaning to our lives in the here and now.

Jewish eschatology is "true" because it teaches me that my individual life in history and society is infinitely valuable; that my body is integral to my sense of self; that I am accountable for who I am and what I do; that my own fulfillment is inconceivable without the simultaneous fulfillment of my people and of all humanity; that the death of my physical body does not mark the total and final end of who I am—I continue to "be" even though I am no longer physically present on earth; that I have an indispensable role to play in the redemption of the world. Finally, it teaches me that history is not simply a "tale told by an idiot . . . signifying nothing," as Shakespeare put it, but a process with a beginning and an end, a process that strives for a realization of all of the potentialities inherent in creation from the outset. Without these convictions, it would be impossible for me to live.

FOR FURTHER STUDY

A good, general overview of Jewish eschatology is in chs. 22 and 23 of Louis Jacobs' A JEWISH THEOLOGY (see ch. 2). For a glimpse of a great scholar at work on a complex set of issues, see the first three chapters of Gershom Scholem's THE MESSIANIC IDEA IN JUDAISM (pb Schocken, 1971), particularly the first essay, which is a masterful overview of Jewish intellectual history. It remains a classic. The distinction between evolutionary and revolutionary messianism is taken from that monograph. Scholem's SABBATAI ZEVI: THE MYSTICAL MESSIAH (Princeton University Press, 1973; pb 1975) is long, frequently technical, but endlessly fascinating. A more accessible version of Scholem's thesis on the relationship of Sabbatian messianism to Lurianic mysticism is in the last two chapters of his MAJOR TRENDS IN JEWISH MYSTICISM (see ch. 4). Moshe Idel's revisionist approach to the material is in his KABBALAH: NEW PERSPECTIVES (Yale University Press, 1988).

The talmudic material is clarified and systematized in part 7 of George Foot Moore's JUDAISM IN THE FIRST CENTURIES OF THE CHRISTIAN ERA: THE AGE OF THE TANNAIM (2 vols. and 1 vol. Notes, Harvard University Press, 1950).

Maimonides' struggle with Jewish eschatology and particularly with the doctrine of the resurrection of the body is in his introduction to Helek (ch. 10 of the Mishnah of Tractate Sanhedrin), collected in A MAIMONIDES READER, edited by Isadore Twersky (see ch. 6). Maimonides' later defense of his position is in "The Essay on Resurrec-

tion" included in CRISIS AND LEADERSHIP: EPISTLES OF MAIMONIDES *(Jewish Publication Society, 1985), translated with notes by Abraham Halkin, with discussions by David Hartman. This compendium of three of Maimonides' shorter works, masterfully translated and cogently discussed, with copious references to all of the traditional and philosophical literature, is indispensable for any student of the medieval giant. See also Louis Jacobs'* PRINCIPLES OF THE JEWISH FAITH *(Basic Books, 1964), a systematic discussion of Maimonides' thirteen principles of Judaism (listed at the conclusion of his introduction to* Helek*). The last two of these principles deal with Maimonides' eschatology, and Jacobs' discussion ranges widely over ancient and contemporary sources.*

Herberg's reworking of traditional Jewish eschatology is in ch. 16 of his JUDAISM AND MODERN MAN *(see ch. 7).*

Afterword:
Doing Your Own Theology

IT IS NATURAL FOR SCHOLARS AND OTHER PROFESSIONALS TO INSIST that their fields remain the private preserve of those who have received advanced, specialized training. After all, what was the purpose of their years of education if just anyone can speak with authority on *their* issues?

If ever this elitism is misplaced, it is in the discipline of theology. More than any other field, theology stems from personal reflection on the core issues of human living. On these issues, every one of us is an authority. There is not a human being who has not wondered about God's existence and nature, who has not speculated about why "bad things happen to good people," who has not worried about the ultimate purpose of human life or about what happens after death, who has not struggled with moral dilemmas. All of these questions are at the heart of any theological inquiry. Together with other specifically Jewish concerns, such as the meaning and purpose of Jewish religious rituals, they are at the heart of Jewish theology as well.

After years of teaching Jewish theology to adult groups across the country, I have discovered that many American Jews are, in fact, "doing" their own theology, but they are doing it in isolation, in the privacy of their own thoughts, or in conversation with spouses and close friends, and sometimes with a rabbi or a teacher. But for the most part, they are not convinced that

275

their personal theology is worth serious consideration by anyone else. Many worry that their ideas are inappropriate, inauthentic, or even heretical. How often has someone come up to me—after a lecture on Mordecai Kaplan's concept of God, for example—and whispered: "Rabbi Gillman, that's just what I have always believed, but I was afraid to tell anyone."

The purpose of this volume is to bring all of this private theologizing into the open, to stimulate further thought and study, and to provide a more systematic context in which it can be pursued. Here's how to get started:

Work in a Group

While there is no reason you can't work on your own, a sympathetic, congenial group can provide a support system, offer helpful criticisms and/or approval, fill in the gaps in your own background, and provide another experience of Jewish community. If you already belong to a *havurah* or a study group, devote some of your group time to Jewish theology.

Put Your Thoughts on Paper

At the outset, don't worry too much about coherence, style, syntax, or spelling. Every writer knows how difficult it is to get those first sentences on paper. Begin wherever you are, even if it means simply making a list of words, phrases, or associations. You will soon find that it gets progressively easier. More important, externalizing your thoughts on paper is the only way to confront them, evaluate them, see what you like, and what you want to change. Until you do this, you will find it easy to deny, avoid, resist, or postpone dealing with the issues.

A Teacher and a Book Can Help

When I work on theology with a group, I usually follow this procedure. Once we have selected a theme—revelation, God, the meaning of the ritual *mitzvot,* suffering, the end of days—I begin by asking the members of the group to write a personal statement on the issue at hand, using whatever resources or data they have already accumulated from reading, classes, sermons, individual reflection, and the like. The statements are then put aside while I outline the various options on the issue in the writings of contemporary thinkers. I emphasize that these options are neither exhaustive nor clear-cut, and that each of the positions has its own inherent strengths and weaknesses. The outline is simply designed to stimulate our thinking on the issue, and help us find the position that seems most sympathetic to us.

This volume can play an important role at this stage of the inquiry. It provides an outline of what our classical (i.e., biblical and rabbinic) sources have to say on a specific issue, traces some of the later formulations in medieval Jewish philosophy and mysticism, and outlines in more detail how contemporary thinkers have dealt with it. I suggest a set of criteria for evaluating each of these contemporary positions, and I conclude each chapter with my own position, indicating why it seems most adequate to me. The "For Further Study" section that concludes each chapter refers the reader back to the original sources that have been discussed. These can be consulted directly. Most of these books are easily available in bookstores or congregational libraries.

I then ask the members of the group to go off to a quiet corner of the room and write a second statement on the issue. I photocopy all of these statements and then share them with the group.

The Sharing of Positions Is Crucial

This is the most difficult step of all. I ask for individual volunteers to read their statements aloud and I encourage the group to react. I have worked very hard to create a certain mood among the members of the group—openness, trust, and a readiness to expose layers of feeling, doubts, and concerns that usually remain private. I try to remain discreetly in the background throughout these exchanges, intervening only to help clarify a question or a response and allowing the discussion to run its course. At the end, I introduce my own comments, pointing out the strengths of the statement and the issues that remain to be resolved or clarified.

Finally, I meet with each member of the group individually and we compare the student's first and second statements. This comparison helps the student gauge the growth that has taken place through the process. We then proceed with the next issue. At the end of the course, each member of the group will have, in fact, written a comprehensive Jewish theological statement of his or her own.

You Can Also Work on Your Own

For any number of reasons, some of us will not be able, or will not choose, to work with a group. Use this volume as your teacher. But make sure to write your own statements, and to compare your later statements with your earlier ones. That step in the process is indispensable.

Write a Theological Will

The process of doing theology never ends. I have students who have rewritten their personal theological statements every few years in the light of their ongoing life experience, reading, and reflection. But there is a point where we feel as satisfied with what we have written as we will ever be. At that point, we may want to put the statement away as part of our heritage for those dear to us.

There is renewed and growing interest among American Jews in the tradition of writing an ethical will—a statement of what we feel most strongly about, a formulation of our value system, of how we want to be remembered, and how we would like our descendants to conduct their lives. In Judaism, ethics is an extension of theology, and it would take but a slight stretching for the ethical will to include a personal theology, a statement of a belief system as well as a value system, of the ideological substructure on which we have built our lives.

Most of all, don't be intimidated. Acknowledge that you have something to say about these questions that has value, at least to you, and write it down on paper. The process may be difficult, even painful, but it can also be exhilarating, and the sense of accomplishment you will feel at the end will make the struggle eminently worthwhile.

—N.G., June 1989

Index

ABRAHAM BEN DAVID, 257
ARISTOTLE
  impact on Judaism, xix,
    xxi, 140–141, 145,
  Umoved Mover, 82–83,
    149–151
ATHEISM
  in existentialism, 171
  in experientialism 124, 135
  in rationalism, 146
AUGUSTINE, 164

BARTH, KARL, 164
BAHYA IBN PAKUDA, 143
BELIEF
  in existentialism, 171–172
  in experientialism,
    123–124, 135
  "in" and "that", 123–124,
    135, 145, 172
  in rationalism, 145–146
  reasons for and grounds
    for, 10–13, 159

BERKOVITS, ELIEZER, 208
BIBLE
  binding of Isaac, 74, 171,
    173
  covenant texts, 42–43, 60
  critical approach to, 15–16
  Elijah on the Carmel,
    176–177
  on eschatology, 195,
    249–254, 260–262
  on experience of God, 65,
    110–116
  as liturgy 7,
  on nature of God, xix,
    3–6, 64–67, 79, 90–95
  on problem of evil,
    189–195, 197–201
  on revelation 13–14,
    23–25
  the Shema 94–95, 223
  social vision, 45–47
BOROWITZ, EUGENE 74, 164,
    186

BUBER, MARTIN, xvi, xix
on belief, 174–178
on eclipse of God, 176,
206–208
as existentialist, 74, 164,
173–178, 184, 269
on God, 79, 94
I and Thou, 23, 84,
173–178, 182
on Jewish law, 23, 178,
180–182
on religion and religiosity,
173, 175
on revelation, 2, 22–23,
180
and Rosenzweig, 22–23,
178, 180–182, 184

CAMUS, ALBERT, xvi
as existentialist, 164, 182
The Myth of Sysyphus,
169–170
The Plague, 170
CHRISTIANITY
the *Credo,* xx, 239
and the death of God,
202–203
as eschatological
movement, 248, 261,
267
the Eucharist, 220–221
on original sin, 29, 46
COMMAND *See also* LAW,
JEWISH; *MITZVAH*
and law, 180–181, 183
and revelation, 47–54, 181

Rosenzweig on, 50–51,
180–181, 183
COMMUNITY, JEWISH
as authority, 56–57
in Kaplan, xvii–xviii,
18–21, 225–226
and *midrash,* 88–90
and myth, 28, 87–88,
230–236,
and ritual, 228–230
CONSERVATIVE JUDAISM,
57–58, 224
COSMOS, 230
and chaos, 116, 209–211
COVENANT, 40–61
biblical texts, 42–43
circumcision as symbol, 41,
55, 235, 242
Hittite forms, 41–44
and the Jewish myth 44,
55
and law, 40–47

DE UNAMUNO, MIGUEL, 164
DOSTOYEVSKY, FEODOR, 164
DURKHEIM, EMIL, 20

EMPIRICISM, RELIGIOUS,
109–137
on atheism, 124, 135
on belief, 123–125
in Bible, 65, 74, 110–116,
120–121
in Halevi, 74, 124–128
in Heschel, 74, 79, 128–135
in Kaplan, 74

on subjectivity, 71–73,
117–124
verification, 120–121,
133
ESCHATOLOGY, 247–273
Amos on, 251, 260, 262
in the Bible, 249–253
centrality, 248
in Christianity, 248, 261,
267
Ezekiel on, 254, 260
gradualist version, 258–264
Herberg on, 269–271
Hosea on, 251, 253
immortality of the soul,
195, 250–251, 255–258,
270
individual dimension, 195,
249–251, 254–258, 268
Isaiah on, 252, 262
Jeremiah on, 251, 253
in Lurianic mysticism,
265–269,
Maimonides on, 257,
262–263
Marxist version, 269
and the Messiah, 252–254,
260
as myth, 264–267, 271
national dimension, 249,
251–253, 268
other worldly version,
253–254, 259–261
and problem of evil,
194–197, 255–258
in Reform Judaism, 268

resurrection of the dead,
195, 255–258, 270
revolutionary version,
258–264
Sabbatai Zevi, 264–269
Scholem on, 264–269
this worldly version,
252–253, 259–260
universal dimension, 195,
249–253, 268
in Zechariah, 248
Zionism, 248, 268
EVIL, PROBLEM OF (see
HOLOCAUST; SUFFERING,
PROBLEM OF)
EXILE
eschatological end, 253,
265–266
in mysticism, 265–266
EXISTENTIALISM, 163–186
on atheism, 171
on belief, 171–172
in Buber, 22–23, 74, 79,
164, 173–178, 184, 269
in Camus, 164, 169–171,
182
as critique, 169–171
in Fackenheim, 74, 164,
176–177, 207
in Herberg, xv–xvi, 74,
164
on Holocaust, 182–184
on Jewish law, 50–51,
180–183
in Kierkegaard, 74, 164,
171–173

leap of faith, 171–173
as philosophical approach,
  163–168
on revelation, 22–24,
  49–51
in Rosenzweig, 22–24,
  49–51, 74, 158, 164,
  178–183, 269
on subjectivity, 76, 172
as temper, 165–166,
  182–184
EXPERIENTIALISM (*see*
  EMPIRICISM, RELIGIOUS)

FACKENHEIM, EMIL, 74
on belief, 207
on eclipse of God,
  176–177, 207
FAITH (see BELIEF)

GOD
attributes, doctrine of,
  96–98
Biblical concept, xix, 3–6,
  64–67, 79, 90–95
in Buber, 174–175
cosmological argument for,
  146, 149–153
death of, 202–205
eclipse of, 176, 206–208
in eschatology, 194–197,
  255–257
and evil, 184–191, 197–21,
  255–258
exile of, 265–266
existence of, 63–67, 146,
  147–156

in Halevi, 9, 124–128
in Heschel, 24, 35, 74, 79,
  93, 129–130, 134,
  208–209
hiding of the face, 176,
  190, 206
and the Holocaust,
  201–211
human perception of,
  67–73
intimacy with, 3–4,
  111–113, 126–127,
  131–134
in Kaplan, 18–19, 74, 82,
  101–104, 198–201,
  204–205, 225
limited, 92–93, 197–201
in Maimonides, 96–98
monotheistic, 90–92, 197
in mysticism, 98–101,
  111–113, 265–266
numinous, 113–114
ontological argument for,
  146, 147–149
pathos of, 35, 79, 93,
  129–130
as personal, 79, 93–96
of the philosophers, 5
and revelation, 3–8
and ritual, 215–244
as sovereign, 90–92
suffering, 208–209
symbols for 80–84, 104,
  106, 203
talking of, 4–6, 25–26, 63,
  79–106
teleological argument for,
  146, 153–156

as Unmoved Mover,
82–83, 149–151
vulnerability of 3–4,
GREENBERG, IRVING, 207–208
GREENE, GRAHAM, 220–221

HAGGADAH, 7, 12, 230
HALAKHA (*see also* COMMAND
and LAW, JEWISH), 40,
56, 59, 121–122, 173,
178, 180–181,
HALEVI, YEHUDA
The Book of the Kuzari,
124–128, 132, 136, 144
on religious experience,
126–127
on revelation, 7
HEGEL, GEORG WILHELM
FRIEDRICH, 167
HASIDISM, 267–269
HEIDEGGER, MARTIN, 164
HERBERG, WILL
on eschatology, 269–271
as existentialist, xvi, 74,
164
as Marxist, xv–xvi, 269
on resurrection of the
dead, 270
on scandal of particularity,
8
HESCHEL, ABRAHAM JOSHUA,
xvi, xix, 128–129
on divine pathos, 35, 79,
93, 129–130
on evil, 208–209, 211
on God, 24, 35, 74, 79, 93,
134, 208–209

on Holocaust, 208–209,
211
on Jewish law, 51–54,
181–182
on prayer, 246
on religious experience,
128–134
on revelation, 24–25, 36
HOLOCAUST, xxii, 89,
182–183, 187, 201–211
in Berkovits, 208
in Buber, 206–208
as chaos, 209–211
in Fackenheim, 176–207
in Greenberg, 207, 208
in Heschel, 208–209, 211
liturgy for, 209–211, 242
ritual for, 209–211, 242
in Rubenstein, 202–205
HUME, DAVID, xvi, 154–155

IDEL, MOSHE, 269
ISLAM, xxi, 139–140

JAMES, WILLIAM, 20
JASPERS, KARL, 164
JOB, BOOK OF, 74, 211
on suffering, 120, 192–194
on religious experience,
115–116

KADDISH, The, 196–197,
210–211, 238
KADUSHIN, MAX
normal mysticism, 121–122
KAPLAN, MORDECAI, xvi, xix,
xxv

on believing, behaving and
  belonging, xvii–xviii
on community, xvii–xviii,
  18–21
on suffering, 198–201
on folkways, 48, 225–226,
  243–244
on God, 18–19, 74, 82,
  101–104, 198–201,
  204–205
on Jewish law, 48
on liturgy, 237, 240
as naturalist, 17–21
on revelation, 17–21
on salvation, 48
on Torah, 17–21
KIERKEGAARD, SOREN, xvi,
  164, 171–172
KUSHNER, HAROLD, xxiii,
  200–201

LAMM, NORMAN
  on Jewish law, 47–48
  on revelation, 14–17, 25
  on ritual, 15
LAW, JEWISH, *see also,*
  COMMAND; *MITZVAH*
  authority behind, 39–60
  in Bible, 39–45
  in Buber, 180–181
  and command, 180–181,
    183
  and covenant, 39–47
  in Heschel, 51–54, 181–182
  joy of, 58–60
  in Kaplan, 48–49
  in Lamm, 47–48

legalism, limits of, 58–60
myth and, 54–58
and revelation, 39–60
in Rosenzweig 50–51,
  180–181, 183
traditionalist view, 47–48
LITURGY
  Ahavah Rabbah, 94–95
  as historical narrative, 7
  as Jewish Credo, 95
  the *Kaddish,* 196–197,
    210–211, 238
  and the Jewish myth,
    95
  and prayer, 239–242
  translations, 237–240
  Yedid Nefesh, 113–114
LURIA, RABBI ISAAC, 98–101,
  265–269,
LOCKE, JOHN, xvi

MAIMONIDES, MOSES
  on eschatology, 257,
    262–263
  on God, xxiv, 96–98,
    151–153
  as rationalist, 73, 143–144,
    156–159
  on resurrection and
    immortality, 257
  on role of Jewish
    philosophy, xviii–xx,
    xxiii
MARCEL, GABRIEL, 164
MENDELSSOHN, MOSES, 144
MESSIAH
  in Bible, 260–262

in Christianity, 261, 263,
267
false, 264–269
other worldly concept,
259–263
Sabbatai Zevi, 264–269
this worldly concept,
259–260
MIDRASH
in eschatology, 258
and Jewish philosophy,
xxv–xxvi
Maimonidean, 157
in mysticism, 99
and myth, 31–32, 88–90,
119–120
MILL, JOHN STUART, 154
MITZVAH (*see also* COMMAND
and JEWISH LAW),
40–59, 180–181,
184
MYSTICISM
on creation, 99, 265
on eschatology, 264–269
God in, 98–101
Idel on, 269
Lurianic version of,
265–269
and religious experience,
111–113
Sabbatianism, 264–269
Scholem on, 264–269
the *Zohar,* 98–101,
MYTH
and community, 28, 87–88,
230–236
definitions, 26–30, 84–88

in eschatology, 265–268,
271
in Freud, 27, 30, 85
functions, 27–30, 85–88
in liturgy, 239–240
and *midrash,* 31–33,
88–90
and *mitzvah,* 54–58
and ritual, 28–29, 56,
87–88, 230–236
in science, 27, 30,
86–87
and symbol, 26, 84–88
in Tillich, 26
truth and falsity, 29–30

NIEBUHR, RHEINHOLD, xvi,
164
NIETZSCHE, FRIEDRICH, 164,
202

ORTHODOX JUDAISM, 56, 224
OTTO, RUDOLF, xvi, 113–114

PHILO, xix, 140
PLATO, xvi, xix, 8, 166–167
PRAYER
communal, 238–239
as expression, 236–238
and liturgy, 239–242
as ritual, 236–242

RATIONALISM, 139–161
Bahya, 143
on existence of God, 73,
146–159
as ideal, 10, 146, 156–159

Maimonides, 73, 143–144,
 156–159
Saadia, 73, 142–143
on subjectivity, 145–146
REFORM JUDAISM, 57, 224,
 226, 268
RESURRECTION
 in Bible, 256
 in Herberg, 270
 in liturgy, 256–257
 in Maimonides, 257
 in Rabbinic literature,
 119–120, 195, 256–257
REVELATION, 1–34
 and authority, 39. 47–54
 in Buber, 2, 36, 180
 and community, 56–57
 dogma of Mosaic
 composition, 13, 15–16
 dogma of verbal, 13, 16–17
 fact of, 2, 6–13, 25
 in Heschel, 24–25, 36
 historicity of, 7–8, 11–13
 in Kaplan, 17–21, 33,
 101–102
 in Lamm, 14–15, 17–18
 and myth, 25–32
 principle of, 2, 3–8
 propositional view, 16–17
 in Rosenzweig, 22–25,
 180–181
 Sinaitic, 7–8, 11–13
 traditionalist views, 5,
 13–17, 33, 35–36, 243
RITUAL, 215–244
 as anachronism, 226–228
 and community, 228–230

and ethics, 242–243
as folkway, 48, 225–226,
 234–235, 243–244
as magic, 217–219
and myth, 28–29, 56,
 230–236
as obedience, 222–224
prayer as, 236–242
sacramentalist view,
 219–222
as structuring space,
 231–234
as structuring time,
 233–234
symbolist view, 224–225,
 230–236, 243–244
ROSENZWEIG, FRANZ, xvi,
 xix, 178–180
and Buber, 22–23, 178,
 180–184
on command and law,
 50–51, 180–182
as existentialist, xvi, 22,
 74, 158, 164, 180–184,
 269
on revelation, 22–25,
 180–181
"The New Thinking", 179
RUBENSTEIN, RICHARD,
 202–205

SAADIA, 73
SARTRE, JEAN-PAUL, xvi, 164,
 202
SCHOLEM, GERSHOM, 107–108,
 264–269
SOCRATES, 164

SOUL
  in Bible, 256
  and body, 254–258
  immortality of, 157–158,
    250–251, 255–258
  perfection of, 157–158,
    257–258
STEINBERG, MILTON, xvi, 200
SUBJECTIVITY, PROBLEM OF,
    67–73
  in existentialism, 76, 172
  in experientialism, 71–73,
    76, 117–124
  in rationalism, 76, 145–146
SUFFERING, PROBLEM OF (*see
    also* HOLOCAUST),
    187–213
  as chaos, 209–211
  coping with, 189
  eschatological resolution,
    194–197, 255–257
  God's responsibility,
    184–191, 197–201,
    255–258
  Heschel on, 208–209, 211
  as hiding of God's face,
    190, 206–208
  human responsibility,
    191–198

Job on, 120, 192–194
Kaplan on, 198–201
Kushner on, 200–201
natural, 187–188
as retribution, 189–192
and theodicy, 188–191, 193,
    196, 255–258
SYMBOL
  and myth, 84–88
  in ritual, 224, 230–236
  and sign, 81–82
  in theology, 80–84

THEODICY (*see* SUFFERING,
    PROBLEM OF)
TILLICH, PAUL,
  and death of God, 202
  Dynamics of Faith, 35–36,
    61, 107
  as existentialist, 164
  on myth, 26
  on theological symbols, 35
TORAH (see also
    REVELATION)
  as authority, 2, 5, 39
  canonization of, 139–140
  and Jewish myth, 3–32

ZIONISM, 248, 268